MATERIALS IN TRIAL ADVOCACY

PROBLEMS AND CASES

ASPEN COURSEBOOK SERIES

MATERIALS IN TRIAL ADVOCACY

PROBLEMS AND CASES

Tenth Edition

THOMAS A. MAUET
Director of Trial Advocacy (retired)
and Milton O. Riepe Professor of Law Emeritus
University of Arizona James E. Rogers College of Law

JUDGE WARREN D. WOLFSON
Distinguished Visiting Professor of Law
DePaul University College of Law

STEPHEN D. EASTON
President
Dickinson State University

Photography by
Amanda Merullo

Cover image credit: Gorodenkoff/Shutterstock.com

To contact Customer Service, e-mail customer.service@aspenpublishing.com, call 1-800-950-5259, or mail correspondence to:

Aspen Publishing
Attn: Order Department
1 Wall Street
Burlington, MA 01803

Printed in the United States of America.

1 2 3 4 5 6 7 8 9 0

ISBN 978-1-5438-5799-3

Library of Congress Cataloging-in-Publication Data

Names: Mauet, Thomas A., author. | Wolfson, Warren D., author. | Easton, Stephen D., 1958- author.
Title: Materials in trial advocacy: problems and cases/Thomas A. Mauet, Director of Trial Advocacy (retired) and Milton O. Riepe Professor of Law Emeritus, University of Arizona, James E. Rogers College of Law; Judge Warren D. Wolfson, Distinguished Visiting Professor of Law, DePaul University College of Law; Stephen D. Easton, President, Dickinson State University; photography by Amanda Merullo.
Description: Tenth edition. | Burlington: Aspen Publishing, 2024. | Summary: "Coursebook for Trials classes in law school"—Provided by publisher.
Identifiers: LCCN 2023042596 | ISBN 9781543857993 (paperback) | ISBN 9781543858006 (ebook)
Subjects: LCSH: Trial practice—United States—Problems, exercises, etc.
Classification: LCC KF8915.Z9 M33 2024 | DDC 347.73/75—dc23/eng/20231002
LC record available at https://lccn.loc.gov/2023042596

About Aspen Publishing

Aspen Publishing is a leading provider of educational content and digital learning solutions to law schools in the U.S. and around the world. Aspen provides best-in-class solutions for legal education through authoritative textbooks, written by renowned authors, and breakthrough products such as Connected eBooks, Connected Quizzing, and PracticePerfect.

The Aspen Casebook Series (famously known among law faculty and students as the "red and black" casebooks) encompasses hundreds of highly regarded textbooks in more than eighty disciplines, from large enrollment courses, such as Torts and Contracts, to emerging electives, such as Sustainability and the Law of Policing. Study aids such as the *Examples & Explanations* and the *Emanuel Law Outlines* series, both highly popular collections, help law students master complex subject matter.

Major products, programs, and initiatives include:

- **Connected eBooks** are enhanced digital textbooks and study aids that come with a suite of online content and learning tools designed to maximize student success. Designed in collaboration with hundreds of faculty and students, the Connected eBook is a significant leap forward in the legal education learning tools available to students.

- **Connected Quizzing** is an easy-to-use formative assessment tool that tests law students' understanding and provides timely feedback to improve learning outcomes. Delivered through CasebookConnect.com, the learning platform already used by students to access their Aspen casebooks, Connected Quizzing is simple to implement and integrates seamlessly with law school course curricula.

- **PracticePerfect** is a visually engaging, interactive study aid to explain commonly encountered legal doctrines through easy-to-understand animated videos, illustrative examples, and numerous practice questions. Developed by a team of experts, PracticePerfect is the ideal study companion for today's law students.

- The **Aspen Learning Library** enables law schools to provide their students with access to the most popular study aids on the market across all of their courses. Available through an annual subscription, the online library consists of study aids in e-book, audio, and video formats with full text search, note-taking, and highlighting capabilities.

- Aspen's **Digital Bookshelf** is an institutional-level online education bookshelf, consolidating everything students and professors need to ensure success. This program ensures that every student has access to affordable course materials from day one.

- **Leading Edge** is a community centered on thinking differently about legal education and putting those thoughts into actionable strategies. At the core of the program is the Leading Edge Conference, an annual gathering of legal education thought leaders looking to pool ideas and identify promising directions of exploration.

SUMMARY OF CONTENTS

CONTENTS

IV

EXHIBITS

IMPEACHMENT AND REHABILITATION

EXPERTS

VII

485

ADVANCED DIRECT AND CROSS-EXAMINATION

VIII

515

CLOSING ARGUMENTS

IX

531

TRIALS

X

611

HISTORIC TRIALS

PREFACE

This book presents a progressive series of problems, cases, and trial files. They can be utilized for semester courses in trial advocacy as well as in post-graduate programs for trial lawyers. The problems are organized to parallel the various stages of a jury trial. Each chapter contains a mix of civil and criminal problems of increasing difficulty, allowing for substantial assignment selection. The problems present situations that commonly occur during civil and criminal trials. They are designed to develop basic trial skills. Chapter 7 contains a dozen cases involving two opposing witnesses that can be used as advanced direct and cross-examination problems, as opening statement and closing argument exercises, and as short trials or hearings. Chapter 9 contains overviews of 16 trial files, each having two to four witnesses per side, that can be used during the semester or as a final trial at the end of the course. Chapter 10 contains five additional trials, based on historic events that can also be used for these purposes. The trial files, like the Chapter 7 problem files, are in the resources section of this book on CasebookConnect. Each trial file can be effectively tried to a jury in approximately three to four hours.

The organization and design of the problems are a result of our experiences as trial lawyers, judges, and trial advocacy teachers. In our view, some of the other available trial advocacy teaching materials are too lengthy and complex. Often these materials base problems on complete case files, requiring the reading of an entire case to prepare one problem. This results in assignments being an exercise in reading and memory, not in trial techniques. The problems in the first six chapters of this book, in contrast, have two principal characteristics. First, they are efficient and self-contained, often being only two or three pages long. Second, each problem emphasizes a specific trial skill that is essential to every competent trial lawyer.

Many of the problems, cases, and trial files are based on actual cases that we have tried during our years as trial lawyers or as judges or those that otherwise have come to our attention. In drafting the materials for this book, we have converted the actual dates into a now commonly used system of stating dates based on their relationship to the present year. For example, "[-1]" means one year ago, "[-2]" means two years ago, and so on. For example, this year being 2023, the date of "6/15/[-1]" is June 15, 2022; "August 1, [-2]" is August 1, 2021. Through this device the dates can be kept realistic.

Finally, we must point out difficulties created by the mock trial setting. Obviously, testimony in that setting gets shaped and at times created by the students. There is perhaps a danger that students will confuse the mock world with the real world. In a mock trial, lawyers cannot know what the truth is because there is no truth: Everything is made up. In the real world, lawyers often know what the truth is and do the best they can to deal with it. Those attempts should lead to serious and important discussions about the nature of the adversary system and a lawyer's ethical obligations and sense of morality.

This book is designed to help teach trial techniques to people who want to learn them and who eventually might get to use them. We do not want to discourage discussion about the lawyer's role and duties in the real trial world; nor do we want our purpose diluted by a confusion of the mock with the real. We rely on the teachers to point out the differences.

What's New in the Tenth Edition

Materials in Trial Advocacy has been used for over four decades. Since 1981 we have received numerous suggestions for additions, deletions, and modifications. We always welcome these suggestions and have incorporated many of them over the years, so that the present edition is substantially different from the first.

There are three major additions to the previous edition, all of them new trial files. The first two are files that have been added to Chapter IX. Trial 9.15 involves a dispute between a landowner and an oil and gas developer. Those from law schools or other trial training programs in or near jurisdictions with substantial oil and gas exploration and production will want to consider using this trial file. This trial demonstrates that a seemingly simple dispute over damages can involve factually complex—and even emotional—underlying matters.

The second addition to Chapter IX, Trial 9.16, is a wrongful death action arising out of a motorcycle accident. It is different than the other Chapter IX trial files because it is designed as a semester-long (or, at least, several week) exercise that takes students from an initial conference with a potential client through the pleading, discovery, and pretrial process, all the way to a jury verdict. It is likely to be of interest to those in advanced trial practice classes or classes that teach both pretrial and trial advocacy.

In the Ninth Edition, we added a then new Chapter X entitled "Historic Trials." Chapter X files are based on actual historical events, which adds elements of realism that are sometimes missing in purely fictional trials. You can use the Chapter X trial files like the Chapter IX files for semester-ending jury trials. But you can also use them to stage community events for your law school or bar organization. Chapter X includes an essay about how to effectively stage historic trials. In this Tenth Edition, we have added a new case, Trial 10.5, which provides a second civil trial option for those who like the historic trial concept.

Acknowledgments

We would like to thank Tara Righetti, Professor, University of Wyoming College of Law and School of Energy Resources, the primary author of Trial 9.15, and her collaborators Charles Nye and Dr. J. Fred McLaughlin. We continue to thank John Mollenkamp, who developed the 9.14 files with one of the co-authors at the University of Missouri School of Law. We thank former University of Missouri School of Law students Elizabeth E. O'Hanlon and James S. Atkins and former University of Wyoming College of Law students Evynne Fair, Mikole Bede Soto, Katelyn Krabbenhoft, and John Fritz, who wrote the Chapter X historic trial files, as well as others who gave us permission to use their materials, as noted in those files. We also thank the Spence Law Firm of Jackson, Wyoming, which provided the financial support for the University of Wyoming College of Law's Spence Law Firm Historic Trial program, which served as the incubator for several of the historic trial files. We would also like to thank Ms. Shannon Snow for her assistance in researching and drafting the medical records for Jennifer Smith v. Kelly Davis, M.D. (9.12). We would also like to thank Professor Mary Rita Luecke of DePaul College of Law for contributing supplemental material, including the drawings in Problems 7.2, 7.6, and 7.9, as well as the defense file memo for Problem 7.7 that is included in the Teacher's Manual. We also would like to thank Professor

Tawnya Plumb, Electronic Services Librarian at the University of Wyoming College of Law's George W. Hopper Law Library, who provided invaluable research assistance and former University of Wyoming Professor Elaine Welle, who provided guidance about the law. Finally, we would like to thank Joe Bevington and Skyler Bagley, students at the University of Wyoming College of Law, for their amazing technical assistance in updating the graphics, and Amanda Merullo, for her diligence and skill in finding and photographing the assorted items in the problems and trials.

Thomas A. Mauet
Tucson, Arizona

Warren D. Wolfson
Chicago, Illinois

Stephen D. Easton
Dickinson, North Dakota

August 2023

MATERIALS IN TRIAL ADVOCACY

PROBLEMS AND CASES

I

JURY SELECTION

Introduction

INTRODUCTION

The problems in this chapter represent common types of civil and criminal cases that are routinely tried to juries. They present recurring issues about which a trial lawyer must reach decisions before and during the jury selection process. In addition, the two-witness cases in Chapter 7 may be used.

For each problem assigned, you should be prepared to make all necessary preliminary decisions and resolve any procedural uncertainties before the jury selection process actually begins. You must be thoroughly familiar with the applicable substantive law, your jurisdiction's procedural rules, and your judge's particular practices during jury selection.

Your instructor may modify the assignments and make specific additional assignments for these exercises.

The suggested background reading is Mauet & Easton, *Trial Techniques and Trials*, Chapter 3.

1.1   CIVIL: AUTOMOBILE NEGLIGENCE

This is a negligence action brought by Sharon Howard against James Walton arising out of a vehicle collision that occurred two years ago during the evening of May 2.

At the time, Howard was driving southbound in the inside lane of Main Street, a four-lane street with two lanes of traffic in each direction. Suddenly, another car, driven northbound in the inside lane by Walton, turned left without signaling and cut in front of Howard. Howard slammed on her brakes but couldn't avoid hitting Walton's car.

Walton maintains that he was driving northbound on Main Street, that he decided to turn left, and that the oncoming car driven by Howard was speeding and crashed into him before he could complete the turn. Walton says he was stopped in the inside southbound lane of Main waiting for a break in the outside lane traffic, so he could finish the turn, when the other car struck him.

The police at the scene gave Walton a Breathalyzer test because they smelled liquor on his breath. The test showed some alcohol but in an amount below the legal presumption-of-intoxication level. The police gave Walton a citation for failing to signal a left turn. The charge was dropped at a later date.

Both drivers were taken to a nearby hospital. Walton was examined and released. Howard was admitted with a broken nose, concussion, and facial cuts. Today she still has visible scarring on her nose and cheeks and complains of periodic headaches. She is 22 years old and single.

Plaintiff's occurrence witnesses are two girls, ages 11 and 12, who were sitting on their front lawn across from where the collision occurred. They will support plaintiff's version of the event, including Howard's claim that she was not speeding.

1. Prepare a juror profile of favorable and unfavorable jurors.
2. Conduct a voir dire examination of prospective jurors and make appropriate cause and peremptory challenges for the plaintiff or defendant.
3. Submit a written list of supplemental questions you wish the court to ask the prospective jurors if the court will conduct the entire voir dire.

1.2   CIVIL: PRODUCTS LIABILITY

This is a products liability case brought by Susan James against the ABC Manufacturing Company.

Three years ago, at a local supermarket, James purchased a standard metal can opener manufactured by the defendant. When purchased, the can opener was in a plastic and cardboard package. The back of the package contained the following words: "WARNING: Use only for opening bottles and cans." James did not read the back of the package at any time.

On May 2, two years ago, James used the can opener to pry open a sticky kitchen drawer. The tip of the can opener broke off and flew into her left eye, resulting in a total loss of vision in that eye.

At the time of the accident, James was 53 years old, married, and had three adult children no longer living with her. She is not formally employed outside of her house, though she is a potter who sells her work at art and craft fairs.

The ABC Manufacturing Company, a Japanese corporation located in Tokyo, defends on the basis of product misuse and the adequacy of the written warning contained on the package. ABC manufactures numerous kitchen utensils and appliances, principally for importation to the United States. It has been in business since 1948. There are several products liability cases pending against ABC based on alleged defects in the can opener, but none has yet been settled or tried.

1. Prepare a juror profile of favorable and unfavorable jurors.
2. Conduct a voir dire examination of prospective jurors and make appropriate cause and peremptory challenges for the plaintiff or defendant.
3. Submit a written list of supplemental questions you wish the court to ask the prospective jurors if the court will conduct the entire voir dire.

1.3   CIVIL: MEDICAL MALPRACTICE

This is a medical malpractice case brought by Juan Gonzalez against Mercy Hospital.

On May 2, two years ago, Gonzalez fell down the stairs of his apartment and fractured his ankle. He was taken to the Mercy Hospital emergency room, where he was examined and treated by the emergency room personnel.

An intern employed by the hospital set the fracture and placed the lower leg in a cast. The next day Gonzalez began to complain of swelling and numbness in the leg, was examined periodically by the hospital staff, and was assured repeatedly by the hospital staff that his complaints were not unusual in injuries of that type.

Five days after the accident the cast was removed, and the leg was found to have significantly impaired circulation. Gangrene had set in. Despite remedial measures, the condition worsened, and the leg eventually had to be amputated just below the knee.

Gonzalez at the time of the accident was 35 years old, married, and the father of two small children. He was employed as a carpenter by a local construction company, but he has not worked at that job or any other since the accident. His employer's health and disability insurance has covered his medical and lost income expenses to date.

Gonzalez, a Mexican national, was a lawful resident alien when the accident happened.

Mercy Hospital, a not-for-profit charitable institution, has been owned and operated for many years by the Jesuits, a Catholic order.

1.   Prepare a juror profile of favorable and unfavorable jurors.
2.   Conduct a voir dire examination of prospective jurors and make appropriate cause and peremptory challenges for the plaintiff or defendant.
3.   Submit a written list of supplemental questions you wish the court to ask the prospective jurors if the court will conduct the entire voir dire.

1.4   CIVIL: WRONGFUL DEATH

This is a wrongful death and survival action brought by William Smith, administrator of the estate of Jennifer Smith, deceased, against the defendants, Frank Jones and the ABC Construction Company.

On May 2, two years ago, Jennifer Smith, age 6, was playing with several other children in the schoolyard of her grade school shortly after school had let out for the day. At the same time, Frank Jones, a 62-year-old carpenter, was driving down the street by the schoolyard in a truck owned by his employer, ABC Construction Company, on his way to a job site.

The school zone is marked with signs. Jones was driving within the posted speed limit. The schoolyard is separated from the street by a fence, which has periodic openings in it.

Jennifer then spotted an ice cream truck parked across the street from the schoolyard. Its lights and music were on. Jennifer suddenly ran through an opening in the fence and across the street toward the truck.

Jones saw the ice cream truck and then saw Jennifer running across the street. He slammed on his brakes and turned his steering wheel but was unable to stop in time. The truck knocked Jennifer down on the pavement.

Jennifer was taken to a nearby hospital where she died five days later without ever regaining consciousness.

1. Prepare a juror profile of favorable and unfavorable jurors.
2. Conduct a voir dire examination of prospective jurors and make appropriate cause and peremptory challenges for the plaintiff or defendants.
3. Submit a list of supplemental questions you wish the court to ask the prospective jurors if the court will conduct the entire voir dire.

1.5 CRIMINAL: ARMED ROBBERY AND AGGRAVATED BATTERY

This is an armed bank robbery and aggravated battery case brought against the defendant, William Hill.

On May 2 of last year, two persons, one of whom was armed with a handgun, robbed the Second Federal Savings and Loan Association. Two tellers and the branch manager were in the bank at the time. Approximately $16,000 was taken.

During the robbery, one of the tellers, Helen Lee, age 37, married, with two teenage children, was shot in the foot. She was taken to a nearby hospital and treated. Today her left leg is slightly smaller in the calf area than the right leg, and she has a noticeable limp.

The police, who obtained the license plate number of the getaway car from a passerby, arrested the defendant one hour later. The defendant, a 20-year-old high school dropout who had been unemployed six months when arrested, had been previously arrested twice for robbery and burglary. The robbery charge was dismissed; the burglary charge is still pending.

Following his arrest, the defendant was placed in a lineup with several other persons. One of the tellers positively identified the defendant as the robber. Helen Lee and the branch manager were unable to make any identification.

The money and handgun were never found. The second offender was never arrested or charged.

1. Prepare a juror profile of favorable and unfavorable jurors.
2. Conduct a voir dire examination of prospective jurors and make appropriate cause and peremptory challenges for the prosecution or defense.
3. Submit a list of supplemental questions you wish the court to ask the prospective jurors if the court will conduct the entire voir dire.

1.6 CRIMINAL: SEXUAL ASSAULT

This is a criminal sexual assault prosecution brought against the defendant, William Jackson.

The victim, Mary Rice, age 22 and single, will testify that she worked as a bartender at Butch's, a local spot popular with college students and young working persons. On May 2 of last year, she left work at 2:00 A.M. and walked to her apartment building one block away. A man followed her onto the elevator and exited on her floor. As she opened her apartment door, the man grabbed her from behind, pushed her into the apartment, told her he had a knife, and sexually assaulted her.

Immediately after the man left, Rice called the police. When they arrived she told them that she had seen the man previously at Butch's. (Based on this and other information, the police arrested the defendant several days later.) The police took Rice to a hospital, where she was examined and released.

When arrested, the defendant told the police that he had accompanied Rice to her apartment, that she had invited him in, and that they had voluntarily engaged in sex.

The defendant, age 22, who is African American, has a prior conviction for burglary. The victim is white.

1. Prepare a juror profile of favorable and unfavorable jurors.
2. Conduct a voir dire examination of prospective jurors and make appropriate cause and peremptory challenges for the prosecution or defense.
3. Submit a list of supplemental questions you wish the court to ask the prospective jurors if the court will conduct the entire voir dire.

1.7   CRIMINAL: TAX EVASION

This is an income tax evasion case brought against the defendant, Joseph Church.

The indictment charges that for the tax year ending December 31, two years ago, the defendant, a physician specializing in orthopedic surgery, intentionally and knowingly understated his gross income. It charges that his unreported gross income for the year was $293,000, resulting in an underpayment of tax in the amount of $70,000.

Church admits that he underreported his gross income in the amounts alleged but denies that this was intentionally and knowingly done. His defense is that he delegated all the financial aspects of his practice to his bookkeeper (since fired), who, he later discovered, was sloppy and did inaccurate work. He claims that he personally had no idea what his gross income for the tax year was when he signed the return.

The bookkeeper will testify that the doctor was satisfied with her work until his tax difficulties began and that she merely did the billings and paid the office expenses. She contends she never did accounting or tax work for the doctor.

1.   Prepare a juror profile of favorable and unfavorable jurors.
2.   Conduct a voir dire examination of prospective jurors and make appropriate cause and peremptory challenges for the prosecution or defense.
3.   Submit a list of supplemental questions you wish the court to ask the prospective jurors if the court will conduct the entire voir dire.

1.8 CRIMINAL: MURDER

This is a murder case brought against the defendant, William Barnes.

On May 2 of last year the victim, Fred Silver, was found in his apartment by police, who were called to the scene by a neighbor who complained of loud voices and noises coming from Silver's apartment. When police arrived, they found Silver already dead, with numerous stab wounds in the neck, chest, and back. At the time of his death, Silver was age 42 and single. He was working for an advertising agency.

Following an anonymous tip, two homicide detectives went to the defendant's home. After a lengthy interrogation, the defendant finally admitted killing Silver, a social friend, after an argument.

The indicated defense is insanity. The defendant's proof will show that during the past five years, the defendant has been admitted two times on a voluntary basis to psychiatric institutions for paranoid schizophrenia. A defense psychiatrist who examined the defendant after his arrest concluded that the defendant was suffering from the same condition at the time of the stabbing. The prosecution has an expert with a contrary opinion.

1. Prepare a juror profile of favorable and unfavorable jurors.
2. Conduct a voir dire examination of prospective jurors and make appropriate cause and peremptory challenges for the prosecution or defense.
3. Submit a list of supplemental questions you wish the court to ask the prospective jurors if the court will conduct the entire voir dire.

II

OPENING STATEMENTS

INTRODUCTION

The trial files summarized in Chapter 9 and included in full in the resources section of this book on CasebookConnect, prepared for use as full trials, may also be used here as representative civil and criminal cases on which to base separate opening statement assignments. In addition, the two-witness cases in Chapter 7 may be used for additional opening statement assignments.

For each problem assigned, you should be prepared to present an opening statement that is logically organized and persuasively delivered to the jury. Your instructor may modify the assignments and make specific additional assignments for these exercises.

The suggested background reading is Mauet & Easton, *Trial Techniques and Trials,* Chapter 4.

III

DIRECT AND CROSS-EXAMINATION

INTRODUCTION

The problems in this chapter represent the kinds of recurring problems routinely encountered during the direct and cross-examinations of common types of witnesses. Each problem focuses on a specific kind of skill, the mastery of which is essential to present the witness's testimony effectively in the courtroom. This chapter focuses on occurrence witnesses, the most common and important witnesses in personal injury and criminal cases. The advanced direct and cross-examination cases in Chapter 7 have a number of witnesses in commercial transactions settings.

You should prepare your specific assignment for each problem as though the case were actually on trial. Accordingly, you should determine whether any admissibility issues exist and anticipate the objections and arguments your opponent is likely to make. In addition, you should structure and execute your direct or cross-examination so that you will effectively present that witness's testimony to the jury.

Most of the witnesses do not have background information. Be prepared to develop realistic, credible backgrounds for them.

Your instructor may modify the assignments and make specific additional assignments for these exercises.

The suggested background reading is Mauet & Easton, *Trial Techniques and Trials*, Chapters 5 and 6.

3.1 CONVERSATIONS AND TELEPHONE CALLS

1. The charge is extortion. Jess Smith is the complaining witness. The defendant is Ed Crosby. Smith has worked with Crosby at Ajax Machine Works for the past five years. They spoke on several occasions, at the plant.

Smith will testify that on January 15 of last year, at 6 P.M., in the 14′ by 20′ Ajax Machine Works coffee room, Crosby said that unless Smith paid him $1,000 by the end of the week, he would put sugar in the gas tank of Smith's new Cadillac. No one else was in the coffee room at the time. Ajax is located at 322 W. Vernon Street.

For the prosecution, call Smith as a witness and put the conversation in evidence.

2. Use the same facts as in No. 1 above, except that the conversation occurred when Crosby called Smith at Smith's home. Smith lives at 3110 S. Crawford Avenue.

For the prosecution, call Smith as a witness and put the telephone conversation in evidence, assuming:

(a) they had talked on the phone many times before January 15 of last year;
or

(b) they had never talked on the phone before January 15 of last year.

3. Assume that Crosby and Smith had never met or spoken before January 15 of last year. Smith will testify that Crosby telephoned him/her at home on January 15, at about 6:00 P.M., and made the threat contained in No. 1 above. Crosby did not give his name during the call. One week later Crosby walked up to Smith outside Smith's house, at 2:15 P.M., and said: "I'm the one who called you last week. Do you have the $1,000?"

For the prosecution, call Smith as a witness and put both conversations in evidence, assuming:

(a) when they talked in front of Smith's house, Smith recognized Crosby's voice;
or

(b) when they talked in front of Smith's house, Smith did not recognize Crosby's voice.

4. For the defense, in each of the above situations, oppose the testimony and cross-examine Smith.

3.2   CONVERSATIONS AND TELEPHONE CALLS

A new client, Kennedy Smith, came to you one year ago today and told you the following story:

One month ago I decided to purchase a new car, so I checked the internet and called Ace Motors. A man answered, said he'd be happy to talk to me, and said I should come in so they could show me the various models and accessories.

The next day I went to Ace Motors and met a salesman, Tim Bonner. I looked at several cars and the accessories, got price quotes, and finally placed my order for a new sports car. I gave him a check for $4,000 as a down payment. The full price of the car was $56,000.

The next day I had second thoughts about the sports car. I decided that it was not the right car for me and that what I really needed was a minivan. I called Ace again and a woman answered. I told her I had ordered a car but wanted to switch my order to a minivan I had looked at the previous day with the same accessories I ordered for the sports car. She asked my name and put me on hold for a few minutes. When she came back she said everything was taken care of; they'd call when the minivan came in. She said the price would be $48,000.

Two weeks later the phone rang. I picked it up and said, "Hello," and the voice said, "Hi, it's Tim Bonner at Ace—your sports car arrived and is ready for pickup." I told him I'd changed the order, and he said he didn't know anything about it. He said I'd better come in.

The next day I went again to Ace Motors and talked to Charles Locker, the owner and manager. He said he had no written record of any order change. In any event, he said, none of the women working for him were sales personnel, and only salespeople were authorized to either write purchase contracts or modify existing orders. Hence, he said, he could only deliver the sports car in accordance with the terms of the written contract.

29

The next day I called Ace Motors and talked to Mr. Locker again. I demanded that he obtain the minivan for me. He refused. I then demanded that he return my $4,000 deposit. He refused, stating that he couldn't return my money since it was a deposit for a sports car, and they were ready to deliver a sports car.

You have brought suit to enforce the oral modification of the contract or, alternatively, for the return of the $4,000. The case is now on trial.

1.   For the plaintiff, conduct a direct examination of Smith.
2.   For the defendant, cross-examine Smith.

3.3 REFRESHING RECOLLECTION AND RECORDED RECOLLECTION

On February 15, [-1], there was a burglary at the Ace Hardware Store, located at 1050 North Main Street.

At about 3:00 A.M. that day, Logan Stone was walking on the sidewalk in front of the store on the way home from the nearby plant where s/he worked the night shift, 5:30 P.M. to 2:30 A.M. Stone saw a man run out of the store and jump into a large black sedan. The car sped away.

Stone, from about ten feet away, saw the license plate number of the car, ZQB-437, as it pulled away from the curb. S/he ran to his/her locked car, which was parked a half-block away, found a pencil and piece of paper in the glove compartment, and wrote down the license plate number. Stone then used a cellular telephone to call the police and report what s/he had just seen. Later, s/he gave Officer Arthur Jones the scrap of paper containing the license plate number.

Now, Fred Miller, the registered owner of the black car, is on trial for the burglary. Stone is called by the prosecution to testify about the license plate number on the black car that left the scene.

1. On direct examination, Stone is unable to remember the license plate number. Use the piece of paper to refresh Stone's memory of the number.

2. On direct examination, Stone cannot remember the license plate number, even after being shown the piece of paper. Get the paper or its contents in evidence.

3. For the prosecution, be prepared to conduct the entire direct examination.

4. For the defense, cross-examine Stone.

5. Assume that Stone testifies that the car s/he saw was a large *white* car. The defendant owns a white Lincoln Continental. For the defense, cross-examine Stone using Jones's police report.

ZQB-437

POLICE REPORT

Re: Burglary at 1050 North Main Street
To: Commanding Officer
From: Patrolman Arthur Jones

Reporting officer arrived at scene of reported burglary at 3:20 A.M. (2/15/[-1]). Interviewed witness Logan Stone. Said witness told reporting officer s/he saw a man run out of the Ace Hardware Store, 1050 North Main, at about 3 A.M. Witness further said the man jumped into a large black car and said car then sped away. S/he did not see the face of the man, but did note the number on the car license plate. Stone said s/he then ran to his/her own parked car and wrote down the license plate number. S/he gave the reporting officer the piece of paper with the license plate number on it.

Arthur Jones
Star number 1424

2/15/[-1]
600 hours

3.4 REFRESHING RECOLLECTION AND RECORDED RECOLLECTION

This is a contract action. Plaintiff, the First National Bank, is suing Smith Brothers Car Sales, a small local car dealer, alleging that the dealership violated its contract with the bank. The contract provided for recurring loans to the dealership each time it bought a new car. When the car was sold, the dealership was required to pay the bank the loan amount on the car, and the bank would then release its lien on the car.

In June, two years ago, the bank's president, Mortimer Jones, suspected that the dealership was selling cars "out of trust"—that is, was selling cars without using part of the proceeds to pay off the bank's loans. He sent one of the loan officers, Mel Jenkins, to the dealership to take a physical inventory of the cars on the lot so that Jones could then compare it with the bank's loan and lien records.

On June 30, two years ago, Jenkins went to the dealership and conducted the inventory and prepared a written record of the inventory results. Based on a comparison of the inventory with the bank's records, Jones directed the bank's attorneys to file this action.

The case is now on trial. The bank calls Jenkins as a witness. Jenkins, before coming to court today, went to the bank's loan records and pulled the inventory sheet, which s/he brought with him/her.

1. On direct examination, Jenkins is unable to remember the number of cars s/he saw on the lot during his/her inventory. Use the inventory sheet to refresh Jenkins' recollection.

2. On direct examination, Jenkins is unable to remember the car models, years, and vehicle identification numbers, even after being shown the inventory sheet. Get the sheet (or its contents) in evidence.

3. For the defendant, cross-examine Jenkins.

FIRST NATIONAL BANK

To: Mortimer Jones, President

        The following are the results of the floor and lot inventory I conducted at Smith Brothers Car Sales on June 30 at your request:

Car Model	Year	VIN
Chevrolet sedan	[-0]	YX43307J
"	"	BZ66237Q
"	"	YX56987J
"	"	GJ44512Q
	"	GJ98002Q
Chevrolet van	"	K4439856
"	"	K6742381
"	"	K9012376
"	"	K4438705
"	"	K6745001
Chevrolet Corvette	[-1]	J22341BX
Ford Mustang	[-2]	FX4409821
Buick Le Sabre	[-2]	B2341821Q

Mel Jenkins,
loan officer

39

3.5   HOMICIDE VICTIM'S WIDOW

This is a manslaughter prosecution. The manslaughter charge arises out of a tavern argument that turned into a brawl, during which the victim was killed when he was stabbed in the chest. The defense is self-defense.

The case is now on trial. To prove the identity of the victim and to show that the victim had no preexisting medical condition that could have caused his death, the prosecution will call the victim's widow, Mary Jones. Mrs. Jones can testify on direct examination that she last saw her husband, Frank Jones, the morning he was killed, May 15 of last year. At that time he was in perfect health. She next saw him late that evening in the county morgue. At that time he was dead.

1. For the prosecution, conduct a direct examination of Mary Jones.
2. For the defense, cross-examine Mary Jones as necessary.
3. For the prosecution, conduct any necessary redirect examination.

3.6 ALIBI WITNESS

This is a criminal case. The defendant, Elmer Barnes, is charged with robbery. The defense is alibi. The defendant claims that at the time of the robbery, June 15 of last year at 10:00 P.M., he was at home, about one-half mile from the scene of the robbery. He claims he didn't feel well that evening and had gone to bed around 9:30 P.M. The defendant, age 17, has no brothers or sisters. One of his parents is deceased. He was arrested and charged on July 3, [-1].

The case is now on trial. To support his alibi defense, the defense intends to call the defendant's mother/father, Peyton Barnes. Mr./Mrs. Barnes can testify that on the night in question, s/he was home all evening. Elmer came home about 7:00 P.M., watched television with him/her in the living room for a while, and went to bed shortly before 10:00 P.M. S/he went to bed a few minutes after he did, after the 9:00 P.M. news program ended.

Peyton Barnes has not previously told this to anyone other than the defense attorney. Police investigators attempted to interview him/her shortly before trial, but s/he told them s/he did not wish to talk to them.

1. For the defense, conduct a direct examination of Peyton Barnes.
2. For the prosecution, cross-examine Peyton Barnes as necessary.
3. For the defense, conduct any necessary redirect examination.

3.7 WITNESS TO CAR COLLISION

This is a personal injury case arising out of an automobile intersection collision that occurred on June 15 of last year. The plaintiff claims that he was driving eastbound on Main Street toward Elm Street, entered the intersection, and was struck by a car, driven by the defendant, that was going northbound on Elm. Plaintiff claims that the defendant ran the red light and was speeding.

The case is now on trial. Plaintiff calls Skylar Howard, who testified as follows, on July 15, [-1], at the Traffic Court case arising from this accident:

I was driving eastbound on Main Street toward the intersection of Elm Street on June 15, [-1], at approximately 8:30 A.M. I was on my way to work, about three miles away. It was the morning rush hour. The car and pedestrian traffic was normal for that time of day. Main Street is a commercial street with four lanes of traffic, two in each direction. Commercial stores and office buildings line Main and Elm.

As I was driving on Main Street, in the outside lane, there was another car ahead of me, perhaps half a block away. Both I and the other car were going perhaps 20 mph. As the car in front of me, a tan Ford sedan, the plaintiff's car, entered the intersection, the light turned yellow. As the Ford reached the far side of the intersection, another car, a beige Toyota, the defendant's car, going from right to left, suddenly entered the intersection and slammed into the right rear side of the Ford. The light was still yellow for Main Street at the moment of impact. The Toyota was speeding as it went into the intersection. I can't tell you how fast the Toyota was going in exact miles per hour, but it was going very fast.

I had worked for my present employer for five years, and my expected work hours were 8:30 A.M. to 5:00 P.M.

1. For the plaintiff, conduct a direct examination of Skylar Howard.
2. For the defendant, cross-examine Howard.

3.8 PEDESTRIAN AT CAR COLLISION

This is a negligence action brought by Leslie Morse against Frieda Smith. Morse gave the following written statement to Smith's insurance company investigator one month after the accident.

On January 15 of this year, at 9:30 P.M., I was walking on the sidewalk on the east side of Main Street northbound toward the intersection of Elm Street. The intersection is controlled by traffic signals.

Both Main Street and Elm Street have one lane of traffic in each direction and parking on both sides of the street. There are walk lights on each corner of the intersection, which is in a single-family residential neighborhood.

As I reached the southeast corner of the intersection, the traffic lights were green for the Elm Street traffic. I waited on the corner looking at the walk lights. When the lights changed and the walk light turned green, I started to cross Elm Street.

Suddenly I heard a loud screech, looked west, and saw a car driven by Smith skidding through the intersection. I tried to jump out of the way, slipped on the pavement, and was struck in the back by the front of Smith's car as I fell. The car was about five feet from me when I first saw it.

It had snowed slightly earlier in the day. At the time of the accident the streets were still wet, and the temperature was approximately 20 degrees.

I was coming from the grocery store, where I bought a quart of milk. I live at 2005 Main Street, about three blocks north of Elm.

Signed

Leslie Morse
_____
Leslie Morse

Date: February 15, [-2]

Witnessed:

James Lavery

James Lavery

Acme Insurance Co.

Investigator

1. For the plaintiff, conduct a direct examination of Morse.
2. For the plaintiff, conduct a direct examination of Morse, using the attached diagram of the intersection.
3. For the defendant, cross-examine Morse.

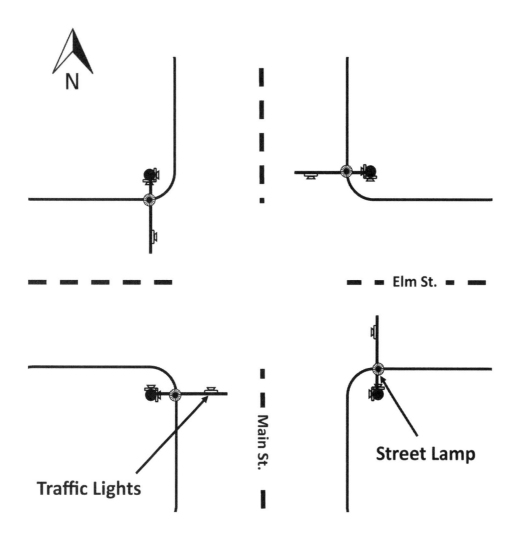

Elm St.

Main St.

Traffic Lights

Street Lamp

N

3.9 POLICE OFFICER ON SURVEILLANCE

This is an attempted burglary case brought against the defendant, Frank Johnson. The events on which the charge is based occurred on January 15 of last year. The principal evidence against the defendant was developed during the surveillance conducted by Officer Tony Barlow. Barlow's report states in pertinent part:

REPORT OF EVENTS: On 1/15/[-1], on midnight shift, assigned to surveillance of Jones's Electronics, a radio and TV repair shop located at 4318 N. Broadway. Store has been burglarized several times in past month, with entry always in the rear. Store is in high-crime area and backs up to large public housing project. Today received tip that another attempt would be made on store.

Arrived at location at 0045 hrs. in unmarked car, parked across street directly in front of store. Streets were lighted, traffic average. (Store is standard small store, with plate glass front, one light on inside. Other similar stores on either side. Narrow alley to left of store, leading to larger alley behind store.) At 0215 hrs. a black Ford sedan, older model, pulled up near front of store, two occupants. They talked for a few minutes, then passenger got out, sedan drove to next corner, lights and motor off. Driver remained in car. Passenger, a male, stood in front of store, apparently casing it, looked around to see if anyone was watching, then turned and walked down an alley adjacent to store, and disappeared behind it. A few minutes passed, then a burglary alarm went off. Moments later the passenger came running down the alley, looked around for the car, ran to the same car still parked on the corner, and jumped in.

Reporting officer made a U-turn, following sedan as it pulled away from the corner. A block later put on siren and lights, sedan speeded up, taking obvious evasive action by ducking down side streets and alleys. Finally curbed sedan at 4700 N. Pearl, arrested two occupants, who said nothing. Passenger identified himself as Frank Johnson, age 17. Driver was juvenile. Car had several empty beer cans on back seat.

51

Both offenders handcuffed, placed in rear of car, and returned to scene of burglary. Inspected rear of store; window broken, apparently setting off alarm. No other persons in area at time.

INVESTIGATION CLEARED AND CLOSED.

Officer Barlow has been a police officer for 12 years, the last 6 as a burglary detective.

1. For the prosecution, conduct a direct examination of Officer Barlow.
2. For the defense, cross-examine Officer Barlow.

3.10   POLICE OFFICER AT SEXUAL ASSAULT SCENE

This is a criminal case that involves the alleged aggravated sexual assault of the victim, Darlene Smith, by the defendant, James Hill. The attack occurred on January 15 of last year. The issue in the case is the accuracy of Ms. Smith's identification of the defendant. Ms. Smith was the prosecution's first witness. She positively identified the defendant as her assailant. She said there was enough light from a nightlight to recognize him. Officer Sean Connors is now called to testify.

You have the police report of Officer Connors. The narrative portion of the officer's report states the following:

NARRATIVE OF EVENTS: On 1/15/[-1] at approx. 0415 hrs., while on routine patrol, received flash message "Rape at 901 Main, 2nd Floor." Proceeded to location, up to 2nd floor of two-story flat (outside doors unlocked), knocked on door, no answer. Pushed door open, saw a woman, now identified as Darlene Smith of same address, sitting on couch. Victim was dressed in nightgown, obviously distraught. As I walked in, she looked up, realized I was a police officer, and immediately said: "I've just been raped." I attempted to comfort the victim, called for an ambulance, and did a quick search of apt.

Victim stated that she was sleeping in her bedroom, heard a noise, looked up, and saw someone moving in the room. She said, "Who's there?" and was suddenly grabbed by the throat. A man with a deep voice said, "Just do as I say and you won't get hurt." She said she saw the man's face for about 30 seconds just after he grabbed her throat. Victim said that the man then sexually assaulted her and ran out the front of the apt. After a few minutes, she got up and called the police from the living room phone.

Ambulance attendants arrived, took victim to St. Mary's Hospital ER. Conducted search of bedroom after turning on overhead light; victim's bed was messed up, obviously the scene of a struggle. A window was broken out on the kitchen door leading to the back porch. (The apt. has a living room off the

53

front stairs, a bedroom, bath, with kitchen in rear.) The kitchen door was the apparent point of entry.

On 1/18/[-1] did follow-up interview of Ms. Smith at her apt. Noted dark blue bruise marks on her neck and face, and moving head carefully. Victim stated the bruises came from the offender grabbing her. She further stated that the hospital discharged her the next morning and that the tests were positive for the presence of semen. She was also positive that she could identify the man if she ever saw him again.

INVESTIGATION CONTINUES. . . .

Officer Connors has been a police officer for six years, always in the patrol division. On the night of the assault s/he was working the first watch (midnight to 8:00 A.M.) on routine patrol in a police car.

1. For the prosecution, conduct a direct examination of Officer Connors.
2. For the defense, cross-examine Officer Connors.

3.11 ROBBERY VICTIM

This is an armed robbery and aggravated kidnapping prosecution brought against the defendant, Charles Tucker. In this jurisdiction, an aggravated kidnapping is a kidnapping committed while the perpetrator is armed with a dangerous weapon. The complainant is Corey Johnson. The alleged crimes occurred on June 15 of last year. You have the police report of the investigating officer, Robert Jones. The narrative portion of his report states the following:

NARRATIVE OF EVENTS: On 6/15/[-1] at approx. 2330 hrs., the victim, Corey Johnson, was walking northbound on the east side of Elm Street. Area is residential w/street lights—victim had left a neighbor's house, where s/he had been playing cards, and was on the way home 2 blocks away.

Suddenly s/he sensed someone behind him/her and started to turn. As s/he turned, s/he saw the offender's face for two or three seconds. That was the only time s/he saw his face, but s/he had a "good look" at him. The offender (later identified as Charles Tucker) grabbed him/her around the neck, choking him/her. S/he tried to scream, but couldn't. The offender said he had a knife and told him/her not to scream or he'd stab him/her. Victim felt a cold hard object pressed against his/her neck. Offender then forced him/her down an alley, still holding him/her by the neck with one hand, to the rear of an adjoining building. (There were no lights in the alley, but victim states that there was enough light from street lights to see the assailant.) Offender ordered victim to lie face down and not move.

Offender threatened to kill him/her if s/he called the police, took victim's backpack, and walked down the alley to the street. Victim then waited a minute and ran to his/her house, where s/he immediately called the police, stating what had happened and describing the assailant as a white male, approx. 20 yrs. old, 5′8″ tall, medium build, wearing dark pants and shirt. Description broadcast.

One squad went to victim's house. About same time another squad saw man fitting description on Elm Street about two blocks from where robbery occurred, in opposite direction from victim's home. Victim was transported in squad car to location where man was detained. As that squad car pulled up to location, victim, who was sitting on back seat of squad car, suddenly blurted out, "That's the man who just robbed me!" and pointed to offender, Charles Tucker.

INVESTIGATION CONTINUES. . . .

The case is now on trial.

1.   For the prosecution, conduct a direct examination of Johnson.
2.   For the defense, cross-examine Johnson.

3.12 ACCIDENT VICTIM

Two years ago Jayden French came to your office with the following statement s/he had given an investigator for Ralph Jones's insurance company:

On June 1, [-2], at approximately 3:00 P.M., I was driving my car northbound on Clark Street toward Division Street. When I reached Division the light turned yellow, so I stopped at the intersection. Just as I stopped my car, a Honda Civic, I heard a loud screeching sound, like brakes being applied hard. I looked into my rearview mirror and saw a large American make of car almost on top of me. Before I could react, the car ran into the rear of my car.

The force of the crash threw me back against the seat and snapped my head backward. I felt a sharp pain at the base of my neck and was momentarily dazed by the force of the crash. After a minute or so, I got out of my car and talked to the driver of the other car, Ralph Jones. We exchanged our names and other information. I was able to drive my car home.

The next morning my neck was painful, and it was too stiff to move. I saw my family doctor, Edmond Gaines, who said I had a classic whiplash injury and prescribed bed rest, heat, and a cervical collar.

For the next week I stayed at home, in bed, applying heat from a hot water bottle at regular intervals. The pain and stiffness prevented me from doing anything and kept me from sleeping. The following week I returned to work, but I still wore the neck brace for two more weeks, and the neck was still painful, especially when I moved it. As the weeks went by the pain gradually decreased in severity, although it still prevented me from doing my usual types of physical activities, such as yard work and sports such as tennis or swimming.

Only in the past week or so has the pain generally subsided, so that I'm finally able to return essentially to normal. I'm still cautious in using my neck, since I'm afraid to strain it and have a relapse. I'm still apprehensive about driving my car, since I obviously don't want the same thing to happen twice.

As far as my financial losses are concerned, it cost $3,800 to repair my car, I lost $2,200 from being out of work for one week, and my doctor's bill was $1,500.

Jayden French
July 15, [-2]

You have brought suit on behalf of Jayden French against Ralph Jones, charging that Jones negligently operated his automobile and caused French's injuries. Your suit asks for all proper damages. The case is now on trial.

1. For the plaintiff, conduct a direct examination of Jayden French.
2. For the defendant, cross-examine French.

3.13   BATTERY VICTIM: CHANGED TESTIMONY

You are the assistant district attorney prosecuting a battery case against the defendant, Phillip Dunn. The victim, Ann Rodd, was standing in front of her home at 4216 S. Ellis on December 11 of last year, at about 6:00 P.M. At that time a man she had never seen before walked up to her and struck her in the face with his right fist. She screamed. Then he ran away. When the police arrived, minutes later, she described her assailant as being a male, about 30 years of age, medium build, and about 5′6″ tall.

The defendant, Phillip Dunn, was arrested a week later based on a description given to a police artist by Rodd. Dunn is 6′ tall, 28 years old, and weighs about 170 pounds. Rodd is 5′4″ tall.

On December 12, the day after the attack, the police prepared a supplementary report on the case, which states:

> SUPPLEMENTARY REPORT—CORRECTION: Victim originally described her assailant as being 5′6″ to Det. James Lanners, #2763, who was preparing information to be used for publication in the daily Police Dept. Bulletin. Reporting officer received a telephone call from Mrs. Rodd on December 12 at about 1930 hours, and she stated that upon standing up in her hospital room at the Swedish Covenant Hospital for the first time since the assault in the presence of her husband she realized that the offender was taller than she had advised Det. Lanners. She stated that based on a comparison with her husband, who is 5′10″ tall, the assailant was approx. 6′ tall. This change was immediately forwarded, enabling the Graphic Arts Section to make the correction in Bulletin #19-314 for December 14.

1. For the prosecution, conduct a direct examination of Rodd. How will you handle the change in height description?
2. For the defense, cross-examine Rodd.

3.14   ACCIDENT INVESTIGATOR AT INTERSECTION COLLISION

On January 15, two years ago, an automobile accident occurred between the plaintiff, Jack Joseph, and the defendant, Charles Frederick, at the intersection of Main Street and Elm Avenue. Plaintiff's insurance company, Universal Casualty Insurance Company, sent a traffic accident investigator, Willy Snoop, to the site of the accident the moment it heard about it. Snoop's report states:

UNIVERSAL CASUALTY INSURANCE CO.

Accident Report

Date: 1/15/[-2]

Time: 8:30 P.M.

Location: Main and Elm

Insured: Jack Joseph

REPORT OF EVENTS: On above date and time, arrived at above location pursuant to home office radio dispatch. On arrival, parties and police still there and interviewed. Measured intersection, location of cars, prepared attached diagram. Car #1 (Joseph) had extensive damage on front. Car #2 (Frederick) had extensive damage on its right side, from rear door to rear bumper. Damage indicated at least moderate speed at impact. Interviewed drivers: Joseph stated he was going through intersection southbound on Main Street with green light when Car #2 suddenly turned left and cut in front of him. Joseph said he tried to stop but couldn't. Frederick stated he was in the intersection, facing north, the light turned yellow, so he made a left turn onto Elm Avenue but the oncoming car (#1) ran the yellow light. Police officer at scene stated that he'd also interviewed Frederick within minutes of the accident, but Frederick never claimed that the light had turned yellow.

Officer gave Frederick ticket for failure to yield right-of-way. (See attached diagram.)

Willy Snoop

Willy Snoop

Snoop, a retired police officer who worked primarily in the traffic division for 18 years, has worked for Universal for three years investigating accidents. The case is now on trial. S/he has no formal training in accident reconstruction.

In this jurisdiction a driver may not enter an intersection on a yellow light. If a driver seeking to make a turn is lawfully in an intersection when the light turns yellow, s/he may complete the turn if s/he can do so safely.

1. For the plaintiff, conduct a direct examination of Snoop.
2. For the plaintiff, conduct a direct examination of Snoop, using the following diagram to illustrate his testimony.
3. For the defendant, cross-examine Snoop.

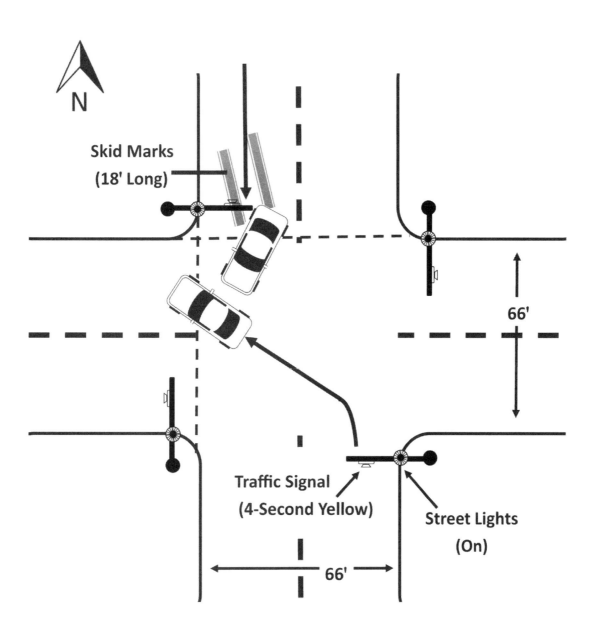

3.15 ROBBERY VICTIM AND BANK DIAGRAM

Avery Stern is the manager of the Second Federal Savings and Loan Association. One year ago today, at about 10:00 A.M., Stern was sitting behind the desk in his/her office in the rear of the bank when s/he heard a gunshot.

S/he jumped up, ran out the door of his/her office and five feet to the left into the hallway. S/he saw a man with a handgun, whom s/he now identifies as the defendant, Ralph Switzer. The defendant was standing about 20 feet away, at one of the tellers' windows.

Stern says that the defendant turned his head, looked momentarily right at him/her, then turned around and ran through the lobby and out the bank's front door.

1. For the prosecution, conduct a direct examination of Stern.
2. For the prosecution, conduct a direct examination of Stern, using the following diagram to illustrate his testimony. The diagram was prepared under Stern's supervision two weeks after the robbery. It is drawn to scale.
3. For the prosecution, conduct a direct examination of Stern, using the diagram to illustrate his testimony. The diagram was prepared under Stern's supervision two weeks after the robbery. It is not drawn to scale.
4. For the defense, cross-examine Stern.

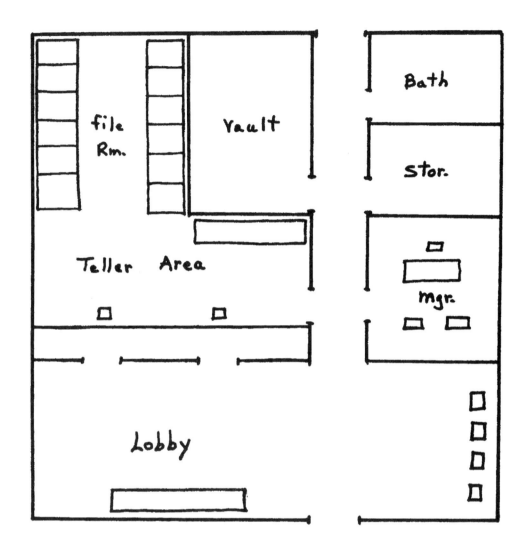

Second Federal Savings and Loan Association

Scale: 1" = 10'

3.16   ROBBERY VICTIM AND LINEUP PHOTOGRAPH

On January 15 of last year, Devon Bradley was robbed of a computer bag by two young men as Bradley was walking at approximately 11:00 P.M. from his/her parking lot to his/her apartment building. The parking lot is next to the building and, while it has no lights of its own, it is illuminated by a street light directly across from the lot.

When the police arrived, Bradley gave them a description of the two men. S/he described each as being about 25 years old, white, approximately 5′10″ tall, 175 pounds in weight, wearing blue jeans and white T-shirts. Neither had a beard, moustache, unusual-looking hair, or other noticeable features.

Three days later the police called Bradley and asked him/her to come to the station to view a lineup. When s/he arrived, Bradley was asked to look at the persons in the lineup and, if s/he recognized anyone as one of his/her assailants, to point him out. After looking at the lineup, Bradley identified the second person from the left, defendant Samuel Jones.

1.   For the prosecution, conduct a direct examination of Bradley.
2.   For the prosecution, conduct a direct examination of Bradley, using the attached photograph to illustrate his/her testimony.
3.   For the defense, cross-examine Bradley.
4.   Assume that Bradley, after viewing the lineup, is unable to identify anyone as the robber. At trial, the prosecution on direct examination introduces no evidence about the lineup, although Bradley does identify the defendant in court as the robber. You have the lineup photograph. For the defense, cross-examine Bradley.

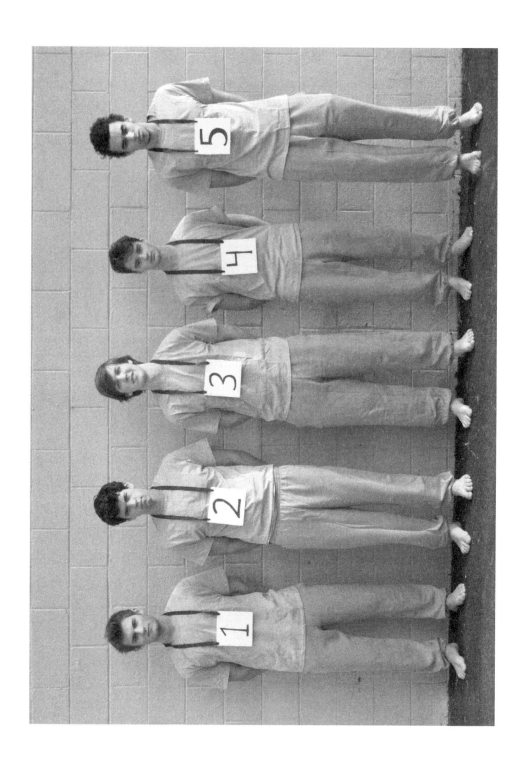

3.17   RECORDS WITNESS AND EXHIBIT

This is a negligence action arising out of an automobile accident on July 27, [-1]. As part of the damages aspects of his case, plaintiff Charles Sampson intends to call Blair Jones, the bookkeeper at his place of work, ABC Warehouse Storage Company, to introduce a payroll record.

Prior to trial you interview Jones, who brings the attached payroll sheet. S/he explains that the warehouse supervisor keeps time cards for each employee and sends him/her the time cards at the end of each work week. Jones computes the gross wages for each employee, based on hours worked and hourly wage rate, then enters the amount on the appropriate payroll sheet. While the number of employees at ABC varies, there is an average of around 40 employees at any given time.

Jones has worked for ABC for nine years; two as a clerk, four as an administrative assistant, and the past three years as the bookkeeper. In addition to preparing payroll sheets, s/he maintains the time cards, prepares payroll checks, and does all the bookkeeping for the company's receipts and expenditures.

1.   For the plaintiff, conduct a direct examination of Jones.
2.   For the defendant, cross-examine Jones.

	ABC Warehouse Storage Company		
	Business Office: 40 E. Congress		
	Warehouse: 4318 Broadway		
	Payroll Sheet, 3rd Quarter, [-1]		
	(warehouse inspectors)		

Week Ending	Tom Fields		Charles Sampson		Ted Smith	
7/5	417.00		424.00			V
7/12	417.00		424.00		410.00	
7/19	417.00		424.00		410.00	
7/26		V	424.00		410.00	
8/2		V		SL	451.00	OT
8/9		V		SL	451.00	OT
8/16	463.00	OT		SL	410.00	
8/23	463.00	OT		SL	410.00	
8/30	444.00	OT		SL	410.00	
9/6	470.00	OT	212.00	PT	410.00	
9/13	453.00	OT	212.00	PT	410.00	
9/20	417.00		424.00			V
9/27	417.00		424.00			V
OV: overtime	PT: part time		V: vacation		SL: sick leave	

3.18   CHARACTER WITNESS

Arthur Bowen has been charged with the crimes of theft and battery. The theft charge is based on Bowen's alleged shoplifting of merchandise from a Sears store. The battery charge is based on Bowen's alleged striking of a Sears security guard, who accused Bowen of shoplifting. These incidents happened one year ago today.

The case is now on trial. Bowen has already testified on his own behalf. He then calls as a witness his next next-door neighbor, Carson Fern, who has known Bowen for six years. Fern has been a social friend and a co-worker of Bowen for those years. Both work as salespeople for Acme Insurance Company.

As next-door neighbors, Fern and Bowen see each other almost every week. They socialize regularly with other neighbors, which includes cookouts in their back yards, going out to dinner at neighborhood places, and being involved in their children's sports events and other school activities. As salespeople for Acme Insurance, Fern and Bowen both work in and out of the office meeting prospective clients and handling established clients' needs. Fern and Bowen are in the office at least one day a week attending sales staff meetings and doing paperwork.

1. For the defense, put in evidence the appropriate character trait of the defendant for each charge. Assume that this jurisdiction has adopted the Federal Rules of Evidence.
2. Use the same information as in No. 1, except that this jurisdiction permits only reputation evidence.
3. For the prosecution, cross-examine Fern.

The prosecution then decides to attack the defendant's testimonial veracity. It calls as a witness Max Palm, another co-worker of Bowen for one year. Palm, also a salesperson at Acme Insurance, has known Bowen for one year.

Palm was assigned to Bowen during his/her probationary training period, which lasted six months. During that time s/he was with Bowen every day, learning how to sell insurance and handle client problems. With the probationary period over, Palm now works on his/her own but still sees Bowen regularly, particularly during the weekly sales staff meetings. S/he believes Bowen is unethical and untruthful. On one occasion, s/he found Bowen had falsified an insurance application in order to earn a commission, but s/he did not report the incident.

4. For the prosecution, put in evidence the appropriate character trait of the defendant. Assume that this jurisdiction has adopted the Federal Rules of Evidence.

5. Use the same information as in No. 4, except that this jurisdiction permits only reputation evidence.

6. For the defense, cross-examine Palm.

3.19 ADVERSE WITNESS

This is a personal injury action brought by Charles Smith against Jamie Watson and the Jacobs Construction Company. Smith was injured when the car he was driving was struck by a truck driven by Watson, a truck driver employed by Jacobs Construction, who was hauling building materials in a company truck to a construction site when the accident happened. The accident occurred June 1, [-2].

Jacobs Construction in its answer admitted Watson was an employee, but denied Watson was on a company job at the time of the accident.

Under the law of this jurisdiction, plaintiff, to establish a prima facie case against Jacobs Construction, must show that Watson was an employee or agent of the company and was working within the scope of his/her employment at the time of the accident. If this is established, any negligence on Watson's part will be imputed to Jacobs Construction.

During discovery, plaintiff took Watson's deposition, part of which is attached. The case is now on trial.

1. For the plaintiff, call Watson as an adverse witness and establish the required proof.
2. For the plaintiff, introduce Watson's deposition for the same purpose.
3. For defendant Jacobs Construction, conduct any further appropriate examination.
4. For defendant Watson, conduct any further appropriate examination.

DEPOSITION OF JAMIE WATSON,

Taken, under oath, on 10/1/[-2]

at office of Frank Tucker,

10 E. Congress St. #500

Jamie Watson, having first been duly sworn, testified
as follows:

p. 14

1 Q. by Thomas Jones, one of the plaintiff's lawyers)
2   Where were you working on June 1, [-2], the day
3   of the collision?
4 A. I was at Jacobs Construction. I'm still there.
5 Q. How long had you worked at Jacobs Construction, as
6   of June 1?
7 A. About five years.
8 Q. What kind of work did you do for the company?
9 A. I was a truck driver supervisor.
10 Q. Was that your job on June 1?
11 A. Yes.
12 Q. What were your hours that day?
13 A. The usual—8:00 A.M. to 4:00 P.M.
14 Q. When did the collision happen?
15 A. Around 3:00 P.M.
16 Q. What were you doing at that time?
17 A. I was delivering some lumber to one of our
18   construction sites.
19 Q. Whose truck was it?
20 A. It was one of the company's flatbed trucks.
21 Q. Who gave you that assignment?
22
23 p. 15
24 A. Bobby Jackson.
25 Q. Who's he?

26 A. He's the dispatcher at the company office that
27   gives out all the jobs for the drivers.
28 Q. Jamie, you no longer work as a supervisor for
29   Jacobs Construction, is that correct?
30 A. Right. I was demoted.
31 Q. When did you stop working as a supervisor?
32 A. June 2.
33 Q. That was the day after the collision?
34 A. Right.
35 Q. Did anyone tell you why they were demoting you?
36 A. Well, Mr. Braverman, he's the head of personnel,
37   told me I was being demoted because "they couldn't
38   afford to keep me as a supervisor anymore."
39 Q. Did anyone else say why they were demoting you?
40 A. Well, the word was that I was going to be the
41   fall guy, to let the other drivers know what would
42   happen if they ever got the company into any
43   lawsuit that would cost it money.
44 Q. Do you know who said that?
45 A. Not really, but I figure somebody in management
46   would have.

3.20   STIPULATIONS

Prepare two written stipulations, in whatever form you consider appropriate, to get the following facts in evidence. You may add any reasonable facts necessary to the stipulation that are not included in the problem. Be prepared to present the stipulation to the jury in the most effective way.

1. Mary Jones has worked in the records department of Rush Hospital for three years. Her job includes filing, retrieving, and copying hospital records.

The records of the hospital are kept in the records department at all times, and include such common records as emergency room reports, progress notes, nurses' notes, reports of operations, and X-ray reports, as well as various laboratory reports. These reports are routinely sent to the records department after they have been prepared at various locations in the hospital.

A subpoena directed to Rush Hospital was sent to Jones. She searched the patient records under "Helen Smith," the name on the subpoena, and found the attached record.

2. Dr. William Burns, a Cook County medical examiner's office pathologist, performed an autopsy on a James Johnson. A copy of his report is attached.

RUSH-PRESBYTERIAN-ST. LUKE'S MEDICAL CENTER 1753 West Congress Parkway

EMERGENCY ROOM / ACUTE CARE

HOSP. # 2

TIME IN: 10:30 (A.M.) P.M. TIME OUT: 1:30 A.M. (P.M.)

PATIENT NAME: Helen Smith	DATE: 2 May (-1)	CLINIC # OR INVOICE #:

ADDRESS: 6000 W. 26st, #100, CITY: Cicero, STATE: Ill. ZIP CODE: TELEPHONE:

EMPLOYER: 22 Federal S + L BIRTHDATE: AGE: SEX: F RACE: W CIVIL STATUS: ☐S ☐M ☐W ☐D ☐SEP

ADDRESS: TELEPHONE: INSURANCE (B.C./B.S. OTHER):

INS. OR B.C./B.S. #: PUBLIC AID #: CASE NAME:

NEXT OF KIN OR EMERGENCY ADDRESSEE NAME: TELEPHONE:

ADDRESS: CITY STATE ZIP CODE

BROUGHT IN BY: CFD ambulance ACCIDENT LOCATION: POLICE INVESTIGATION: ☒Yes ☐No

ATTENDING DOCTOR OR SOURCE OF PRIMARY CARE: ☐IN AREA ☐OUT OF AREA

SUBJECTIVE:

Patient stated she was shot in lower left leg near ankle, by the same man who robbed the bank that morning.

OBJECTIVE: T 98.6 P 72 R 18/min. B/P 110/70

Physical Exam:

Pallor, with organsystems (HEENT, h, l, abd) within normal limits.

· Open wound (0.5 x 0.5 cm) anterior-lateral aspect distal third left lower leg with venous oozing. Marked tenderness and swelling of wound area with crepitation of bone.

CONSULTATION:

PROBLEM(S):

Gunshot wound distal lower left leg, Fx left tibia and fibula.

PLAN:

Admit.

DIAGNOSTIC STUDIES:

CBC, u/A, EKG, chest X-ray, lytes X-ray; left lower leg

Campbell
Physician's Signature

_____
Nurse's Signature

INSTRUCTION TO: _____ DATE: _____
(Patient's Name) (Hospital #)

NEXT VISIT TO: _____
(Physician or Institution)

IMPRESSION AND INSTRUCTION:

PHYSICIAN'S OR NURSE'S SIGNATURE: _____ PATIENT'S _____

FORM # 3797 3/77

MEDICAL RECORDS

85

MEDICAL EXAMINER

Ellis Smith, M.D., Medical Examiner

Report of Findings
Name: James Johnson, of 3318 W. Congress
       5'8", 167 lbs., M/W

Identifying witness: Myrna Johnson, 3318 W. Congress,
                              (wife of deceased)

Date of Examination: October 30, [-1], at 1:45 p.m.

Date of Injury: October 28, [-1]

Location: 3318 W. Congress

How occurred: Multiple injuries to head-chest

Nature of injury: Accident____; Suicide____; Homicide__x__;
                   Unknown____.

Death was caused by: a.___Multiple injuries_____

                      b._____

                      c._____

Pathological findings: (external and internal)

        1. Multiple contusions, face-head-neck-chest
        2. Multiple fractures, larynx-cricoid
        3. Multiple fractures, anterior ribs, third through
            eighth
        4. Multiple contusions, brain
        5. Subdural and epidural hemorrhage
        6. Intraorbital hemorrhage, left and right
        7. Intramuscular hemorrhage, anterior and posterior
            to chest and abdominal areas, extensive
        8. Multiple contusions, heart

                          Examination performed by:

                          ___William Burns_____
                          William Burns, M.D.
                          Forensic Pathologist

3.21 JUDICIAL NOTICE

1. Get the following facts in evidence through judicial notice. Assume that each fact is relevant to the issues in the case on trial, which is a civil case.

(a) Broadway in midtown Manhattan is a busy street during rush hour.

(b) In January, the ground in Montana is usually frozen.

(c) On October 5, [-2], the moon was full.

(d) November 11 is a legal holiday on which banks are closed.

(e) The life expectancy of a white male presently 40 years of age is 36.3 years.

(f) On June 1, [-1], the blood alcohol content limit under Illinois law for a driver over the age of 21 was 0.08. (Assume that the trial is in a jurisdiction other than Illinois.)

(g) The government of Kazakhstan has no extradition treaty with the United States.

2. How will you get the judge to inform the jury of the judicially noticed facts?

3. What differences would result if the trial were criminal?

4. As the opponent, oppose the introduction of the facts in each instance.

IV

EXHIBITS

Introduction

4.1   Gun

4.2   Monogrammed Card Case

4.3   Knife

4.4   Sexual Assault Evidence Collection Kit

4.5   Brake Tube

4.6   Photograph of Police Officers and Plaintiff

4.7   Photographs of Accident Victim

4.8   Photograph of Building

4.9   Photograph of Building

4.10 Photograph of Building

4.11 Diagram of Intersection

4.12 Diagram of House

4.13 Map

4.14 Promissory Note

4.15 Contract

4.16 Photocopies of Check

4.17 Letters

4.18 Stock Purchase Order

4.19 Theft Report

4.20 Accident Report

4.21 Time Card

4.22 Deposit and Withdrawal Slips

INTRODUCTION

The problems in this chapter deal with the kinds of exhibits that are commonly introduced in evidence during civil and criminal trials.

For each problem, you should be prepared to establish a foundation that is legally sufficient to admit the exhibit in evidence and that maximizes its persuasive effect. In addition, you should be prepared to introduce the exhibit at a time when it reinforces and complements the witness's direct examination. Finally, you should be prepared to publish the exhibit to the jury at the most advantageous time and in the most persuasive way.

Most of the witnesses do not have background information. Be prepared to develop realistic, credible backgrounds for them.

Your instructor may modify the assignments and make specific additional assignments for these exercises.

The suggested background reading is Mauet & Easton, *Trial Techniques and Trials*, Chapter 7.

4.1　GUN

This is an unlawful possession of a concealed weapon prosecution. A police officer, Fran Smith, arrested the defendant, Earl Jones, after a search that produced a revolver from his coat pocket.

Officer Smith recorded the following information about the seized revolver in his/her report: a .38 caliber Smith and Wesson revolver, 2″ barrel, stainless steel with wood handle.

Before giving the weapon to the police department's evidence section, Officer Smith placed his/her initials and date on the revolver: "2/8/[-1]—FRS."

1. For the prosecution, get the gun in evidence. (Prepare and bring an appropriate exhibit to class.)
2. Assume that this is an armed robbery prosecution. Officer Smith has testified to the seizure of the gun from Jones. The victim, Sandy Wilson, is now testifying. S/he identifies the defendant as the man who took his/her wallet at gunpoint on February 6, [-1]. The victim describes the defendant's gun as a "shiny revolver with a short barrel" but can only say that the exhibit "looks similar to" the one used by the defendant during the robbery. For the prosecution, get the gun in evidence during Wilson's testimony.
3. For the defense, oppose the offers.

4.2 MONOGRAMMED CARD CASE

This is a burglary prosecution. Someone broke into the home of Dakota Fran Dickinson, the burglary victim, sometime during the day on June 15 of last year. Three weeks later, the police found the attached item in a trash barrel in the defendant's backyard.

When the item was shown to Dickinson, s/he stated that it was a brass business card case with his/her initials monogrammed on it, given to him/her as a Christmas present two or three years ago by his/her husband/wife. S/he kept it on the dresser in his/her bedroom.

1. For the prosecution, get the card case in evidence. (Prepare and bring an appropriate exhibit to class.)
2. For the defense, oppose the offer.

4.3 KNIFE

This is an armed robbery prosecution. On June 15 of last year at about 11:00 P.M., Lee Thompson was robbed at knifepoint in the 1900 block of Clark Street. The robbery occurred on the sidewalk in the middle of the block at the entrance to an alley.

Thompson described the knife to the police as a "small dark pocketknife with a blade about two inches long." Dallas O'Leary, a police officer who arrived at the scene of the robbery, found a knife fitting that description in an open trash barrel in the alley, about 30 feet down the alley from the sidewalk where Thompson told the officer s/he had been robbed. When it was shown to him/her, Thompson stated that this knife looked "just like" the one used to rob him/her, but s/he couldn't say for sure it was the same one. Thompson has identified the defendant, Marshall Harris, as the man who robbed him/her with a knife.

Now, at trial, both Thompson and O'Leary are available as witnesses. Since finding the knife, Officer O'Leary has kept it in his/her locked locker at the police station and has brought it to court today. S/he did not place any labels or markings on the knife.

1. For the prosecution, get the knife in evidence. (Prepare and bring an appropriate exhibit to class.)
2. For the defense, oppose the offer.

4.4 SEXUAL ASSAULT EVIDENCE COLLECTION KIT

This is a criminal sexual assault prosecution. The defendant is accused of sexually assaulting Phyllis Moore on September 20, [-1], in Springfield, Massachusetts.

After the alleged assault, Moore was treated and examined by Dr. Ralph C. Tucker of Western New England Hospital. Dr. Tucker took a vaginal swab of the victim. He then placed the specimen onto a slide that he sealed into an envelope with the printed kit number 46740, initialed the slide "RCT," and checked the box for "yes" in response to the question, "Was sample collected?"

Dr. Tucker then sealed the envelope into a Sexual Assault Evidence Collection Kit box with the same number, 46740. In response to the "Incident Reported to Police?" question on the kit's cover, Dr. Tucker checked the box for "Yes: If yes, record victim's name here" and wrote the name "Phyllis Moore." He then checked the box for "No" in response to the question "Other evidence (e.g., clothing) submitted in transport bag?" Then he filled in the following information, in his handwriting: For "Hospital/Clinic," he wrote "Western New England Hospital"; for "Phone number/ext.," he wrote "(413) 787-2903"; for "Clinicians," he wrote "N/A"; for "Kit sealed by," he wrote "Dr. Ralph Tucker"; for "Placed by," he wrote "Hand delivered to Officer Robert Jacobs"; for "Date," he wrote "Sept. 20, [-1]"; for "Time," he wrote "11:32," and then he circled "P.M."

Dr. Tucker then handed the sealed box to Springfield Police Officer Robert L. Jacobs, who was in the emergency room waiting area. When Officer Jacobs received the sealed box, he wrote the following information on it: For "Received from," he wrote "Dr. Ralph Tucker"; for "Medical Facility," he wrote "Western New England Hospital"; for "Police identification no.," he wrote "Badge No. 4264," which is his badge number; for "Date," he wrote "9/20/[-1]"; for "Time," he wrote "23:32"; for "Received by," he wrote "Off. Robert Jacobs."

Officer Jacobs then drove to his precinct headquarters. At the precinct headquarters, he wrote the phrase "To precinct vault, 9/21/[-1], 0:12 A.M., RLJ" next to "Agency"; then "9/21/[-1]" after "Date," and "0:12" after "Time." He then placed the sealed box in the precinct's locked vault.

On September 27, [-1], Officer Jacobs removed the sealed box from the vault, drove to the State Crime Lab, and delivered it to Dr. Ashton Jones, the laboratory pathologist. Just before handing the sealed box to Dr. Jones, Officer Jacobs wrote the following entries on the outside of the box: For "Received from," he wrote "Officer Robert Jacobs"; for "Medical Facility," he wrote "Springfield P.D."; for "Police Identification No.," he wrote "Badge No. 4264"; for "Date," he wrote "9/27/[-1]"; for "Time," he wrote "9:24."

After receiving the box from Officer Jacobs, Dr. Jones wrote the following entries on the bottom of the box: For "Received by," s/he wrote "Dr. Ashton Jones"; for "Agency," s/he wrote "State Crime Lab"; for "Date," s/he wrote "Sep. 27, [-1]"; for "Time," s/he wrote "9:24," then s/he circled "A.M."

After receiving the box, Dr. Jones opened it. S/he then opened the envelope and examined the slide under a microscope. Dr. Jones's examination indicated the presence of semen in the specimen. Dr. Jones had not seen the specimen before September 27. After examining the slide, Dr. Jones put it back into the envelope. S/he kept the envelope containing the slide in his/her laboratory until today, when s/he brought it to court.

Two weeks before this trial began, Officer Robert Jacobs died of a heart attack. No other police officer saw the box in question.

Assume that Dr. Tucker has testified to preparing the vaginal swab and slide and to sealing the slide into the envelope, then sealing the envelope into the box. He says he delivered the box to Officer Jacobs. He does not know what Officer Jacobs did with the box.

There are no other documents concerning this specimen.

The case is now on trial. Phyllis Moore has already testified. The witness is Dr. Jones.

1. For the prosecution, get the kit in evidence, assuming that Dr. Tucker testified he sealed the envelope and box and recognizes the box as the one he delivered to Officer Jacobs on September 20. (Prepare and bring an appropriate exhibit to class.)

2. For the defense, oppose the offer.

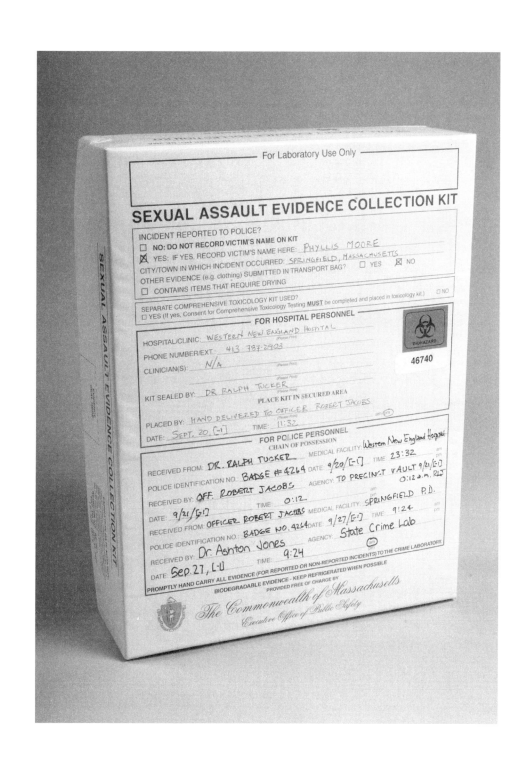

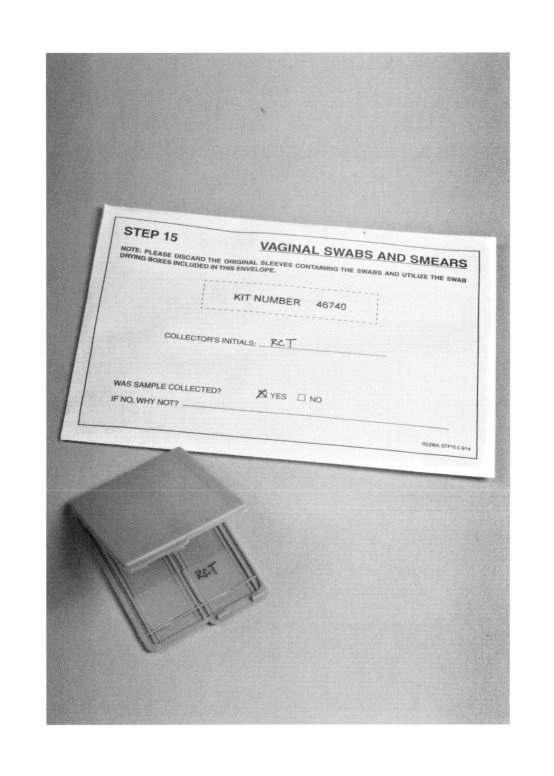

STEP 15

VAGINAL SWABS AND SMEARS

NOTE: PLEASE DISCARD THE ORIGINAL SLEEVES CONTAINING THE SWABS AND UTILIZE THE SWAB
DRYING BOXES INCLUDED IN THIS ENVELOPE.

KIT NUMBER   46740

COLLECTOR'S INITIALS: RCT

WAS SAMPLE COLLECTED?   ☒ YES   ☐ NO
IF NO, WHY NOT?

RE2MA: STP15.5 3/14

4.5   BRAKE TUBE

This is a products liability action brought against an automobile manufacturer. The plaintiff alleges that a rubber brake hose was defectively designed and manufactured, resulting in a brake failure and accident.

On June 15 of last year, Riley Schmidt, an accident investigator, went to the corner of Maple and Elm Streets, where a collision between two cars had just occurred. S/he prepared the following report:

> I examined one of the two cars involved, a [-3] Ford sedan, Vehicle Identification No. AZ4180772. During my examination I removed a rubber brake hose from the brake assembly of the car's left rear wheel.
>
> After removing the hose, which was about 12″ long, I wrapped it in a plastic bag, then placed it in a small cardboard box. I put shipping tape on all the edges of the box, prepared an address label, which I then glued to the box, put proper postage on it, and dropped it in a mailbox.

A few days later Morgan Smith, a professor of chemistry at the University of Illinois, received the box in his/her university mailbox. Professor Smith put the box in his/her desk. Some days later s/he removed the box from her desk, took it to the laboratory, cut open one side of the box, and removed the plastic bag and hose. After examining the hose, s/he cut a 4″ section off. The remaining 8″ section s/he photographed and put back in the box; s/he then closed the cut side of the box with shipping tape. S/he next put the box back in his/her desk, where it was left until s/he removed it and brought it to court.

On November 1, [-1], Professor Smith photographed the 4″ section and performed a variety of microscopic and chemical tests on it. That section was entirely destroyed during the testing process.

1.   For the plaintiff, get the box and contents in evidence. (Prepare an appropriate exhibit and bring to class.)
2.   For the defendant, oppose the offer.

113

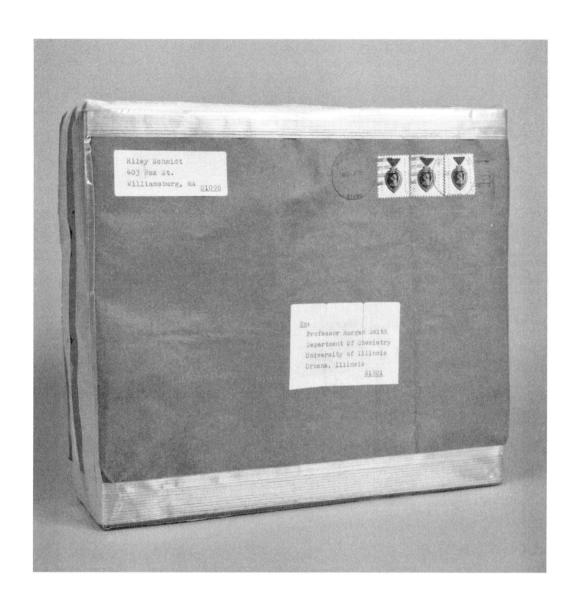

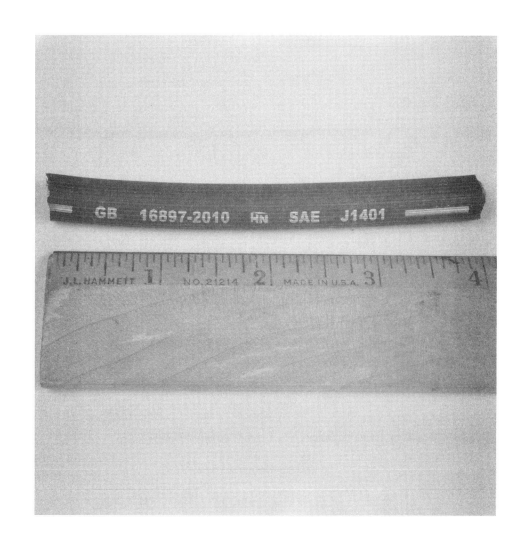

4.6 PHOTOGRAPH OF POLICE OFFICERS AND PLAINTIFF

This is a civil rights action brought against the city police department by Charles Jackson, who was arrested by the police on March 15 of last year. Jackson alleges that the police arrested him on that date without reason and physically assaulted him, depriving him of his civil rights.

Plaintiff's witness, Mickey Mars, was standing on the southeast corner of Clark and Madison Streets at about noon on March 15 and saw police officers on that corner forcing Jackson to the ground. Mars was about five feet away from the scene. The weather was clear and sunny. S/he was on his/her way to lunch from his/her office, one block south on Clark Street. One of the officers, s/he says, held Jackson while another officer poked his nightstick in Jackson's neck. Jackson then shouted: "Help, they're killing me!"

Mars "did not like what the officers were doing," according to the e-mail s/he sent to Jackson's attorney. Therefore, s/he took out her cell phone and took a picture of the scene. The next day, s/he noticed a story in the local newspaper about the arrest. The story said Jackson was the person being arrested. It also identified his attorney. Mars e-mailed his/her cell phone photo to the attorney.

1. For the plaintiff, get the photograph in evidence and use it in conjunction with the witness. This is the first time during the trial that the photograph has been mentioned.

2. For the defendant, oppose the offer.

119

4.7 PHOTOGRAPHS OF ACCIDENT VICTIM

This is a wrongful death action brought by Earl Sanders, executor of the estate of Frances Sanders.

On June 15 of last year, Frances Sanders was struck and instantly killed by a car driven by Karl Schmidt. A police officer, Jules Monroe, can testify that s/he was on patrol duty, received a radio message about the accident, and arrived at the scene moments later, at 2:15 P.M. When s/he arrived, s/he found Frances Sanders lying motionless on the pavement, as portrayed in the attached photographs taken by police investigators called to the scene by Monroe. Other testimony will show that Ms. Sanders was crossing Main Street at its intersection with Elm Street when she was struck.

1. For the plaintiff, get the photographs in evidence.
2. Assume that Sanders was not killed and has brought a negligence action against Schmidt. For the plaintiff, get the photographs in evidence.
3. For the defendant, oppose the offers.

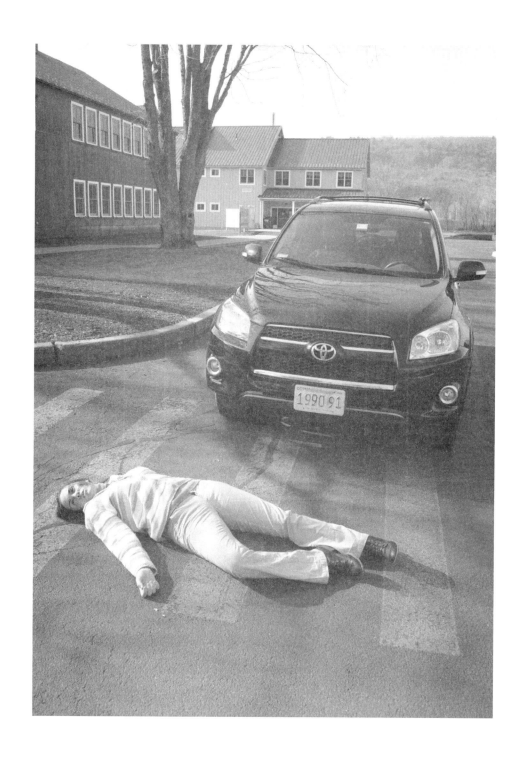

4.8   PHOTOGRAPH OF BUILDING

This is a burglary prosecution. The condition of the Whiskerz Pub on January 15, two years ago, is an issue in this case. The tavern, located at 1610 Maple, was torn down last year, and the location is now a vacant lot.

You have a photograph of the Whiskerz Pub taken in January of last year. [Note: This photograph is available in the resources section of this book on CasebookConnect.] In addition, you find a witness, Jaime Mendez, who lived in an apartment above the tavern in January, two years ago.

1. For the prosecution, get the photograph in evidence.

2. Assume that the sign that extends from the building was not there when Mendez lived in the building. For the prosecution, get the photograph in evidence.

3. Assume that Mendez lived in the apartment at the two windows on the left side of the photograph, to the north, at 1612 Maple. S/he has told the police that on the day of the burglary, at about 3:00 P.M. on a sunny day, s/he was looking out the right of the two windows when s/he saw the defendant, Carl Dunn, run out of the Whiskerz entrance, look up at him/her "for a moment," then run north past his/her window. The distance from the window to the place where Dunn was standing when he looked up is approximately 15 feet. For the prosecution, elicit Mendez's identification of the defendant, making use of the photograph.

4. For the defense, oppose the offers.

4.9 PHOTOGRAPH OF BUILDING

This is a burglary prosecution. On June 15 of last year someone broke into Robin Smith's house, located at 1234 Halsted Street. Entry was apparently made through a side door, as shown by pry marks on the frame and door.

Officer Quinn Jackson, who was called to the scene when the owner discovered the break-in, saw the marks and recovered a crowbar lying in some shrubs and grass, approximately five feet from the door. Technician Kaden Jones took the attached photograph later that same day.

1. For the prosecution, get the photograph in evidence via the testimony of either Jackson or Jones, and then use it in any way you deem appropriate.
2. For the defense, oppose the offer.

4.10   PHOTOGRAPH OF BUILDING

This is an armed robbery prosecution. The witness, Bobbie Cleary, saw an armed robbery taking place at about 11:30 P.M. one year ago today. Cleary was standing on the wooden porch in front of 3002-04 Elm Street, the doorway in the left side of the photograph. The armed robber was standing on the wooden porch in front of 3006-08 Elm Street, the doorway in the right side of the photograph. The victim of the robbery was standing just to the right of the robber on the porch of the 3006-08 doorway. Cleary has identified the defendant as the man who committed the armed robbery. The two doorways are approximately 30 feet apart.

1.   For the prosecution, get the photograph in evidence, have the witness describe the distance between the doorways, and use the photo in any way you deem appropriate.

2.   For the defense, oppose the offer and cross-examine the witness.

4.11 DIAGRAM OF INTERSECTION

A police officer, Emerson Tatum, was in his/her squad car on June 15 of last year at 3:00 P.M. observing traffic at the intersection of Maple and Elm Streets. Tatum had parked in a parking lot on the northwest corner of the intersection, facing southeast. There are no traffic control signals at the intersection.

Tatum saw a pedestrian, Elmer Franks, cross Elm Street, going northbound, on the east side of Maple. As Franks entered the crosswalk, a car driven northbound on Maple by Robert Dixon made a right-hand turn on Elm and failed to stop for Franks. The car's front bumper struck Franks as he was in the crosswalk, knocking him several feet east, where he fell down on the pavement, facing east. The car then stopped at Franks's feet.

Franks has brought a negligence action against the driver of the car. The defense is that the pedestrian was not in the crosswalk at the time of the accident.

Plaintiff now calls Officer Tatum as a witness. Two weeks before trial Tatum went to the intersection, made the necessary measurements, and prepared a diagram of the intersection, which is attached.

1. For the plaintiff, get the diagram in evidence and use it to illustrate Tatum's testimony.
2. For the plaintiff, have Tatum illustrate his/her testimony by making a sketch of the intersection on a blackboard.
3. For the defense, oppose the offer and cross-examine Tatum.

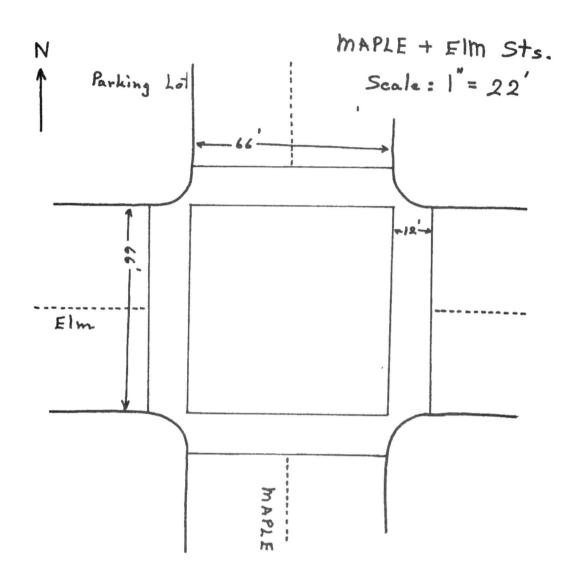

MAPLE + Elm Sts.

Scale: 1" = 22'

Parking Lot

N

66'

66'

12'

Elm

MAPLE

143

4.12 DIAGRAM OF HOUSE

This is a criminal sexual assault prosecution. The victim, Shirley Rice, was attacked at approximately 2:00 A.M. on June 15 of last year by a man who apparently gained entry to her home through an open living room window.

At the time of the attack, the bedroom lights were off but the lights in the living room and kitchen were on. Rice awoke when she heard a sound in the living room, sat up, and saw a man standing in the doorway to the bedroom. He stood there for about ten seconds. That was the last time she saw his face clearly.

The issue at trial is the identification of the attacker. Rice identified the defendant, Sam Moore, during a lineup one week after the attack.

A police officer, Fred Miller, sketched a diagram of Rice's house that day. The diagram, which is attached, is not to scale.

1. For the prosecution, use the diagram during Rice's direct testimony in any way you deem appropriate. Confine the examination to the identification issue.
2. For the defense, oppose the offer and cross-examine Rice.

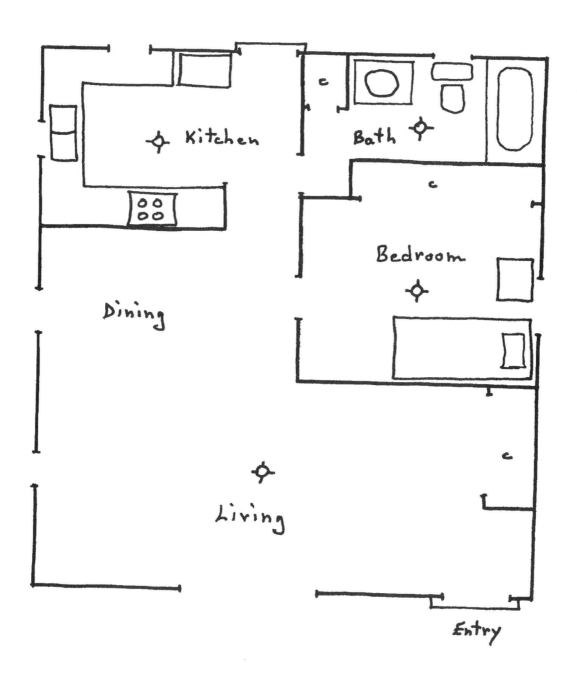

Kitchen

Bath

c

c

Dining

Bedroom

Living

c

Entry

Rice House — 6/15/[-1]

4.13 MAP

This is a robbery prosecution. The defendant is accused of robbing a concession stand in the state capitol in downtown Phoenix at 5:00 P.M. on June 15 of last year. However, evidence will also establish that the defendant "punched in" at his place of work, the dining hall at the Mesa Community College near downtown Mesa, at 5:30 P.M. and that he customarily drives his car to work.

To prove that it is possible to drive from the state capitol to Mesa Community College within 30 minutes, the prosecution calls Madison Wilson, a police patrolman, as a witness. Wilson will testify that s/he took two possible routes from the state capitol to the College: first, south on 19th Avenue and east on Southern Avenue, the local route; second, using Interstate 10 and Highway 360, the expressway route. Both routes are approximately 15 miles long.

Wilson will testify that s/he drove both routes at 5:00 P.M. on the same day of the week as the robbery. S/he drove both routes in a squad car, going as quickly as s/he reasonably could, given the traffic conditions. His/her time for the local route was 35 minutes; the expressway route took 25 minutes.

1. For the prosecution, get the map in evidence and use it to illustrate Officer Wilson's testimony.
2. For the defense, oppose the offer and cross-examine Wilson.

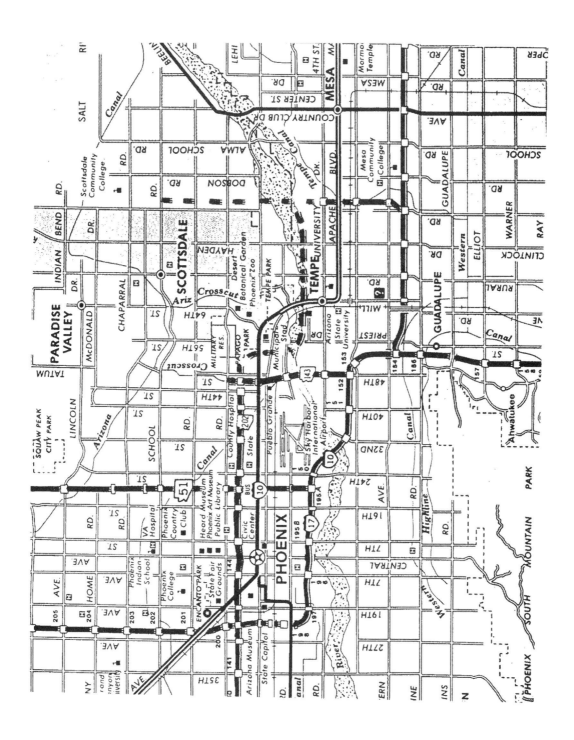

151

4.14   PROMISSORY NOTE

This case involves a suit brought by Fran Smith on a promissory note allegedly signed by William Burns. Burns denies signing the note.

Your witnesses are Fran Smith, the plaintiff, who says that s/he was present when Burns signed the note, and Reese Jones, who was not present when the note was signed but is familiar with Burns's signature through previous correspondence and business dealings.

1. For the plaintiff, get the promissory note in evidence, using Fran Smith as the witness.

2. For the plaintiff, get the promissory note in evidence, using Reese Jones as the witness.

3. Assume that the promissory note is payable to Household Loan Company and is one of the company's regular forms. Call a custodian of the records from Household to get the note in evidence.

4. For the defendant, oppose the offer(s).

```
              PROMISSORY NOTE


                         Date:  June 30, [-2]


For value received, the undersigned hereby promises

to pay to Fran Smith the sum of twelve thousand

($12,000.00) dollars on or before December 31, [-2]


                    Signed: William Burns
                            William Burns
```

4.15 CONTRACT

This is a contract action, brought by Charlie Joiner against Fred Turner, which alleges that Turner failed to perform in accordance with a written contract they had previously executed. The case is now on trial.

According to Joiner, the contract, which is attached, was executed by them in Turner's office on the date shown on the contract. Joiner claims that s/he personally saw Turner sign his name on the contract. Turner denies signing it.

1. For the plaintiff, introduce the contract in evidence, using Joiner as the witness.

2. What other methods can be used to authenticate the contract?

3. Assume that after executing the contract, Turner kept the signed original and gave Joiner an unsigned photocopy of the contract. Assume also that Turner has denied the existence of the contract and has not produced the original. For the plaintiff, get the unsigned photocopy in evidence. (Assume that the attached contract is the unsigned photocopy.)

4. For the defendant, oppose the offer.

CONTRACT

The parties, Charlie Joiner ("Joiner") and Fred Turner ("Turner"), hereby enter into the following agreement:

1. Joiner for the past five years has been in the business of building custom homes, a business that requires substantial amounts of sand and gravel earthfill.

2. Turner for the past five years has been in the business of obtaining and selling sand and gravel earthfill to contractors and other customers.

3. Joiner hereby agrees to purchase, and Turner agrees to sell, all sand and gravel earthfill in such quantities as Joiner will require, for a period of five years from the date of this contract.

4. Joiner will notify Turner, either orally or in writing, of his/her requirements as they shall arise from time to time. Turner will fill the orders and deliver them to any job site within a radius of fifty (50) miles of Turner's present business headquarters, within the shortest practical period of time, and in any event within a commercially reasonable period of time.

5. Joiner will pay Turner in full for any deliveries within ten (10) days of delivery, at a rate that will be identical to the most preferred rate Turner has given to any other customer within ninety (90) days preceding the order, and in any event shall not be higher than the average rate in the industry during the same time period.

Date: 1 June [-1]

Charlie Joiner

Charlie Joiner

Fred Turner

Fred Turner

4.16   PHOTOCOPIES OF CHECK

This is a contract action. Shannon Smith sues Jordan Jones for failure to pay a $2,000 debt. Jones claims s/he paid off the debt through the check that is photocopied in the proposed exhibit. The issue is whether the debt is discharged.

Jones will testify that s/he prepared the check and dropped it off at Smith's place of work, the Hasty Tasty Restaurant at 1400 Main Street. S/he will say that Smith was not there at the time. Jones is not familiar with Smith's handwriting. S/he did not see the check again, but the bank statement that s/he received at the beginning of March [-1] included photocopies of the front and back of the check that s/he now intends to introduce into evidence.

Smith has testified that s/he does not remember ever seeing the check. S/he has admitted that the signature on the back of the (photocopied) check "looks like" his/her signature, but s/he does not recall endorsing the check or doing anything with it. S/he admits to having an account at the Second National Bank.

The plaintiff has rested. Jones is on the stand.

1. For the defendant, get the check in evidence to prove that Jones made the payment and that Smith received the payment.
2. For the plaintiff, oppose the offer.

Jordan Jones
221 N. LaSalle St.
Phone: 626-9982

648

Date 2-7-[-1]

PAY Shannon Smith
TO THE ORDER OF

$ 2000.00

Two Thousand Dollars and No Cents

DOLLARS **FBIC**

Continental Bank
Continental Illinois National Bank and Trust of Chicago

FOR Full Payment – Smith Debt

Jordan Jones

⑆⑆1234567890⑆ ⑆23 ⑈890 ⑈ 90 2345

Shannon Smith

2d Nat. Bk.
2/21/[-1]

PAID
Cont. Bk.
2/14/[-1]

4.17 LETTERS

This is a contract action brought by Alex Jones against Fred Neal and Acme Wholesale Distributors. Jones alleges that Neal and Acme violated their agreement when they refused to deliver a quantity of folding chairs.

The alleged contract is contained in the attached letters. Neal's letter is the original received by Jones. Jones's letter is an unsigned photocopy obtained from Jones's files. Neal denies ever receiving the original of Jones's letter.

Assume the following facts:

(a) Hilda Frank, who had been Jones's secretary for 15 years at the relevant time, died before this trial.

(b) Jones cannot testify that s/he is able to recognize Neal's signature, but Jones can recognize Neal's voice from prior conversations.

(c) Jones will say that s/he personally did not mail the August 6 letter, nor did s/he see it mailed.

(d) Jones will say that for the 15 years before August 6, [-1], Hilda would not file an unsigned photocopy until she had mailed the original and that she always mailed the original on the same day it was dictated and signed.

(e) On August 8, [-1], the wholesale price charged by Acme for its metal folding chairs was increased to $30.00 each.

1. For the plaintiff, conduct a direct examination of Jones and get the two letters in evidence.

2. For the defendants, oppose the offers and cross-examine Jones.

ACME WHOLESALE DISTRIBUTORS
2933 East Congress

June 15, [-1]

Alex Jones
Ace Office Supply Company
418 E. Broadway
Toledo, Ohio

Dear Alex:

   In accord with our phone conversation of last
Wednesday, we hereby offer to sell you metal folding
chairs (Catalogue item #A-417) at $23.00 each, plus
freight charges, carrier of your designation, payable
C.O.D., delivery at your place of business within 30 days
of your acceptance of this offer.

   This offer will remain an open firm offer until
August 7,[-1]. Any acceptance must be in writing and our
offer will be deemed accepted only when your written
acceptance addressed to this firm is duly deposited in
the United States mail.

                              Very truly yours,

                              Fred Neal

                              ACME WHOLESALE DISTRIBUTORS

                              By: Fred Neal

ACE OFFICE SUPPLY COMPANY
418 E. Broadway

August 6, [-1]

Acme Wholesale Distributors
2933 E. Congress
South Haven, Michigan

Att'n: Fred Neal

Dear Mr. Neal:

    In accord with your offer contained in your letter of
June 15, [-1], we hereby order one thousand (1,000) metal
folding chairs (Item #A-417), total price of $23,000.00, on
terms specific in your letter.

    Please give us 48 hours notice of anticipated delivery
so we can make arrangements here.

                        Sincerely,

                        ALEX JONES

4.18   STOCK PURCHASE ORDER

This is a contract action brought by the Zoom Corporation, a creditor of Jamie Z. Wilson. The issue is whether Wilson bought 300 shares of General Foods Organic Products stock on March 1, two years ago. S/he denies that s/he did.

To prove that the transaction took place, you subpoena Andy Jones, district manager of the local office of MWE Investing Services. Your subpoena calls for him/her to produce MWE records that deal with the transaction in question.

Jones comes to court with the attached record. S/he had never seen it before receiving the subpoena and had no hand in its making. S/he will say that the document is referred to at the company as a "purchase order." It is created by the person who takes the order, whether in person, on the phone, or otherwise. After the order is typed, it is sent to the purchase order department, where the actual purchase is made. Once the purchase is made, a copy of the order, along with a request for payment, is sent to the buyer. Jones cannot say who filled out the purchase order. At least 15 people were in the order department in March [-2]. S/he has been unable to locate any other records concerning the transaction.

1. For the plaintiff, conduct a direct examination of Jones and get the document into evidence.

2. Assume that Jones searches the records but cannot find any records showing any transactions concerning Wilson during the year in question. For the defendant, conduct a direct examination of Jones to demonstrate the absence of any such records.

3. Assume that Jones will testify that the company's regular procedure was to destroy original purchase orders after one year, but that at the end of the year the records department feeds the purchase information into its computer records. S/he brings to court the computer document created when the trial subpoena was received. For the plaintiff, get the document into evidence.

4. Assume that the words "Wilson is a liar and a thief" are handwritten on the document, as in the second version of the document included here. Offer it into evidence.

5. For the defendant, oppose all the plaintiff's offers.

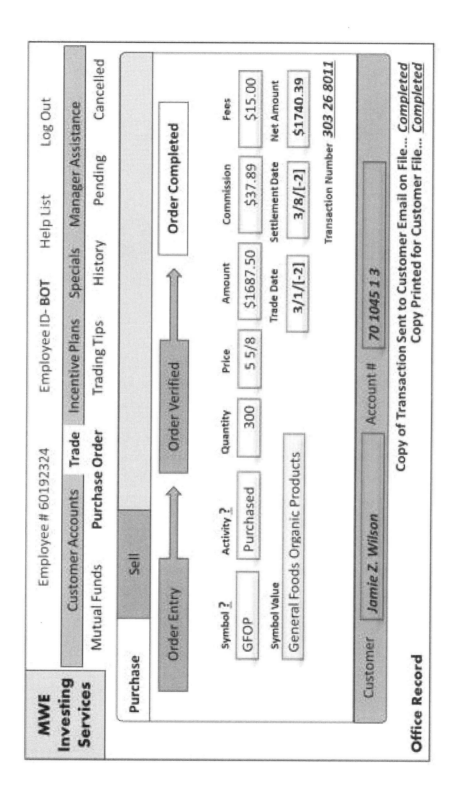

173

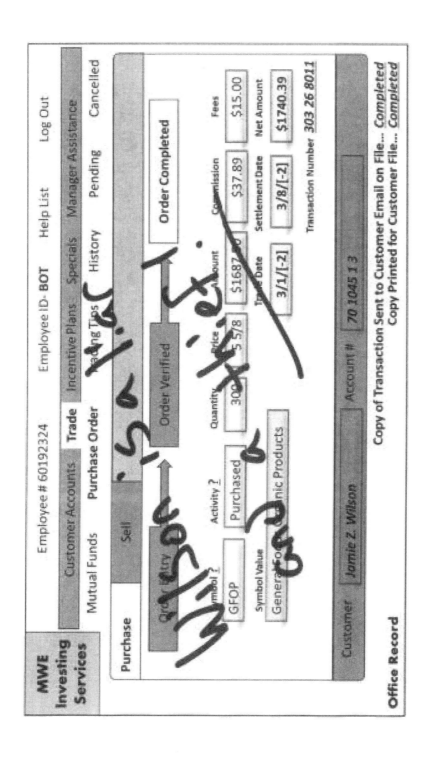

4.19 THEFT REPORT

This is a theft prosecution. The defendant, Fred Riley, is on trial for the theft of Sandra Franklin's car on September 25 of last year. When the trial begins, the prosecution learns that Franklin is somewhere in Europe and cannot be located in time to call her as a witness.

In order to prove the theft of the car and the ownership of the car, the prosecution subpoenas London Maxwell, general manager of the Maxwell Insurance Company. S/he brings the attached form. Ralph Sturdley, the agent who signed the form, cannot be located.

1. For the prosecution, get the form in evidence to prove the theft and ownership of the car.

2. Assume that this is an action by Franklin against Maxwell Insurance on the insurance policy. To prove that she reported the theft on October 1 of last year, Franklin intends to introduce the attached form. For the plaintiff, get the form in evidence for the stated purpose, using London Maxwell as a witness.

3. Use the same information as in No. 2, except that Maxwell Insurance denies Franklin was insured at the time of the theft. For the plaintiff, get the form in evidence to establish that Franklin was insured.

4. For the defense, oppose the offers.

AUTO THEFT REPORT FORM

PERSON REPORTING: Sandra Franklin

DATE OF THIS REPORT: October 1, [1]

INSURED: Sandra Franklin

VEHICLE: Toyota Prius
                                     LICENSE NUMBER 123-899

SERIAL NUMBER: Y257831670

DATE OF THEFT: September 25, [-1]

PLACE VEHICLE TAKEN FROM: Greyhound Parking Lot,
                                     Clark and Lake
                                     Streets, Chicago

WERE POLICE NOTIFIED: Yes

IF YES, DATE POLICE NOTIFIED: September 27, [-1]

                 MAXWELL INSURANCE COMPANY

        BY: _Ralph Sturdley_
            Ralph Sturdley, Agent

4.20   ACCIDENT REPORT

This case involves a two-car collision resulting in personal injury and property damage. The collision occurred on July 1, two years ago. The plaintiff, Frank Jones, the driver of the first car, is suing Sharon Walker, the driver of the second car, for negligence in allegedly crossing the center line of a highway on a curve and driving too fast for conditions.

The case is now on trial. Plaintiff calls Sandy Smith, the custodian of records of Acme Casualty Company, the defendant's insurance carrier. Pursuant to a subpoena, Smith brings the attached accident report prepared by one of the company's accident investigators, Charles Franklin, who was at the scene after the accident. Franklin is unavailable for trial.

1. For the plaintiff, get the report in evidence.
2. Assume that the state highway department accident investigator prepared the attached report pursuant to his statutory duty. For the plaintiff, get the report in evidence.
3. For the defendant, oppose the offer.

ACCIDENT REPORT FORM

Acme Casualty Company, Inc.

Date of this report:	July 1, [-2]
Investigator at scene:	Charles Franklin
Insured: Policy:	Sharon Walker Standard casualty policy, $100,000 max. coverage
Insured vehicle:	[-4] Chrysler sedan Illinois license # 987-654
Date of accident: Time of accident: Location of accident:	July 1, [-2] 4:00 p.m. Sheridan Road, 1/4 mile N. of Town Rd., Glencoe (curve at bottom of ravine)
Parties involved:	(1) insured (2) Frank Jones, driving a [-5] Cadillac Seville
Other witness(s):	(1) Fred Minelli, Glencoe Police Dept. Patrolman, at scene after accident.
Condition of vehicle(s):	(1) Walker vehicle had damage to left front bumper, headlight and wheel area (2) Jones vehicle had damage to left side of body from front headlight to rear door.
Accident scene:	Sheridan Rd., at accident scene is a right hand curve, going northbound. (1) Walker car stopped at shoulder of road on east side of road. Skid marks for approx. 45' from rear of car. Skid marks for left wheels crossed center line near point of origin. (2) Jones car stopped at shoulder of road on west side of road, approx. 60' from Walker car. Skid marks for 15', beginning in west lane directly opposite from Walker car skid marks origin.
Statements:	(1) Walker said she was sorry about the whole thing, that she wasn't familiar with the road and the curve was sharper than she thought. (2) Jones said he was driving in his customary safe manner when he was hit by the Walker car when it crossed the center line and veered into his outside lane.

183

4.21 TIME CARD

This is a criminal prosecution. The whereabouts of the defendant, John Hudson, on February 9 of last year at 10:30 A.M.—the date and time of the crime involved—is the principal issue in the case. Evidence has been presented showing that the robbery occurred three miles from Brenner Metal Works and that it would take about ten minutes to drive between the two places at 10:30 in the morning.

Hudson says he was at work at the time. His lawyer subpoenas Terry Brenner, president of Brenner Metal Works. Brenner brings, as the subpoena commands, Hudson's time card with machine-stamped time entries for the pertinent time period. The time cards are kept in a rack next to the time clock by the employee entrance to the plant. At the end of each two-week period the cards are collected and given to the bookkeeper.

Brenner has no personal knowledge of Hudson or of Hudson's activities on the relevant date.

1. For the defense, conduct a direct examination of Brenner, get the time card in evidence, and present it to the jury in the most effective way.

2. Assume that Brenner brings to court a computer printout of all employees' in and out times for the February 1 to 15 time period. S/he tells you that all time cards are summarized at the end of each quarter on computer memory banks and the time cards are then destroyed. S/he ordered the computer printout from the records department when s/he received the subpoena.

    For the defense, conduct a direct examination of Brenner, getting into evidence the computer printout and testimony about the relevant date. (Use the attached record as if it were the computer printout.)

3. For the prosecution, oppose the offers and cross-examine Brenner.

185

Brenner Metal Works

Employee Time Card

Employee Name: John Hudson

Signature: *John Hudson*

Pay Period: 2/1 to 2/14

Date	2/1	2/2	2/3	2/4	2/5	2/6	2/7
In:	5:58 A.M.	6:02 A.M.	6:05 A.M.	5:58 A.M.	5:55 A.M.		
Out:	10:02 A.M.	10:05 A.M.	10:02 A.M.	10:01 A.M.	10:02 A.M.		
In:	10:30 A.M.	10:35 A.M.	10:30 A.M.	10:35 A.M.	10:30 A.M.		
Out:	2:35 P.M.	2:35 P.M.	2:35 P.M.	2:40 P.M.	2:35 P.M.		

Date	2/8	2/9	2/10	2/11	2/12	2/13	2/14
In:	5:50 A.M.	5:58 A.M.	5:55 A.M.	6:02 A.M.	6:00 A.M.		
Out:	10:05 A.M.	9:50 A.M.	10:02 A.M.	10:05 A.M.	10:01 A.M.		
In:	10:35 A.M.	10:25 A.M.	10:31 A.M.	10:35 A.M.	10:35 A.M.		
Out:	2:40 P.M.	2:30 P.M.	2:40 P.M.	2:35 P.M.	2:32 P.M.		

4.22 DEPOSIT AND WITHDRAWAL SLIPS

The Valley National Bank was robbed shortly after opening on June 1 of last year. Following the robbery the branch manager, Gale Atkins, performed an audit of the bank to determine the amount of the loss. Included in the audit were the previous day's cash count, the cash count after the robbery, and the records of transactions conducted on June 1. The robbery occurred at one teller station. The previous day's cash count at that station was $3,500. An audit after the robbery showed a cash count at that station of $250. From these figures Atkins was able to compute the cash taken during the robbery.

The only transactions conducted on June 1 before the robbery are represented by the attached documents, which Atkins found in the usual compartments in the tellers' drawers.

1. For the prosecution, get the records in evidence via the testimony of Gale Atkins.

2. For the defense, oppose the offers.

Valley National Bank of Arizona

SAVINGS DEPOSIT

DATE 6-1-[-1]

DEPOSITS MAY NOT BE AVAILABLE FOR IMMEDIATE WITHDRAWL

SIGN HERE IF CASH RECEIVED FROM DEPOSIT

GERALD THEIRS

NAME (PRINTED)

1307 GARFIELD AVE.

ADDRESS

⑅⑈1234567890⑈ ACCOUNT NUMBER 7 9 2 1 - 9 4 6 0

CURRENCY	100	0	0
COIN			
CHECKS	289	4	3
SUBTOTAL			
LESS CASH RECEIVED			
NET DEPOSIT	389	4	3

Valley National Bank of Arizona

SAVINGS DEPOSIT

DATE 6-1-[-1]

DEPOSITS MAY NOT BE AVAILABLE FOR IMMEDIATE WITHDRAWL

Terry Jones

SIGN HERE IF CASH RECEIVED FROM DEPOSIT

TERRY JONES

NAME (PRINTED)

201 E HAWAII

ADDRESS

⑅⑈1234567890⑈ ACCOUNT NUMBER 3 7 0 1 - 3 3 5 7

CURRENCY			
COIN			
CHECKS	243	5	7
SUBTOTAL			
LESS CASH RECEIVED	100	0	0
NET DEPOSIT	143	5	7

Valley National Bank of Arizona

SAVINGS DEPOSIT

DATE 6-1-[-1]

DEPOSITS MAY NOT BE AVAILABLE FOR IMMEDIATE WITHDRAWL

SIGN HERE IF CASH RECEIVED FROM DEPOSIT

FRANCIS WINCHESTER

NAME (PRINTED)

1343 E. PINE ST

ADDRESS

⑅⑈1234567890⑈ ACCOUNT NUMBER 8 8 2 1 - 9 3 9 1

CURRENCY	300	0	0
COIN (Check)	288	0	1
CHECKS	415	3	7
SUBTOTAL			
LESS CASH RECEIVED			
NET DEPOSIT	1,003	3	8

Valley National Bank of Arizona

SAVINGS WITHDRAWAL

DATE O6OI[-1]   BRANCH ☐ MAIN ST. ☒ UNIVERSITY ☐ $ 127.00

One hundred twenty-seven and no _____ DOLLARS

CHARGED TO BELOW LISTED ACCOUNT
Pat Smith
SIGNATURE
1501 S Taylor
ADDRESS

⑆1234567890⑆ ACCOUNT NUMBER 8 5 2 1 - 0 6 7 8

Valley National Bank of Arizona

SAVINGS WITHDRAWAL

DATE 6/1/[-1]   BRANCH ☐ MAIN ST. ☒ UNIVERSITY ☐ $ 500.00

_____ DOLLARS

CHARGED TO BELOW LISTED ACCOUNT
Freddie Jackson
SIGNATURE
453 Terrace
ADDRESS

⑆1234567890⑆ ACCOUNT NUMBER 6 2 1 7 - 4 9 8 0

Valley National Bank of Arizona

SAVINGS WITHDRAWAL

DATE 6/1/[-1]   BRANCH ☐ MAIN ST. ☒ UNIVERSITY ☐ $ 100.00

One Hundred dollars and 00/100 _____ DOLLARS

CHARGED TO BELOW LISTED ACCOUNT
Haley Jackson
SIGNATURE
2119 S. Pulaski, AS
ADDRESS

⑆1234567890⑆ ACCOUNT NUMBER 6 2 8 7 - 1 3 4 0

4.23   SUMMARY CHART

This is a warranty action. The XYZ Car Rental Company purchased numerous vehicles from General Motors during the past four calendar years. XYZ claims that the four-speed automatic transmissions that came with some of the cars it bought from General Motors during that time period were defective and is suing for the cost of replacing the transmissions and other consequential damages.

To determine the full extent of the loss, XYZ hired a temporary employee from a secretary service, Kelly Services. For five weeks, from November 1, [-1], to December 7, [-1], the employee, Sammy Sparks, went through numerous records to determine which of XYZ's purchased automobiles had the special four-speed automatic transmission in them. This transmission was the purportedly defective part (General Motors stock item #T33-413).

After going through all the records (order forms, shipping orders, invoices, etc.), Sparks produced the following document and gave it to Wilbur Theis, the general manager of XYZ. (The underlying documents have already been examined by the defendants but have not been introduced in evidence.)

1. For the plaintiff, conduct a direct examination of Sparks and get the document in evidence.

2. Assume that all of XYZ's records are computerized. The exhibit was created by comptroller Hayden Johnson, who conducted a computer search for all vehicle purchases involving GM Stock Item #T33-413. For the plaintiff, conduct a direct examination of Johnson and get the document in evidence.

3. For the defendant, oppose the offer(s).

SUMMARY OF XYZ CAR RENTAL COMPANY'S PURCHASES OF VEHICLES FROM GENERAL MOTORS DURING THE PERIOD 1/1/[-4] THROUGH 11/1/[-1] DEFECTIVE FOUR-SPEED AUTOMATIC TRANSMISSIONS
(GM Stock Item #T33-413)

Car Type	VIN	Purchase Date	Invoice Cost
Chevrolet	VX23816	Jan. 1, [-4]	$2,413
Buick	QT31620	May 1, [-4]	2,508
Buick	QT4140	June 30, [-4]	2,508
Chevrolet	VX33016	Aug. 4, [-4]	2,413
Chevrolet	VX33493	Aug. 30, [-4]	2,413
Chevrolet	PX4407	Feb. 1, [-3]	2,483
Chevrolet	PX5996	March 1, [-3]	2,483
Buick	J337	March 10, [-2]	2,543
Buick	J40077	June 1, [-2]	2,543
Buick	J59338	July 1, [-2]	2,543
Buick	J88710	Oct. 15, [-2]	2,543
Chevrolet	AB99-6110	Feb. 1, [-1]	2,576
Chevrolet	AB10-16217	March 1, [-1]	2,576
Chevrolet	AB17-73556	June 15, [-1]	2,576
Chevrolet	AB20-66137	Aug. 1, [-1]	2,576
Total: 15 cars			$37,697

4.24   PRISON LOGBOOK

This is a prosecution for conspiracy to commit three murders. The defendant, Jerry Stone, was an inmate at the Ironside Correctional Center at the time of the acts alleged in the indictment. The prosecution's theory is that the actual killer, Victor Raines, committed the murders on instructions from Stone. The prosecution has the prison visitors' logbook that reflects Raines's visits with Stone one day before each murder. It seeks to introduce the logbook to prove that Raines had in fact visited Stone at the prison on those particular dates.

In order to introduce the logbook into evidence, the prosecution relies on the testimony of Gabbie McMann, the Inmate Records Coordinator at Ironside. An FBI agent interviewed McMann after the murder, and the agent's report contains the following:

Gabbie McMann has been employed by the Department of Corrections for eight years. S/he is responsible for maintaining and storing the prison visitors' logbook. S/he is familiar with the procedure for admitting visitors and has personally observed the procedure from time to time. S/he states that normal prison procedure is that visitors are required to show identification to the lobby officer and to sign their names and record their addresses on a sheet in the logbook. The lobby officer is required to check a visitor's identification against the entry in the book. McMann has no personal knowledge of whether the lobby officer checks each entry in the logbook against the identification that has been shown to the officer, but s/he can say that lobby officers are required to follow the prescribed procedure. S/he has no personal knowledge of the entries that reflect visits by a Victor Raines.

1.   For the prosecution, conduct a direct examination of McMann and get the logbook entries into evidence.

2.   For the defendant, oppose the offer and cross-examine McMann.

IRONSIDE CORRECTIONAL CENTER

Date: March 15 [2]

Inmate visited: Richard Jefferson
Name of visitor: Sam Everett
Address of visitor: 1642 Thomas   City

Time in: 1045
Time out: 1210

Inmate Visited: Jerry Stone
Name of visitor: Victor Olaine
Address of visitor: 6030 S. White
City

Time in: 1150
Time out: 1410

Inmate Visited: Ralph Henry
Name of visitor: Felix Sampson
Address of visitor: 2017 Hale   City

Time in: 1315
Time out: 1420

Date: June 2 [-2]

Inmate visited: Jerry Stone
Name of visitor: Victor Raines
Address of visitor: 6030 S. White
City
Time in: 945
Time out: 1115

Inmate Visited: Sidney Berg
Name of visitor: Ralph Stein
Address of visitor: 400 N. Michigan City

Time in: 1020
Time out: 1215

Inmate Visited: Arthur Blane
Name of visitor: Thelma Bledsoe
Address of visitor: 1640 W. Taylor City

Time in: 1045
Time out: 1340

203

Date: Aug 7 [-2]

Inmate visited: Sonford Stark
Name of visitor: Louise Stark
Address of visitor: 3630 Belmont City

Time in: 940
Time out: 1145

Inmate Visited: Harry Fields
Name of visitor: Sam Fields
Address of visitor: 4012 W Harper City

Time in: 1015
Time out: 1220

Inmate Visited: Terry Stone
Name of visitor: Victor Raines
Address of visitor: 6230 S. White
City

Time in: 1030
Time out: 1045

4.25   E-MAIL AND WEBSITE MESSAGES

This is a breach of contract case arising out of an attempt to purchase a car advertised on a website. On July 14, [-1], defendant Corey Cain placed an ad on the website Jackie's Jalopies offering to sell a [-4] Chevy SUV for $20,000.

On July 19, [-1], plaintiff Alex Abel sent an e-mail to the address listed in the ad offering to pay $18,500 for the SUV. The defendant admits receiving this e-mail. The plaintiff claims that defendant sent a return e-mail accepting the offer on July 20, [-1]. The defendant's deposition is attached.

The key exhibits in this case are the two e-mails, one sent by the plaintiff to the defendant, and the other allegedly sent by the defendant to the plaintiff. Plaintiff claims that s/he printed these two e-mails from his/her computer without altering them in any way.

The case is now on trial.

1. For the plaintiff, introduce the ad and the two e-mails in evidence.
2. For the defendant, oppose the admission of the claimed e-mail from the defendant to the plaintiff.

Web Advertisement

reply below ☐ **Prohibited**   Posted 07-14 1:54 PM_DT

◀ prev ▲ next ▶

⭐ **[-4] Chevy SUV $20,000**

A great vehicle at a steal of a price!

Reply to: cuinsept@mmsn.com

LS Sport Utility 4 Door with 4WD
$20,000 firm

This is a terrific deal!! I am headed to grad school in the city and need the money more than a vehicle, otherwise I would keep it.

Chevy	SUV
4WD	

Bluebook value is $22,900 so $20,000 is the lowest price I want to go. I am wiling to transport a reasonable distance upon payment.

Contact Corey Cain at cuinsept@mmsn.com for more information!

Details:
Mileage: 52,000
Engine: 6-Cyl, 4.2 Liter
Transmission: Automatic
Drive Train: 4WD
Color: Silver

post id: 123456789   posted: 7-14   email to friend   report abuse

E-mail from Plaintiff Abel to Defendant Cain

To: Corey Cain <cuinsept@mmsn.com>

From: Alex Abel <aabel@aaol.com>

Re: Vehicle listed for sale on *Jackie's Jalopies*

Date: July 19, [-1]

Time: 2:32 P.M.

I want to buy the Chevy SUV you listed for sale on *Jackie's Jalopies*.

I will pay you $18,500 for it immediately after my mechanic inspects it and finds it to be in proper working order.

You can contact me at aabel@aaol.com.

Alleged E-mail from Defendant Cain to Plaintiff Abel

To: Alex Abel <aabel@aaol.com>

From: Corey Cain <cuinsept@mmsn.com>

Re: Vehicle listed for sale on *Jackie's Jalopies*

Date: July 20, [-1]

Time: 10:47 A.M.

Thank you for your offer to buy my Chevy SUV for $18,500. It's a great vehicle and $18,500 is more than a steal of a price. Although your offer is lower than I wanted to go, I need to complete this transaction now to pay for grad school, so I will accept your offer.

I will contact you soon with details about where and when we can meet to complete this transaction.

Excerpts from Transcript of Deposition of
Corey Cain, Defendant
October 25, [-1]

Conducted at Howard, Fine & Howard, Inc.,
Office of plaintiff's attorney

410 Grand Avenue
Corey Cain, having been first duly sworn, testified
as follows:

p. 3

1   Q. State your name, please.
2
3   A. Corey C. Cain
4
5   Q. What is your e-mail address?
6
7   A. C U IN SEPT @ MMSN.COM
8
9   Q. Do you have any other e-mail accounts?
10
11 A. No, I do not.
12
13 Q. Do you share this e-mail account with anyone else?
14
15 A. No, I do not.
16
17 Q. Do you ever use public computers to send e-mails?
18
19 A. Yes, I use the ones on campus and also the ones in
20   the public library.
21
22 Q. Did you place an ad on the website *Jackie's*
23   *Jalopies* offering to sell a Chevy SUV?
24
25 A. Yes, I did.
26
27 Q. Using your cuinsept@mmsn.com e-mail address?
28
29 A. Yes.
30
31 Q. Is Exhibit 1 a copy of the ad you placed?
32
33 A. Yes, it is.

34 Q. And is Exhibit 2 a copy of the e-mail response you
35   received from the Plaintiff, Alex Abel?
36
37 A. Yes, it is.
38
39 Q. Is this the only response you received to the
40   *Jackie's Jalopies* ad?
41
42 A. No, I received several others over the course of
43   about 10 days after I placed the ad. But all but
44   one were offers for less than the offer from Abel.
45
46 Q. Did you sell the vehicle to one of the people who
47   responded?
48
49 A. Yes, on July 23rd I received an offer for the full
50      $20,000 I asked for and I sold that person the car.
51
52 Q. What about Exhibit 3, the e-mail presented by
53   Abel, saying that you would sell the car to the
54   plaintiff for $18,500?
55
56 A. I did not send that e-mail.
57
58 Q. Is the "from" e-mail address on this
59   correspondence your e-mail address?
60
61 A. Yes, it is, but I never sent that e-mail.
62
63 Q. Did you send any e-mails to the plaintiff?
64
65 A. No.
66
67 Q. You never responded to this offer to buy the car
68   for $18,500?
69
70 A. No. I really didn't want to sell it for less than
71      $20,000. It was worth a lot more than that so
72   I was already losing money with that price and
73   I didn't want to go lower.
74
75 Q. But you didn't reject the offer either?
76
77 A. No, I didn't want to say yes or no right away.
78   I was afraid it might be my only chance to sell
79   the car so I just ignored it hoping I would get a
80   better offer, and I did.
81
82 Q. Did you ever respond to the plaintiff's e-mail?

83 A. Not individually. I sent a message via *Jackie's*
84   *Jalopies* to everyone who used the ad service
85   saying the car was sold.
86
87 Q. Where do you think this e-mail came from?
88
89 A. I think Alex Abel created a phony e-mail to try to
90   force me to sell the car at the lower price and
91   used my words from the ad to make it sound like
92   me. If I was going to answer a specific e-mail
93   offer, I would have just hit the reply button, not
94   started a whole new message.

This is to certify that I have read the transcript of
my deposition taken on October 25, [-1], and that the
transcript accurately states the questions asked and the
answers given.

Corey Cain
Corey Cain

Subscribed and sworn to
Before me on this 14th
day of November, [-1]

Donald Marshall
Notary Public

4.26   CHAT ROOM TRANSCRIPT

Defendant, Wade Sampson, is charged with arson and murder. The state alleges that on July 19, [-1], Sampson intentionally started his house on fire, and that the fire killed Nellie Sampson, his daughter. Sampson denies starting the fire and claims that the fire was started by a faulty electrical appliance.

The key evidence in the case is an alleged "Booze Busters" chat room discussion. The police received alleged transcript(s) of this chat room discussion from Mitch Bronson, who says he is a regular participant in the chat room. Bronson says that "Booze Busters" is an Internet group of problem drinkers who support each other through the chat room. The defendant denies making any of the statements in the alleged transcript(s) of the chat room discussion.

Attached are transcripts of interviews of Mitch Bronson and the defendant's girlfriend, Gloria Wilbur, and an alleged printout of the chat room conversation.

The case is now on trial.

1. For the state, introduce the "cut and paste" transcript of the chat room conversation in evidence. For this version of the exercise, assume that the only version of the transcript available is the one with the title "Booze Busters Chat Room Excerpts, November 12, [-1]." Assume that this is the version of the transcript delivered by Mitch Bronson to Detective Shelby Moore. According to Bronson, he produced this version by cutting and pasting the conversation from the chat room to a word processing document, then printing the word processing document. For this version of the exercise, assume that neither Bronson nor Moore made any attempt to produce a screenshot version of the chat room discussion, and that it is no longer possible to produce such a version. In other words, assume that a screenshot version of the transcript does not exist.

2. [As an alternative:] For the state, introduce the screenshot version of the chat room conversation. For this version of the exercise, assume that, after

meeting with Mitch Bronson, Detective Shelby Moore went with Bronson to his home. Bronson printed a screenshot of the chat room conversation and gave it to Moore.

3. For the defense, oppose the offer(s).

Booze Busters Chat Room Excerpts, November 12, [-1]

20:15:01	<SlamminSammy> Slammin' Sammy here. What's up? Anyone in?
20:15:06	<TheMitchster> TheMitchster here. Not Much. How about you?
20:15:12	<SlamminSammy> I'm way down. I'm mourning the loss of people I've rejected all my life. My sweetheart watched me go to jail twice. And I killed Nellie because her mother stood between us.
20:15:26	<TheMitchster> Sammy, what are you talking about, you killed Nellie? Is this a cold fact? Are you getting help?
20:18:40	<SlamminSammy> I don't know if this is so smart. They could trace this back to me somehow. My handle is no big secret. But I guess everyone here promised each other confidentiality, so I guess I can open up. You might think that I'm flailing myself for some sort of weird self gratification. But this is as real as it gets. After I divorced her mother, I tried to get custody of Nellie, and we agreed to joint custody. She used joint custody to jerk me around, using Nellie to make my life miserable. So the last night when Nellie was still with me, before she had to go back to her mother, I got totally wasted. I just kept thinking that my ex was ruining both my and Nellie's lives. I knew I had to end that. So after Nellie went to sleep, I set the house on fire. I got outside, and made a big show of how distraught I was, so nobody would know what I did. In the emergency room in Piney River, I bawled my eyes out. After a while the booze wore off, and I realized what I had done. They were so worried about me that they flew me to Springfield Hospital. I got released a while ago, and I've been dwelling on it ever since.
20:20:55	<TheMitchster> Sammy, do the cops know you did this?
20:22:05	<SlamminSammy> No, they think the fire was caused by an electrical appliance. At least that's what they said the fire marshal told them. Thank god the fire marshal was such an idiot.

221

The screenshot version of the chat room dialogue is shown below.

Booze Busters Chat Room	Date: November 12, [-1]

File   Edit   View   Friends   Help

ADD

SlamminSammy

TheMitchster

20:15:01 <SlamminSammy> Slammin' Sammy here. What's up? Anyone in?

20:15:06 < TheMitchster> The Mitchster here. Not Much. How about you?

20:15:12 <SlamminSammy> I'm way down. I'm mourning the loss of people I've rejected all my life. My sweetheart watched me go to jail twice. And I killed Nellie because her mother stood between us.

20:15:26 < TheMitchster> Sammy, what are you talking about, you killed Nellie? Is this a cold fact? Are you getting help?

20:18:40 <SlamminSammy> I don't know if this is so smart. They could trace this back to me somehow. My handle is no big secret. But I guess everyone here promised each other confidentiality, so I guess I can open up. You might think that I'm flailing myself for some sort of weird self gratification. But this is as real as it gets. After I divorced her mother, I tried to get custody of Nellie, and we agreed to joint custody. She used joint custody to jerk me around, using Nellie to make my life miserable. So the last night when Nellie was still with me, before she had to go back to her mother, I got totally wasted. I just kept thinking that my ex was ruining both my and Nellie's lives. I knew I had to end that. So after Nellie went to sleep, I set the house on fire. I got outside, and made a big show of how distraught I was, so nobody would know what I did. In the emergency room in Piney River, I bawled my eyes out. After a while the booze wore off, and I realized what I had done. They were so worried about me that they flew me to Springfield Hospital. I got released a while ago, and I've been dwelling on it ever since.

20:20:55 < TheMitchster> Sammy, do the cops know you did this?

20:22:05 <SlamminSammy> No, they think the fire was caused by an electrical appliance. At least that's what they said the fire marshal told them. Thank god the fire marshal was such an idiot.

SEND

223

Transcript of Interview of Mitch Bronson
on November 13, [-1]
at Buffalo Police Department
Statement of Mitch Bronson, age 42, of 414 Maple
Street, Buffalo, regarding possible homicide, pursuant
to interview by Police Detective Shelby Moore.

1 Q. Please state your name.
2
3 A. Mitch Bronson.
4
5 Q. And your address?
6
7 A. 414 Maple Street, here in Buffalo.
8
9 Q. We just met, Mr. Bronson, but you know that I am
10   Detective Shelby Moore of the Buffalo Police
11   Department, right?
12
13 A. Yes.
14
15 Q. And you came to the police station today of your
16   own free will?
17
18 A. That is correct.
19
20 Q. In fact, you came in on your own, without me or
21   anyone else from the Buffalo Police Department
22   asking you to do so.
23
24 A. Yes. I came to report my concerns about a possible
25   crime. I wish I did not have to be here, but
26   I could not sleep at all last night, so I decided
27   I had no choice but to come to tell you about this.
28
29 Q. Before we get into the reason why you are here, let
30   me cover one more preliminary matter. Mr. Bronson,
31   you have agreed to answer my questions and to have
32   those questions and your answers recorded, so that
33   an electronic transcript can be produced.
34
35 A. That is correct.
36
37 Q. Okay, I think that is all of the preliminary stuff.
38   Tell me why you are here.

225

39 A. Like I said, I could not get any sleep last night
40   after what happened yesterday.
41
42 Q. What happened yesterday?
43
44 A. Something crazy happened in the chat room.
45
46 Q. Chat room?
47
48 A. You know. A place in cyberspace where people can go
49   to communicate with each other online. Each person
50   can add to the conversation. The chat room that
51   I use is for a group called Booze Busters.
52
53 Q. What is Booze Busters?
54
55 A. It is sort of like Alcoholics Anonymous, only
56   different. All of us in Booze Busters know we have
57   a drinking problem, but we don't agree with the AA
58   folks that you have to give up drinking completely.
59   We know we have a problem, but we believe we can
60   reduce our drinking without totally eliminating it.
61
62 Q. So this chat room is sort of an electronic version
63   of a support group?
64
65 A. Yep. Sometimes I go there when I need help
66   controlling my drinking, like when I am upset.
67   Other times, like yesterday, I go there to support
68   other members of Booze Busters who might need help.
69
70 Q. Is it anonymous?
71
72 A. It is supposed to be. All of us use made-up names,
73   instead of our real names. But some of the made-up
74   names are pretty close to people's real names.
75
76 Q. What is your name in this chat room?
77
78 A. The Mitchster. See what I mean?
79
80 Q. So it is not really all that anonymous?
81
82 A. Well, when you join the group, you promise to never
83   tell anyone outside the group what anybody said
84   in the chat room. That is why I feel so bad about
85   being here talking to you today. But I couldn't
86   live with myself if I did not tell somebody in law
87   enforcement about what happened yesterday, so here
88   I am.

89 Q. What happened in the chat room yesterday?
90
91 A. Yesterday evening I was online, checking sports
92   scores, so I decided to log into the chat room for
93   a while. And Slammin Sammy said some things that
94   were really disturbing.
95
96 Q. Who is Slammin Sammy?
97
98 A. Well, I guess I am not supposed to know, because of
99   all that anonymous stuff. But I do know. Slammin
100   Sammy is Wade Sampson.
101
102 Q. How do you know that?
103
104 A. I am the one who invited him into the Booze Busters
105   group in the first place, a couple of years ago. At
106   the time, Wade was my business partner.
107
108 Q. How so?
109
110 A. He and I owned a bunch of sandwich shops together.
111   He had invented a sandwich with roast beef, ham,
112   and turkey that he just loved, so we called it
113   the Slammin Sammy on our menu. When he joined the
114   group, he used that as his group name.
115
116 Q. Why did you invite him to join the group?
117
118 A. Both of us drank too much. He had a better excuse
119   than I did, to tell you the truth, as some bad
120   things happened to him. He went through a horrible
121   divorce in his hometown of Piney River. And then
122   his daughter died in a house fire. I felt really
123   bad for him. Well, I used to, anyway.
124
125 Q. Getting back to yesterday, what happened in the
126   chat room?
127
128 A. I printed out the important part. Here it is.
129
130 Q. And you are handing me a one-page document that
131   says Booze Busters Chat Room Excerpts, November 12,
132   [-1] at the top?
133
134 A. That is correct. I cut and pasted the key parts
135   into a word processing document, then I added the
136   title.

137 Q. Okay. But how do you know that Wade Sampson typed
138   these things?
139
140 A. First of all, Wade is Slammin Sammy, like I said.
141   Second, this post has language that sounds just
142   like Wade.
143
144 Q. Like what?
145
146 A. He loves the phrase "weird self gratification."
147   I have never heard anyone else use that phrase.
148   And see that reference to "sweetheart" at the top?
149   Nobody calls their girlfriend that anymore, but
150   Wade does.
151
152 Q. Who is his girlfriend, by the way?
153
154 A. Gloria Wilbur.
155
156 Q. Does she live here?
157
158 A. Yeah. Over by Midtown Park. I don't know the
159   address, but I am sure you can look it up.
160
161 Q. I will do that. Anything else that tells you Wade
162   Sampson wrote this?
163
164 A. Well, he has gone to jail twice that I know of.
165   So he got that right. And he obviously knows his
166   daughter's name, Nellie. And all of that stuff
167   about her dying in a fire is just like he has told
168   me when he has talked about it. Well, almost all
169   of it. Before this, he had always said it was an
170   accidental fire. So the stuff about him setting it
171   and pretending to be horrified is new.
172
173 Q. Leaving that out of the equation for the moment,
174   what has he told you before about this fire?
175
176 A. That there was a fire, for one. That the fire
177   marshal said it was caused by an electrical
178   appliance. That he went to the emergency room in
179   Piney River. That they took him in for observation
180   at Springfield Hospital. Of course, when he said
181   that before, I thought he really was distraught,
182   not just faking it.
183
184 Q. Anything else?
185
186 A. Well, he really does hate his ex-wife. I can assure
187   you of that.

228

188 Q. And you are his ex-partner. Does he hate you?
189
190 A. Well, we aren't on the best of terms. You know
191   how it is when you are former partners. We don't
192   exactly consider ourselves best friends anymore.
193   And we are still fighting a bit over splitting up
194   the assets. But it is nothing out of the ordinary.
195   I still wish him the best. Well, I used to. Now
196   I don't know what to think.
197
198 Q. Is there anything else you want us to know?
199
200 A. Not that I can think of. Other than I really hate
201   to break the confidentiality pledge. But I had to
202   do that, because somebody has to look into this
203   stuff.
204
205 Q. Okay, then, let's wrap this up. You understand that,
206   using our electronic transcription technology, a
207   written version of this statement will be produced,
208   and you will be asked to review it and, if it is
209   correct, sign it?
210
211 A. Yes.
212
213 Q. And you are willing to sign it, freely and
214   voluntarily?
215
216 A. Sure. I wish I did not have to be involved in any
217   of this, but I want to do the right thing here.
218
219 Q. This will end the recorded interview of Mitch
220   Bronson.

This is to certify that I have reviewed this
transcript of my recorded interview on November 13,
[-1], and that the transcript accurately states the
questions asked and the answers given.

Mitch Bronson
_____
Mitch Bronson

Transcript of Interview of Gloria Wilbur
on November 15, [-1]

at Buffalo Police Department

Statement of Gloria Wilbur, age 36, of 1428 Parkside
Road, Buffalo, regarding pending investigation
of potential homicide in Piney River, pursuant to
interview by Police Detective Shelby Moore.

1   Q. State your name and address, please.
2
3   A. Gloria Wilber. 1428 Parkside Road in Buffalo.
4
5   Q. Is that by Midtown Park?
6
7   A. Right across the street.
8
9   Q. And I introduced myself when I called you this
10   morning and again when you came to the station,
11   but just to get it on the record, you realize that
12   I am Detective Shelby Moore of the Buffalo Police
13   Department, right?
14
15 A. Yes.
16
17 Q. And you came to the police station today of your
18   own free will?
19
20 A. That is correct.
21
22 Q. You drove here yourself?
23
24 A. Yes, after you called. I am glad you did. I heard
25   rumors about that creep Mitch Bronson trying to
26   say my Wade said something about the fire that
27   killed his daughter. I hope you don't believe a
28   word that jackass Bronson has said.
29
30 Q. Let's slow down just a minute. Let me cover
31   one more preliminary item. As I explained to
32   you before we turned on the recorder, this
33   interview is being recorded. And you have agreed
34   to answer my questions while being recorded. So
35   you know that my questions and your answers are
36   being recorded, so we can produce an electronic
        transcript of this interview.

231

37   A. Sure. And I am glad that you are doing that,
38   because we need to set the record straight here.
39

40   Q. Why do you say that?
41

42   A. Like I said, you should not believe a word or even
43   a syllable that comes out of the mouth of that
44   creep Bronson.
45

46   Q. Why not?
47

48   A. He hates Wade.
49

50   Q. Because of their business?
51

52   A. Well, that is part of it. He is trying to cheat
53   Wade out of his fair share of the assets, now that
54   Wade had finally had enough of him stealing the
55   proceeds from the Fairview store.
56

57   Q. Stealing the proceeds? Didn't he own that store?
58

59   A. He owned half of it. But we found out that he
60   was taking about half of the cash from the cash
61   register from that store almost every day and
62   pocketing it. He admitted it and said he would
63   never do it again, but then he did, so Wade told
64   him they were through.
65

66   Q. That is why Bronson hates Wade?
67

68   A. Part of it. The other part is about me, I guess.
69

70   Q. How so?
71

72   A. I am embarrassed to say this, but that creep has a
73   crush on me, I guess. Every time he gets drunk, he
74   puts his hands all over me.
75

76   Q. Have you ever done anything to encourage him?
77

78   A. Are you kidding? That creep? Never. I love Wade.
79

80   Q. By the way, does Wade have any special names for
81   you?
82

83   A. No. He just calls me his sweetheart. Isn't that
84   cute? Nobody calls anyone that anymore, but he
85   does. He is just a great guy.

```
86   Q. How long have you been dating him?
87
88   A. For about four years. We have been living together
89      for ten months. Well, off and on.
90
91   Q. Off and on?
92
93   A. I moved out once.
94
95   Q. Why?
96
97   A. He threatened to push me down the stairs once when
98      he was drunk. I am not going to put up with that,
99      so I moved out.
100
101  Q. So you thought he was serious?
102
103  A. When he drinks too much, sometimes he loses his
104     temper a bit. I had to have him arrested.
105
106  Q. Has he ever gone to jail on any other occasion?
107
108  A. Only one other time. For a driving while
109     intoxicated conviction a couple of years ago. See,
110     that's the whole thing. As long as he does not
111     drink too much, he is fine.
112
113  Q. When was the last time he had a drink?
114
115  A. It is not every time he drinks. Most of the time he
116     only drinks a little, and he is fine then. He has
117     not gone on a binge since the time he threatened to
118     push me down the stairs and I had him arrested.
119
120  Q. So you feel safe with him now?
121
122  A. Of course I do. I would not be there if I did not
123     feel safe. I am not one of those kind, detective.
124     Wade is a kind soul. Timid, even. Which is why
125     that jerk Bronson could take advantage of him.
126     Poor Wade is so peaceful. He will do anything to
127     avoid a fight or an argument.
128
129  Q. But you did have him arrested for domestic
130     violence.
131
132  A. Potential domestic violence, detective. He never
133     touched me. Looking back, I realize that was a
134     mistake by me. He was not going to do anything to
135     me. I overreacted.
```

```
136  Q. Getting back to Mr. Bronson, you think he has it
137     in for Wade?
138
139  A. I don't think so. I know so. He took advantage of
140     Wade when they had those sandwich shops. For one
141     thing, he always ran the books and the computers,
142     while Wade handled the personnel stuff and
143     actually did all the work of running the shops.
144     I have to give this to that creep, he really knows
145     computers. He can do anything with them. He even
146     created a phony set of reports from the Fairview
147     store that fooled Wade for a long time.
148
149  Q. Is there anything else you want to tell us?
150
151  A. No. Just don't believe anything that creep Mitch
152     Bronson tells you.
153
154  Q. Let's wrap this up, then. You know that I will now
155     use our electronic transcription technology to
156     produce a written version of this statement, then
157     I will ask you to review it and sign it?
158
159  A. Yes.
160
161  Q. Are you willing to sign it, freely and voluntarily?
162
163  A. Absolutely. Everything I have said is the complete
        truth.

     Q. This is the end of the recorded interview of
        Gloria Wilbur.
```

This is to certify that I have reviewed this
transcript of my recorded interview on November
15, [-1], and that the transcript accurately
states the questions asked and the answers given.

Gloria Wilbur

Gloria Wilbur

4.27 SOCIAL MEDIA POST

In each of its permutations, this problem concerns the admissibility or other use of a "status update" posted to the Mule Strong Group of SocialNet, a social media service. The November 24, [-1], status update said, "Okay, I get it. I need money and I need to get out of this dump of a town. It is time to kill too birds with one stone." The proponent of this evidence claims that Brett L. Waye wrote this status update. For each version of the problem outlined below, the proponent wishes to use this status update, along with other evidence, to convince the fact finder (usually the jury, but in some instances the judge) that Waye committed insurance fraud and arson by burning his house two days after posting the status update.

Other evidence in the case has established, will establish, or could establish, the following:

Brett L. Waye married Hannah Goings on July 21, [-12]. They have a daughter who is ten years old and a son who is eight years old.

From July, [-12], to November 26, [-1], they lived at 1917 5th Avenue in Chillicothe, Missouri, in a home that they owned (subject to 30-year mortgage). However, in September, [-1], Hannah Goings-Waye, a CPA, accepted a job as the Chief Financial Officer of the Metro Area Hospital in Kansas City, Missouri. After accepting this position, she spent Mondays through Fridays, and sometimes weekend days, in Kansas City.

From June, [-12], to May, [-1], Brett L. Waye worked as a production manager at Bushwhacker Brewery in Chillicothe. Bushwhacker declared bankruptcy in May, [-1], and shut down its plant. Because the brewery had been the largest employer in Chillicothe, its demise has had a major negative impact on that town's economy. As of the time of the trial, many homes are on the market, and those that have sold since the brewery closure have sold for less than half of their value before the brewery's closure.

Despite a constant attempt to find work, Brett Waye has been unemployed since the demise of Bushwhacker Brewery. On January 2 of this year, he and his two children moved to Kansas City. He is now looking for work in Kansas City.

On November 26, [-1], a fire that started at about 2:00 A.M. destroyed the house at 1917 5th Avenue in Chillicothe. Nobody was in the home at the time the fire destroyed it.

You will be assigned a specific context for the proposed use of the November 24 status update. Please concentrate on that specific context and ignore all other contexts. For example, in your case, perhaps only Exhibit 6 exists, so you can make no use of the other exhibits.

In each of the specific contexts below, the proponent (i.e., the person discussed in subparagraph "i") wishes to introduce or make some other use of the November 24 post, to try to convince the jury or the judge that it establishes, or helps to establish, that Waye committed insurance fraud and arson by burning his house. The proponent should focus on this task. This problem is NOT designed for a comprehensive examination of the witness by the proponent. In each instance, the opponent should object to the proponent's use of the status update or otherwise lessen its impact, perhaps (but not necessarily) via cross-examination.

(1) *Waye v. West Is Best Insurance*: In this case, Brett L. Waye has sued West Is Best Insurance to recover under the homeowner's policy for the loss of the home. West Is Best refuses to pay the claim because it asserts that Waye burned down the house and is therefore ineligible to recover, due to the arson exclusion in the homeowner's policy.

(a) [Background for (1)(a), (b), and (c); (2)(a), (b), and (c); and (3)(a), (b), and (c):] West Is Best calls Hannah Goings-Waye as a witness. She testifies that she and Brett were under substantial financial strain after he lost his job. She also testifies that the two of them were conversing via SocialNet's private message option on November 23, [1], because Brett no longer had a cell phone. In many of her "dozens" of messages during the "back and forth" SocialNet conversation that day, she tried to convince Brett to move to Kansas City to look for work. She testifies that the last message on November 23 was from Brett to her, saying something like, "I will think it over and get back to you tomorrow." On the evening of the next day, November 24, [-1], she saw the message at issue, which Brett probably accidentally posted to the Mules Strong Group, thinking he was sending a private message to her. She is also prepared to testify that Brett often uses the expression "two birds with one stone" and, when typing or writing, often makes errors in selecting the wrong version of to/two/too.

Problem (a): If asked, Hannah would testify that the November 24 message said something like, "Okay, I get it. I need money and I need to get out of this dump of a town. It is time to kill too birds with one stone."

(i) For West Is Best Insurance, use Hannah's testimony to prove that Brett burned his house and committed insurance fraud.

(ii) For Brett, resist the offer and, if necessary, cross-examine Hannah.

(b) [See above for Background.] When she is asked what the November 24 message said, Hannah will say "I do not remember." Your file contains Exhibit 1. It looks like a screenshot from a computer, though you have no idea how it got into your file or who put it there.

(i) For West Is Best Insurance, use Hannah's testimony and Exhibit 1 to prove that Brett burned his house and committed insurance fraud.

(ii) For Brett, resist the offer and, if necessary, cross-examine Hannah.

(c) [See above for Background.] When she is asked what the November 24 message said, Hannah will say, "I do not remember. But I do remember that the message seemed important enough that I should talk to Brett about it when I next saw him. So I cut-and-pasted it into a word processing document, then printed it out and put the printout into my purse. I did not save the electronic version of that file, but I did save the printout." That printed page is Exhibit 6.

(i) For West Is Best Insurance, use Hannah's testimony and Exhibit 6 to prove that Brett burned his house and committed insurance fraud.

(ii) For Brett, resist the offer and, if necessary, cross-examine Hannah.

(d) West Is Best calls Lynn Wallenstein, who brings Exhibit 5 (and its attachments, Exhibits 1-4) to the stand. Wallenstein's testimony, if allowed, will be consistent with Exhibit 3, the report s/he drafted.

(i) For West Is Best, use Wallenstein's testimony and, if useful, some or all of Exhibits 1-5, to prove that Brett burned his house and committed insurance fraud.

(ii) For Brett, resist the offer(s) and, if necessary, cross-examine Wallenstein.

(e) West Is Best brings the original of Exhibit 5 (and its attachments, Exhibits 1-4) to court.

(i) For West Is Best Insurance, use Exhibit 5 and its attachments to prove that Brett burned his house and committed insurance fraud.

(ii) For Brett, resist the offer.

(2) *State v. Waye*: In this case, the state is prosecuting Brett for arson and insurance fraud.

(a) [See above for Background. This background should be modified only to reflect that the state calls Hannah Goings-Waye as a witness.]
If asked, Hannah would testify that the November 24 message said something like, "Okay, I get it. I need money and I need to get out of this dump of a town. It is time to kill too birds with one stone."

(i) For the state, use Hannah's testimony to prove that Brett burned his house and committed insurance fraud.

(ii) For Brett, resist the offer and, if necessary, cross-examine Hannah.

(b) [See above for Background. This background should be modified only to reflect that the state calls Hannah Goings-Waye as a witness.] When she is asked what the November 24 message said, Hannah will say, "I do not remember." Your file contains Exhibit 1. It looks like a screenshot from a computer, though you have no idea how it got into your file or who put it there.

238

(i)   For the state, use Hannah's testimony and Exhibit 1 to prove that Brett burned his house and committed insurance fraud.

(ii) For Brett, resist the offer and, if necessary, cross-examine Hannah.

(c) [See above for Background. This background should be modified only to reflect that the state calls Hannah Goings-Waye as a witness.] When she is asked what the November 24 message said, Hannah will say, "I do not remember. But I do remember that the message seemed important enough that I should talk to Brett about it when I next saw him. So I cut-and-pasted it into a word processing document, then printed it out and put the printout into my purse. I did not save the electronic version of that file, but I did save the printout." That printed page is Exhibit 6.

(i)   For the state, use Hannah's testimony and Exhibit 6 to prove that Brett burned his house and committed insurance fraud.

(ii) For Brett, resist the offer and, if necessary, cross-examine Hannah.

(d) The state calls Lynn Wallenstein, who brings Exhibit 5 (and its attachments, Exhibits 1-4) to the stand. Wallenstein's testimony, if allowed, will be consistent with Exhibit 3, the report s/he drafted.

(i)   For the state, use Wallenstein's testimony and, if useful, some or all of Exhibits 1-5, to prove that Brett burned his house and committed insurance fraud.

(ii) For Brett, resist the offer(s) and, if necessary, cross-examine Wallenstein.

(e) The state brings the original of Exhibit 5 (and its attachments, Exhibits 1-4) to court.

(i)   For the state, use Exhibit 5 and its attachments to prove that Brett burned his house and committed insurance fraud.

(ii) For Brett, resist the offer.

(3) *Goings-Waye v. Waye*: In this case, Hannah is suing Brett for divorce and for custody of the couple's two children. She asserts that Brett's alleged burning of the house and insurance fraud helps to prove that he is unfit to be the custodial parent.

(a) [See above for Background. This background should be modified only to reflect that Hannah Goings-Waye calls herself as a witness.]

If asked, Hannah would testify that the November 24 message said something like, "Okay, I get it. I need money and I need to get out of this dump of a town. It is time to kill too birds with one stone."

    (i) For Hannah, use her testimony to prove that Brett burned his house and committed insurance fraud.

    (ii) For Brett, resist the offer and, if necessary, cross-examine Hannah.

(b) [See above for Background. This background should be modified only to reflect that Hannah Goings-Waye calls herself as a witness.] When she is asked what the November 24 message said, Hannah will say, "I do not remember." Your file contains Exhibit 1. It looks like a screenshot from a computer, though you have no idea how it got into your file or who put it there.

    (i) For Hannah, use her testimony and Exhibit 1 to prove that Brett burned his house and committed insurance fraud.

    (ii) For Brett, resist the offer and, if necessary, cross-examine Hannah.

(c) [See above for Background. This background should be modified only to reflect that Hannah Goings-Waye calls herself as a witness.] When she is asked what the November 24 message said, Hannah will say, "I do not remember. But I do remember that the message seemed important enough that I should talk to Brett about it when I next saw him. So I cut-and-pasted it into a word processing document, then printed it out and put the printout into my purse. I did not save the electronic version of that file, but I did save the printout." That printed page is Exhibit 6.

(i)   For Hannah, use her testimony and Exhibit 6 to prove that Brett burned his house and committed insurance fraud.

(ii) For Brett, resist the offer and, if necessary, cross-examine Hannah.

(d) Hannah calls Lynn Wallenstein, who brings Exhibit 5 (and its attachments, Exhibits 1-4) to the stand. Wallenstein's testimony, if allowed, will be consistent with Exhibit 3, the report s/he drafted.

(i)   For Hannah, use Wallenstein's testimony and, if useful, some or all of Exhibits 1-5, to prove that Brett burned his house and committed insurance fraud.

(ii) For Brett, resist the offer(s) and, if necessary, cross-examine Wallenstein.

(e) Hannah brings the original of Exhibit 5 (and its attachments, Exhibits 1-4) to court.

(i)   For Hannah, use Exhibit 5 and its attachments to prove that Brett burned his house and committed insurance fraud.

(ii) For Brett, resist the offer.

(4) *Sullivan v. Focks*: In this case, Brett has testified as a fact witness to a car accident, on behalf of plaintiff Sullivan.

(a) The cross-examination of Brett is underway.

(i)   For Focks, cross-examine Brett. You have a copy of Exhibit 5 and its attachments (Exhibits 1-4).

(ii) For Sullivan, resist the use of Exhibits 1-5 and, if necessary, conduct related redirect examination.

(b) Plaintiff Sullivan's case, including Brett's testimony, is completed. In her case-in-chief, defendant Focks calls Hannah to the stand. If allowed to do so, she will testify in a manner consistent with version (1)(a) of the problem, *supra*.

(i)   For Focks, conduct a direct examination of Hannah to attack Brett's credibility.

(ii) For Sullivan, object to Hannah's testimony and, if necessary, cross-examine her.

(c) Plaintiff Sullivan's case, including Brett's testimony, is completed. In her case-in-chief, defendant Focks calls Wallenstein to the stand.

    (i) For Focks, conduct a direct examination of Wallenstein to attack Brett's credibility. You have a copy of Exhibit 5 and its attachments (Exhibits 1-4).

    (ii) For Sullivan, resist the use of Exhibits 1-5 and, if necessary, cross-examine Wallenstein.

(5) *United States v. Waye, I*: In this case, the federal government is prosecuting Brett for alleged tax fraud. The government claims that Brett overstated his charitable deductions by claiming donations that he did not make. The alleged tax fraud concerns his [-5] tax return. Brett has not, and will not, testify in the case.

(a) The government calls Hannah to the stand during its case-in-chief. If allowed to do so, she will testify in a manner consistent with version (1) (a) of the problem, *supra*.

    (i) For the government, conduct a direct examination of Hannah.

    (ii) For Brett, object to Hannah's testimony and, if necessary, cross-examine Hannah.

(b) The government calls Wallenstein to the stand during its case-in-chief.

    (i) For the government, conduct a direct examination of Wallenstein. You have a copy of Exhibit 5 and its attachments (Exhibits 1-4).

    (ii) For Brett, resist the use of Exhibits 1-5 and, if necessary, cross-examine Wallenstein.

(6) *United States v. Waye, II*: In this case, the federal government is prosecuting Brett for alleged tax fraud. The government claims that Brett overstated his charitable deductions by claiming donations that he did not make. The alleged tax fraud concerns his [-4] tax return. Brett has testified in his defense.

(a) The cross-examination of Brett is underway.

  (i) For the government, cross-examine Brett. You have a copy of Exhibit 5 and its attachments (Exhibits 1-4).

  (ii) For Brett, resist the use of Exhibits 1-5 and, if necessary, conduct related redirect examination.

(b) The defense has rested. In its rebuttal case, the government calls Hannah to the stand. If allowed to do so, she will testify in a manner consistent with version (1)(a) of the problem, *supra*.

  (i) For the government, conduct a direct examination of Hannah.

  (ii) For Brett, object to Hannah's testimony and, if necessary, cross-examine Hannah.

(c) The defense has rested. In its rebuttal case, the government calls Wallenstein to the stand.

  (i) For the government, conduct a direct examination of Wallenstein. You have a copy of Exhibit 5 and its attachments (Exhibits 1-4).

  (ii) For Brett, resist the use of Exhibits 1-5 and, if necessary, cross-examine Wallenstein.

(d) The defense has rested. In its rebuttal case, the government has offered Exhibit 5 and its attachments (Exhibits 1-4) into evidence.

  (i) For the government, articulate the argument for admission of Exhibit 5 and its attachments.

  (ii) For Brett, resist the offer.

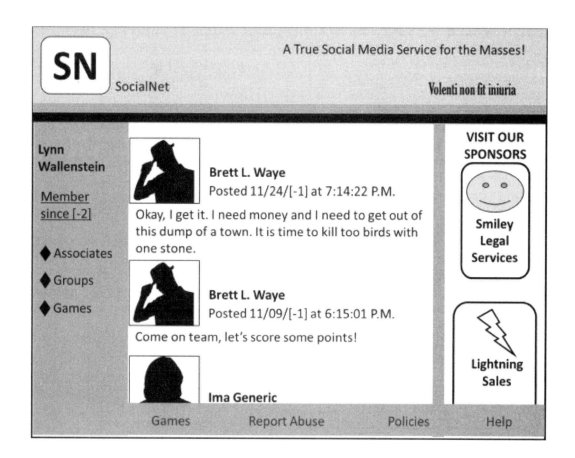

EXHIBIT
1

LSM

November 28, [-1]
Via Certified Mail

Claims Department
West Is Best Insurance
1846 Vine
Kansas City, MO

RECEIVED
Claims Dept.
11/29/[-1]
Claim#: 54A4734F

An accidental fire completely destroyed my home at 1917 5th Avenue in Chillicothe, Missouri, on November 26. I have moved with my to children into the Local Stay Motel, so the kids can stay in school here, at least for the rest of [-1]. But I expect to move, probably to Kansas City, after the first of the year.

Please let me know what I need to do to get paid for the loss to my home and for temporary living quarters here.

As you can imagine, my life is a shambles now. Please act on this immediately.

Sincerely,

Brett L Waye

Brett L. Waye

Local Stay Motel, 114 West Highway 36, Chillicothe, MO 64601 (660) 646-8822

EXHIBIT
2

247

West Is Best Insurance

Sensitive Matter Report

To: Dale Jessen, Vice President of Claims

From:Lynn Wallenstein, Claims Adjuster II, Computer Specialist

Date: December 5, [-1]

RE: Insured Brett L. Waye, Claim No. 54A4734F, Policy G283B9Home

When I arrived back to work today after a two-week family vacation, I noticed a SocialNet status update that was apparently posted by Brett L. Waye on November 24, [-1], stating, "Okay, I get it. I need money and I need to get out of this dump of a town. It is time to kill too birds with one stone."

Brett Waye, his wife Hannah, and I were college fr classmates. We are members of the Mule Strong Group at SocialNet. That group consists largely of our classmates from the University of Central Missouri. Brett and I knew each other well in college. This helped me to sell him a homeowner's policy in Febuary of this year, when I was a sales agent.

Thus, I knew was probably our insured and I knew that any claim against his policy would hurt my loss rating from my days in sales and, therefore, reduce or eliminate my year-end bonus. I ran a quick check of the electronic file, which I am authorized to do as the Claims Department's Computer Specialist, for Brett L. Waye. In that file, I saw a letter from Waye on the stationary of the Local Stay Motel, 114 West Highway 36, Chillicothe, MO 64601, to the Claims Department, dated November 28, [-1], notifying the company of a fire at the Waye home at 1917 5th Avenue, Chillicothe, MO, on November 26, [-1]. Receipt of this letter resulted in our assignment of Claim No. 54A4734F to the claim on the homeowner's policy.

After seeing this letter, I realized that the November 24 status update could be of svalue, as it seemed to indicate that Waye was planning to start his house on fire. When I received training after transfering to the Claims Department in April of this year, company lawyers told us that one issue we face in litigation is proving that a particular person is the author of an email, social network status update, or other electronic communication, because people often claim that they did not write electronic

EXHIBIT

3

communications that others assumed were from them. Thus, I realized that it would be helpful if I could establish that Waye wrote the November 24 status update.

I am a friend of Brett Waye, but I do not condone insurance fraud. So I decided to see if I could tri entice him into disclosing his location. As you might know, at my suggestion the company paid to join a service called www.jokes and cartoons.com in October. That service, which we and other insurance companies subscribe to, helps us to find people.

At approximately 10:00 a.m. this morning, I sent a private em message replying to the November 24 message, saying "Brett: Hope all is okay. To cheer up, check this out: www.jokes and cartoons.com." Pursuant to our subscription, I sent a blind cc of my reply message too the Skip Tracing Department of www.jokes and cartoons.com.

A few Twenty minutes after I sent the private reply message, the original poster of the November 24 status update, presumably Brett Waye, clicked on www.jokes and cartoons.com. As soon as that person clicked on the www.jokes and cartoons.com website, the Skip Tracing Department at www.jokes and cartoons.com automatically sent me an email with the IP (Internet Protocol) address that was being used by that person to access the www.jokes and cartoons.com site. [The person who clicks on the www.jokes and cartoons.com site does not realize that this email with his or her IP address is being generated. That person just sees a website with jokes and cartoons.]

I copied the IP address I received via the automatic email from www.jokes and cartoons.com to my computer clipboard. Then I composed an email to FindEmNow, another computer service that we subscribe to, asking them to provide locat geographical information for the IP address, which I copied into my email.

As you may know, the IP address is associated with the internet service provider that the person using the internet is using. Thus, the IP address does not provide a precise location, such as a street address, for the person using the computer. But it does provide some information about that person's location, by providing information about the internet service provider the person was using.

Shortly after my email to FindEmNow, I received an automatic email from FindEmNow indicating that the IP address that I had provided was associated with the following geographical data:

West Is Best Insurance

Sensitive Matter Report

Probable State: Missouri   Probable County: Livingston

Probable City: Chillicothe Approx. Coordinates: 39.76° N, 93.56° W

I did a quick internet search for the latitude and longitude of Chilicothe, Missouri. That search revealed the coordinates to be 39.7931° north and 93.5519° west. My internet search also showed that the main highway through Chillicothe, U.S. 36, is south of the center of town. Thus, the approximate coordinates provided by FindEmNow are consistent with the probable location of the Local Stay Motel in Chillicothe. Thus, it appears that the writer of the November 24 status report was using an internet service provider, very possibly via free service provided by a motel like the Local Stay, in Chillocothe.

Because the process of locating physical addresses via IP addresses is not foolproof, one can never say with certainty that an IP address is associated with a particular physical location. However, based upon my expertise and experience, including familiarity with both the www.jokes and cartoons.com and FindEmNow services, it is my opinion that it is over 90% probable that the person who sent the November 24 status update referenced above was in Chillicothe, Missouri, probably at or near the Local Stay Motel, this morning when he linked to www.jokes and cartoons.com.com.

That person clicked the www.jokes and cartoons.com link because I sent it to him. Almost certainly, that person was Brett Waye. Waye knows me, so he trusted me when I sent him this link. Therefore, with the use of our www.jokes and cartoons.com and FindEmNow subscriptions, it is my opinion, to a level of certainty well over 90%, that we have established that the person who sent the November 24 status update was Brett L. Waye.

I hope you agree that this experience establishes the value of services like www.jokes and cartoons.com and FindEmNow. These are expensive services, to be sure. But we in the Claims Department often need to find witnesses, insureds, and others and to link emails and other electronic communications to specific persons.

Pursuant to company policy regarding sensitive matters, I have typed this report on one of the typewriters in our office, not on word processing software, and I have sent all emails regarding this

matter to the "Destroy Now" delete box, which makes them essentially untraceable (though, as we know, it is folly to ever suggest that something could never be restored). Pursuant to company policy regarding sensitive matters, I will run this manual report through the scanner, to create a pdf version that will be filed under the above-referenced matter, then place this original in your physical mailbox. I will make no paper copies.

I took a screenshot of the November 24 message and added it to the electronic file for Claim No. 54A4734F.

Brett L. Waye
1917 5th Avenue
Chillicothe, MO 64601

2345

Date _Feb 21 [-1]_

PAY _West or Best Insurance Company_ $ 982 46/100

TO THE ORDER OF

Nine hundred eighty two and 46/100 _____ DOLLARS   **FBIC**

MWE Bank of the State
101 Main St
Chillicothe, MO 64601

FOR _Annual Premium Polley #6283139 Home_   _Brett L. Waye_

⑈ ⑈2345678901⑈   123 ⑈⑈890 ⑈⑈ 90   2345

EXHIBIT 4

AFFIDAVIT OF TERRY SANDERSON
On January 4, [-0]

Terry Sanderson, having been first duly sworn, testified as follows:

1)   I am the custodian of records at West Is Best Insurance Company of Kansas City, Missouri.

2)   In [-8], our company completed its transition to an electronic records system, whereby we retain records in electronic format, not paper. When we determine that a paper record should be maintained, we scan the document into a pdf file and retain the pdf version. In most instances, we discard the original paper version.

3)   Whenever possible, records produced by our company are created by a person who has knowledge of the information contained in the record, at or as close as reasonably possible to the time the person made the observation or received the information contained in the record.

4)   Our records are maintained and used in the ordinary course of our business, which involves marketing and issuing insurance policies and resolving claims under those policies.

5)   Today, i.e., January 4, [-0], I searched the electronic records for Claim No. 54A4734F, Policy G283B9Home, Insured: Brett L. Waye. That search revealed the following records, which are attached in printed form:

    (1) Screen Shot of Social Net Post from Brett L. Waye, 11/24/[-1], 7:14:22 p.m.

    (2) November 28, [-1], handwritten letter from Brett L. Waye, c/o Local Stay Motel, 114 West Highway 36, Chillicothe, MO 64601, to West Is Best Insurance

    (3) West Is Best Insurance Sensitive Matter Report from Lynn Wallenstein, Claims Adjuster II, Computer Specialist, to Dale Jessen, Vice President of Claims

    (4) Check for $982.46 from Brett L. Waye to West Is Best Insurance Company, dated February 21, [-1].

FURTHER AFFIANT SAYETH NOT.

DATED this the ___4___ day of __January__ 20[-0]

Terry Sanderson
Terry Sanderson

SWORN to subscribed before me, this ___4th___ day of __JANUARY__ 20[-0]

Pat Wozney PAT WOZNEY
NOTARY PUBLIC

My Commission Expires:

___9-16-[+4]___

Comm. Exp. 9/16
NOTARY PUBLIC NOTARY SEAL
HOWELL COUNTY, STATE OF MISSOURI
Commission # 0000000

EXHIBIT 5

259

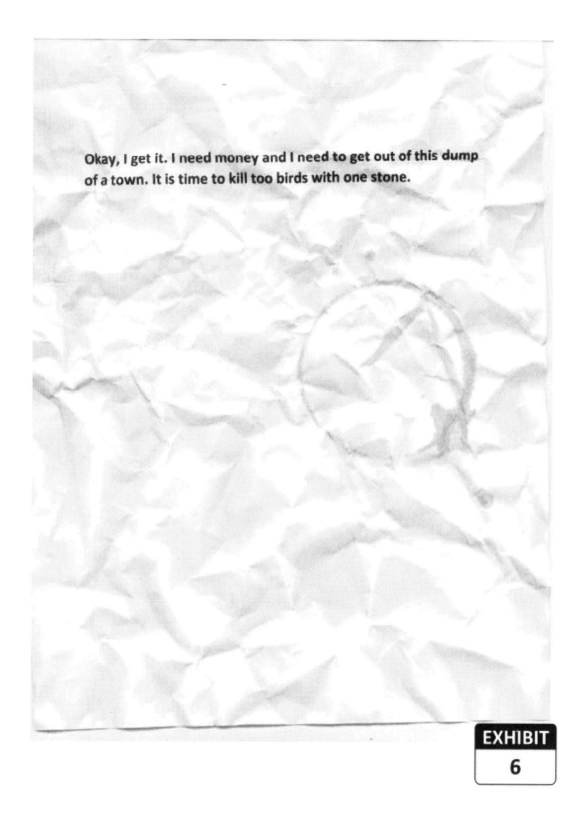

Okay, I get it. I need money and I need to get out of this dump of a town. It is time to kill too birds with one stone.

EXHIBIT

6

V

IMPEACHMENT AND REHABILITATION

Introduction

INTRODUCTION

The problems in this chapter represent cross-examination situations commonly encountered at trial. The problems principally involve impeachment with prior inconsistent statements, since these are the most common impeachment sources during trials.

For each problem assigned, you should be prepared to cross-examine or impeach the witness in a way that effectively presents the discrediting or impeaching evidence to the jury. If the witness does not admit to making an impeaching statement, be prepared to complete the impeachment by calling an appropriate prove-up witness. On redirect examination, be prepared to rehabilitate the witness by repairing or minimizing any damage done during the cross-examination.

Your instructor may modify the assignments and make specific additional assignments for these exercises.

The suggested background reading is Mauet & Easton, *Trial Techniques and Trials*, Chapter 6.

265

5.1 ORAL STATEMENT

This is a personal injury suit. Plaintiff, Charles Smith, charges that on June 1, [-2], the defendant, William Barnes, was driving his car in excess of the speed limit and that his speeding caused the car to leave the road, injuring Smith, who was a passenger in Barnes's car.

The case is now on trial. Plaintiff calls Rory Fletcher, a witness to the accident. Fletcher testifies that s/he had been sitting on the porch of his/her house at 4000 N. Clark Street for one hour when the Barnes car sped by. Fletcher says that the car was traveling 70 mph in a 55 mph zone. Fletcher says during that hour s/he drank a glass of iced tea, read the local newspaper, relaxed, and just watched the traffic.

You know from the police reports that a police officer, James Watson, interviewed Fletcher a few minutes after the accident. According to the report, Fletcher stated that the Barnes car was "traveling about 65 to 70 mph," and that s/he (Fletcher) "had just gone out on the porch moments before Barnes's car came by."

1. For the defendant, cross-examine Rory Fletcher.
2. Assume that Fletcher on cross-examination denies making the statements to Officer Watson. For the defendant, prove up the impeachment.
3. For the plaintiff, conduct any necessary redirect examination.

5.2   ORAL STATEMENT

This is a personal injury suit. One year ago today, at 2:00 P.M., the car the defendant was driving struck a pedestrian, Mark Jones, as he was crossing Clark Street, a north-south street, at Elm Street. Jones claims that he was crossing Clark Street on the south side of Elm and was in the marked crosswalk at the time he was struck. The defendant says that Jones was outside the crosswalk.

The case is now on trial. Jones's friend, Rowan Tucker, testifies for the plaintiff on direct examination that s/he was walking directly behind Jones when the car struck Jones. Tucker says that Jones was within the crosswalk at the time of the collision.

You know from your investigation that about 20 minutes after the accident, Tucker told the investigating police officer, Sam Smith, that Mark Jones was "about five feet out of the crosswalk" at the time he was struck by the car.

1. For the defendant, cross-examine Rowan Tucker.
2. Assume that on cross-examination Rowan Tucker denies making the statement to Officer Smith. For the defendant, prove up the impeachment.
3. For the plaintiff, conduct any necessary redirect examination.

5.3 ORAL STATEMENT

This is a personal injury suit. The defendant, Alex Bevernick, struck the plaintiff, a pedestrian, with his/her car on June 15, [-1].

The case is now on trial. Bevernick testified on direct examination that s/he had the green light as s/he approached on Juniper Street and as s/he entered the intersection with Maple Street. S/he said that the light for his/her car was green when s/he struck the plaintiff. Bevernick claims the plaintiff was crossing against the red light.

You previously interviewed the owner of a hot dog stand located on the southwest corner of the intersection where the accident took place. The hot dog stand owner, Luigi Roviaro, told you that seconds after the accident, Bevernick walked over to the hot dog stand and said, "I should have stopped when the light started to change to red." Roviaro also told you that the plaintiff was sitting on a nearby curb holding his leg when Bevernick said that, but that the plaintiff was too far away to have heard the words. No one else was in the immediate vicinity.

1. For the plaintiff, cross-examine Alex Bevernick. Assume that Luigi Roviaro is available as a witness.

2. Assume that Bevernick, if asked, will deny saying those words to Roviaro. If asked what s/he did say, s/he will reply, "I told him that man was a fool to cross against the red light." For the plaintiff, cross-examine Bevernick. Prove up any impeachment.

3. For the plaintiff, cross-examine Alex Bevernick. Assume you have learned that Luigi Roviaro died one week ago.

4. For the defendant, conduct any necessary redirect examination.

5.4 WRITTEN REPORT OF ORAL STATEMENT

You represent Michael Morgan, who is accused of the murder of Bridget Wilson. On direct examination, Officer Kim O'Leary testified to an oral confession by Morgan. The officer's testimony was exactly the same as his/her report. Only O'Leary and Morgan were present at the time of the interview.

Morgan is 17 years old. This was his first arrest. He finished one year of high school before he dropped out to find work as a day laborer.

Morgan will testify later and will admit telling Officer O'Leary he went to Bridget Wilson's house and found Wilson asleep on the couch. However, he will deny saying any of the other things in the statement. Morgan will testify that he told O'Leary that when he found Wilson asleep on the couch, he turned around and walked out, going to the party by himself.

1. For the defense, cross-examine Officer O'Leary.
2. For the prosecution, conduct any necessary redirect examination.

INTERVIEW OF MICHAEL MORGAN

PLACE OF INTERVIEW: Homicide division
                                headquarters
                                2426 N. Damen Avenue

TIME INTERVIEW INITIATED: 2210 hours, 6/15/[-1]
TIME INTERVIEW TERMINATED: 2240 hours, 6/15/[-1]
PERSON CONDUCTING INTERVIEW: Investigator Kim O'Leary

Subject named above was given Miranda warnings and stated he understood and voluntarily waived his rights and wanted to speak to reporting officer and did not desire presence of lawyer.

Subject then was asked extent of his knowledge concerning death of Bridget Wilson. Subject responded by saying he entered Bridget Wilson's home at approximately 1300 hours. By prearrangement, subject and Wilson were to attend a party at a friend's house. When subject arrived at Wilson's home, he found Wilson asleep on a couch. Subject said he woke Wilson and asked her why she was not ready for the party. He said she responded that she was not going to the party or anywhere else with him. Subject then became enraged and struck Wilson with an ash tray. She fell to the floor, unconscious. When subject observed her condition, he ran out of the house.

BY: *Kim O'Leary*
Reporting Officer

275

5.5 WRITTEN REPORT OF ORAL STATEMENT

William Hill has been charged with armed robbery. Robin Jacobs was a victim of the robbery. The case is now on trial.

On direct examination, Jacobs pointed to Hill and said, "That's the man who held us up. There's no doubt in my mind."

During direct examination, the prosecutor did not ask Jacobs about the lineup (although Helen Smith, the other victim, did testify about the lineup and her identification of the defendant). The lineup took place on May 6 of last year, the day of the robbery. Jacobs has not seen Hill since the lineup was conducted.

You have the attached FBI report about the lineup.

1. For the defense, cross-examine Robin Jacobs.
2. Should the prosecutor have asked Jacobs about the lineup on direct examination? If so, what questions should have been asked?
3. Assume that Jacobs on cross-examination denies making the statement noted in the police report. Complete the impeachment.
4. For the prosecution, conduct any necessary redirect examination.

FD-302 (10-6-[-5])

FEDERAL BUREAU OF INVESTIGATION

Date of transcription <u>5/6/[-1]</u>

On 5/6/[-1] a lineup was conducted by FBI Special Agent Thomas Barnett at the Robbery headquarters building at Harrison and Kedzie, at approximately 4:00 p.m. (1600).

Individuals in the lineup were:

#1:	James Hudgins	IR# 362143
#2:	William Hill	IR# 482563
#3:	James Rhoades	IR# 482571
#4:	Frank Williams	IR# 399688
#5:	Richard Long	IR# Unknown

Viewing the lineup were Helen Smith and Robin Jacobs.

Each individual stepped forward, said the words: "This is a stickup. Don't do anything stupid," then stepped back. All five then made turns in unison.

Helen Smith and Robin Jacobs viewed the lineup through a one-way window. Immediately after the lineup each witness was interviewed separately. Smith stated that #2 was the robber. Jacobs said that #2 looked like the robber, but s/he couldn't be sure.

Investigation on <u>5/6/[-1]</u>   at <u>Robbery Headquarters Building at Harrison and Kedzie</u>

File # <u>195-PX-87457-ROB</u>   Date dictated <u>5/6/[-1]</u>

By _____ FBI Special Agent Thomas Barnett

This document contains neither recommendations nor conclusions of the FBI. It is the property of the FBI and is loaned to your agency. It and its contents are not to be distributed outside your agency.

279

5.6 JOB APPLICATION FORM

This is an action brought under this state's labor laws. Tracy Burke has sued TITE Security Co., Inc., claiming that s/he was unlawfully fired from his/her job because of union organizing activities.

TITE Security defends on the grounds that it fired Burke because s/he misrepresented certain material facts on his/her employment application.

It is the law of this jurisdiction that an employer may defend a wrongful discharge claim on the basis of facts unknown at the time of the discharge. However, the unknown facts must be sufficient for the trier of fact to reasonably conclude that the employee would not have been hired had the facts been known at the time of hiring. That is, the employee's misrepresentations or omissions must be material, directly related to measuring a candidate for employment, and relied on by the employer in making the hiring decision.

At trial, on cross-examination, Burke will admit the following:

(a)   S/he received a dishonorable discharge from the Marines in [-17].

(b)   While in the Marines his/her only duties were as a division clerk.

(c)   S/he was convicted of a battery charge in [-11].

Attached is the employment application form Burke submitted to TITE Security.

1.   For the defendant, cross-examine Tracy Burke.
2.   For the plaintiff, conduct any necessary redirect examination.

Tite Security, Inc.

APPLICATION FOR EMPLOYMENT

GENERAL INFORMATION

Name (Last)	(First)	(Middle Initial)	Telephone
Burke	Tracy		(555) 862-6920

Address (Mailing Address)	(City)	(State)	(Zip)	Other Telephone
1776 Reed Road	Lost Prairie	Blackacre	17742	( ) -

Previous Address (Mailing Address)	(City)	(State)	(Zip)	E-Mail
13 Maple Drive	Lost Prairie	Blackacre	17742	jarhead@www.com

POSITION

Position Desired	How did you learn about this position?
Guard	Saw Tite guards

EDUCATION AND TRAINING

High School Graduate ☐ Yes ☒ No   Name of Last High School Attended: Lost Prairie

College, Business School, Military (Most recent first)

Name and Location	Dates Attended Month/Year	Credits Earned Quarterly or Semester Hours	Credits Earned Other (Specify)	Graduate	Degree & Year	Major or Subject
Construction	From [-17] To			☐ Yes ☐ No		
M.P. in Marine Corps	From [-29] To [-17]			☐ Yes ☐ No		

VETERAN INFORMATION (Most recent)

Branch of Service		Date of Entry	Date of Discharge
Marine Corps		[-29]	[-17]

Highest Rank	Rank at Discharge	Special Training or Duties
PFC	PFC	M.P.

Do you receive any type of disability? If so, please describe	Type of Discharge
No	Honorable

Motor Vehicle Information

Do you have a valid driver's license?	State	Driver's License Number:	Expiration:
☒ Yes ☐ No	BLKACRE	12-76-45-3	[+2]

Do you own a vehicle?	Make and Year:	Is the vehicle insured?	Type of Insurance:
☒ Yes ☐ No	RAV 4 [-4]	☒ Yes ☐ No	☒ Collision ☒ Liability

Name of Insurance Company:	Name of Insurance Agent:
EDNA Ins. Co.	I. N. Shorinse

Other

Have you ever been refused a surety bond?	If yes, please provide details:
☐ Yes ☒ No	

Have you ever been convicted of a crime?	If yes, please provide details:
☒ Yes ☐ No	Minor traffic violations

I certify the information contained in this application is true, correct, and complete.

Signature of Applicant _Tracy Burke_   Date _7/15/[-8]_

Please use the reverse side of this application to list the names of all your employers, dates of employment, and contact information of employers (you may list volunteer positions as well as paid positions, if you wish). List present or most recent employer first.

283

5.7 LETTER

This is a personal injury action arising out of an automobile accident that occurred on June 15 of last year at 3:00 P.M. Mackenzie Richardson, the plaintiff, sued the defendant, claiming that s/he had the green light at an intersection and that the defendant ran the red light, causing the accident.

The case is now on trial. Richardson testified on direct examination that s/he was traveling west on Maple toward the intersection with Main at 25 mph, the legal speed limit, and that the light for his/her street was green. As s/he was in the middle of the intersection s/he saw the light turn yellow. A split second later, the defendant's car, traveling southbound at a high rate of speed, crashed into the right side of his/her car.

You have subpoenaed records from the plaintiff's casualty insurance company, Acme Insurance. Among the records the company produces is a signed photocopy of the following letter to Richardson's lawyer. Richardson will admit that the signature is his/hers.

1. For the defendant, cross-examine Richardson.
2. For the plaintiff, conduct any necessary redirect examination.

July 18, [-1]

William Martin
Attorney at Law
404 Main Street

Re: Accident of 6/15/[-1]

Dear Mr. Martin:

As you requested during our previous discussions in your office, I am writing to tell you the basic facts surrounding the accident on June 15, [-1], in which I was injured.

I was driving in my usual manner toward the intersection. I was going west on Maple, approaching Main Street. The light for me was green. I don't recall the speed I was driving although I certainly don't make it a habit of speeding. As I got near the intersection, the light suddenly turned yellow. I couldn't really stop without entering the intersection, so I kept going. The light must still have been on yellow when the other driver plowed into me, although I really didn't see the light after I entered the intersection. He hit me on the right side.

I trust when you have reviewed the matter you will file suit against the other driver, since he refused to pay for any of my expenses.

I am sending a copy of this letter to Elmer Jackson, my insurance agent, since he wants to stay informed about this.

Very truly yours,

Mackenzie Richardson

cc: Elmer Jackson
     Acme Insurance Company
     4403 Summit Ave.

287

5.8   Q AND A SIGNED STATEMENT

This is a murder prosecution. The case involves a fatal shooting that occurred on March 16 of last year at approximately 2:00 A.M., to which Angel Chaparro was a witness.

The case is now on trial. On direct examination, Angel Chaparro has testified to the following:

(a)   "One of the men who was shot was in my tavern one week before all this happened."

(b)   "I saw a man come out of the alley. He had a gun in his hand. He fired his gun at the men."

(c)   "The man who fired the gun was someone I had never seen before that night. I have not seen him since. But I had a good look at him that night."

Chaparro identifies the defendant, Julio Vega, as the shooter.

You have the attached statement of Angel Chaparro, given the same night of the shooting.

1.   For the defense, cross-examine Angel Chaparro.
2.   For the prosecution, conduct any necessary redirect examination.

16 Mar., [-1], 0430 hrs.

Statement of Angel Chaparro, age 49, of 852 W. Fletcher, second floor, #549-4575, Owner of the Grand Slam tavern, 3740 W. Clark, #231-9555, relative to the fatal shooting of Karl Ulrick, M/W age 42, of 1910 W. Fullerton, and also the serious shooting of Wolfgang Ulrick age 35, of 3817 N. Lakewood, incident occurred at 3740 W. Clark St. (on Street) on 16 Mar., [-1], at about 0200 hrs.

Typed and questioned by Inv. Richard Daletski #12123. Statement taken at the Area #6 Homicide office, 3801 N. Damen.

1 Q. What is your name, address, occupation, and
2   telephone?
3
4 A. Angel Chaparro, 852 W. Fletcher, I own a tavern,
5   the Grand Slam tavern, 549-4575.
6
7 Q. Do you understand the English language?
8
9 A. I understand the language pretty well; if I don't
10   understand a word I'll ask you the meaning.
11
12 Q. How long have you owned the tavern called the Grand
13   Slam, located at 3740 W. Clark St.?
14 A. For six years.
15
16 Q. Do you own a gun, or keep a gun in your tavern?
17
18 A. No, sir.
19
20 Q. Do you know of any of your customers who own a gun?
21
22 A. No. I wouldn't allow that. Guns make trouble.
23   I don't want no trouble with police. I have a
24   license to protect.
25 Q. Did anything unusual happen in your tavern tonight,
26   and can you recall how many customers were in your
27   tavern at closing time?
28
29 A. Everything was smooth; there were six customers
30   sitting at the bar.
31
32 Q. Did you know the six customers by name?
33
34 A. No. Not all of them. I knew four of them.

291

Continued statement of Angel Chaparro relative to
the fatal shooting of Karl Ulrick, and the serious
shooting of Wolfgang Ulrick.

1 Q. Are you referring to the four men that were taken
2   into custody by the police on the street in front
3   of your tavern?
4
5 A. Yes, Santos, Joe, Angel, and Manuel. We left the
6   tavern at the same time when I was closing.

7 Q. Calling your attention to the time you were closing
8   your tavern today at about 0200 hours, 16 Mar., [-1],
9   did anything unusual happen outside of your tavern?
10
11 A. Yes, I was putting the key in the tavern door to
12   lock it and I heard shooting, about four or five
13   shots. I then turned around and saw the blue light
14   flashing on the police cars. The police told me to
15   put my hands up, and handcuffed me. The Lieutenant
16   then came and I identified myself, and the police
17   took the handcuffs off and drove me to the station.
18
19 Q. Did you see where the shots came from, and did you
20   see anyone with a gun?

21 A. No.
22
23 Q. Did you see the men who were shot, and if so did
24   you ever see them before tonight?

25 A. No, I never saw the men before.
26
27 Q. Other than hearing the four or five shots you
28   mentioned, did you see anything?
29
30 A. No, the entrance to my tavern is about four feet
31   from the sidewalk, and I could not see to either
32   side of me.
33 Q. Do you have any idea who might have done this
34   shooting?
35
36 A. No.

292

Continued statement of Angel Chaparro relative to the
fatal shooting of Karl Ulrick, and the serious shooting
of Wolfgang Ulrick.

1 Q. Are there any questions relative to this shooting
2   that I may have failed to ask you?
3
4 A. Not to my knowledge.
5
6 Q. After reading this statement, which consists of
7   three pages, and you find the statement correct as
8   you dictated, will you sign this statement?
9 A. Yes, I will.
10

Angel Chaparro
_____
Angel Chaparro

5.9 DEPOSITION TRANSCRIPT

This is a negligence action. Martha Rose has sued Remy Brock for injuries she incurred when she was struck by the car Brock was driving on January 15, [-2], at the intersection of Belden Avenue and Clark Street. Belden Avenue runs east-west; Clark Street runs north-south. There are no traffic control signals or street markings at the intersection.

At trial, Rose has testified that before she stepped off the northeast corner of the intersection she looked to her left and saw no cars coming. She said she was walking slowly across Belden Avenue, moving directly south, and had reached the middle of the westbound lane when Brock's car "came out of nowhere" at a high rate of speed, hitting her and throwing her in the air about 20 feet in a due west direction.

At trial, Brock testified as follows on direct examination:

Q. Which lane of Belden Avenue were you in?

A. I was traveling in the westbound lane closest to the north curb of Belden Avenue. I was going about ten mph.

Q. As you approached Clark Street, what happened?

A. I saw the woman standing on the northeast corner of Clark and Belden. She just stood there for a few seconds. Then she suddenly ran off the curb and darted right into the path of my car. I could not avoid hitting her. There was simply no time.

Q. What part of your car struck her?

A. About the middle of the front.

Q. How much time passed from the time you first saw her until you came into contact with her?

A. It was just a few seconds.

You have the attached transcript of a deposition that Brock gave on January 15, one year ago.

1. For the plaintiff, cross-examine Brock.

2. For the defendant, conduct any necessary redirect examination.

3. Assume that Brock will not admit giving the answers contained in the deposition transcript. Prove up any impeachment.

Taken, under oath, on January 15, [-1], at office of
John Sawyer, 180 North LaSalle Street, Suite 630

p. 16

1 Q. (by John Sawyer, plaintiff's attorney) How fast were
2 you driving at the time you struck the pedestrian?
3
4 A. About 20 mph.
5 Q. What was the highest speed you reached in the block
6 you traveled before the accident?
7
8 A. I never went more than 25 mph.
9
10 Q. When is the first time you saw the woman whom you
11 struck with your car?
12 A. When I hit her.
13
14 Q. Before the impact, did you ever see the woman?
15
16 A. No.
17 Q. (by Richard Jones, defendant's attorney) I want to
18 be sure I understand you. Did you see anything before
19 your car came into contact with the plaintiff?
20
21 A. Yes, I did.
22
23 Q. I am talking about the time just before the
24 accident. What did you see?
25 A. I saw her come off the curb, running fast, and
26 before I knew it, I hit her.

p. 47

I have read the questions and answers contained in
this 47-page deposition transcript and they truly
and accurately represent the questions asked and the
answers given.

Remy Brock
_____
Remy Brock

5.10 DEPOSITION TRANSCRIPT

This is a products liability action. Plaintiff is suing General Motors (GM), claiming he was injured because the hydraulic brake system on his [-7] car ruptured and failed during an emergency stop, causing an accident and resulting in injuries to himself and his car.

Plaintiff claims that the brake system on his car was defectively designed and was not the best and safest design that GM was capable of manufacturing in [-7]. GM's defense is based on "state of the art." It claims that the brake system design was the best one that GM was capable of incorporating into its [-7] production models.

The case is now on trial. The defense in its case calls as a witness Jess Reston, a GM design engineer whose principal work has been on brake systems, to testify on the design aspects of the [-7] GM brake system.

On direct, Reston testified to the following facts: GM spends millions of dollars each year on design research, its purpose being to design the most reliable and safe vehicle possible for the buying public. In its [-7] models, all GM cars had a single hydraulic brake system, using one master cylinder that connected to the brake drums on all four wheels. This design was a standard one in the industry, had been used for many years, was extremely reliable, and, viewing the brake system as a whole, was the best one readily available at that time. Through ongoing research, GM was able to modify that system to one using a dual hydraulic system, but that new system was not fully developed until the [-4] production model.

You have the attached deposition transcript of Jess Reston, given on July 14 of last year.

1. For the plaintiff, cross-examine Jess Reston.
2. For the defendant, conduct any necessary redirect examination.

Taken, under oath, on July 14, [-1],

at office of Frank Jones,

221 N. Dearborn St., #800

p. 47

1 Q. (by Frank Jones, one of plaintiff's lawyers) Mr./
2   Ms. Reston, you've been devoting your efforts to
3   brake systems designs for the past 15 years, is
4   that correct?
5
6 A. Yes.
7
8 Q. So, it's fair to say that you're familiar with the
9   progress of brake systems design at GM, as well as
10   the other manufacturers in the U.S., isn't it?
11 A. I like to think I am.
12
13 Q. If someone else came up with a new design or
14   system, you'd certainly consider it for use by GM,
15   wouldn't you?
16 A. Certainly, if it was feasible.
17
18 Q. Mr./Ms. Reston, in [-7] you knew that Alta Motors
19   had been working on a dual hydraulic brake system,
20   didn't you?
21
22 A. Yes.
23 Q. You were familiar with the design?
24
25 A. Yes.
26
27 Q. Its advantage is that if one of the two hydraulic
28   systems ruptures, the other one still functions,
29   doesn't it?
30 A. Yes.
31
32 Q. So a car can still be braked, right?
33
34 A. Yes, although obviously not as quickly or safely.
35 Q. Insofar as a rupture in any hydraulic brake line
36   was concerned, the dual system was a safer design
37   than GM's single brake system, wasn't it?
38
39 A. It was safer only in the event of a rupture in the
40   system.

41 Q. Well, if there was a rupture in one of the lines,
42　　the Alta Motors car could still brake, while the GM
43　　would have a total brake failure, wouldn't it?
44
45 A. Yes.
46 Q. The Alta Motors dual system, which was safer in the
47　　event of a rupture, was known to you and GM in [-7],
48　　right?
49
50 A. Well, we'd heard of it.
51
52 Q. Was there a reason GM didn't use the Alta Motors
53　　system in [-7]?
54 A. We considered it, but we found that it simply
55　　wasn't cost-effective.
56
57 Q. How much would it have cost to incorporate a dual
58　　system in the GM cars in [-7]?
59
60 A. We estimated that it would be around $185.00 extra
61　　per car.
62 Q. GM didn't install the dual system in its models
63　　until the [-4] models, right?
64
65 (by William Smith, one of the defendant's lawyers)
66 Objection. Subsequent remedial measures are inadmissible.
67
68 Q. (by Frank Jones) Please answer the question.
69 A. That's correct.
70
71 Q. That was the same year the federal government first
72　　required the dual system on all U.S. cars, isn't it?
73
74　　(by William Smith) Objection. Same basis.
75 Q. (by Frank Jones) Please answer.
76
77 A. Yes.

1 Q. (by William Smith, one of the defendant's lawyers)
2   What year did you first hear about the dual brake
3   system?
4
5 A. I think it was in [-9] or [-8].

6 Q. How long does it take GM to get a new design
7   concept actually included in a production model?
8

9 A. It usually takes three or four years from preliminary
10   design through inclusion in actual production.
11
12 Q. Was cost the only reason why you didn't incorporate
13   the dual system in [-7]?

14 A. No. It just wasn't ready for production. There just
15   wasn't enough time.

Jess Reston
July 28, [-1]

303

5.11   DEPOSITION TRANSCRIPT

This is a negligence action. Frank Johnson has sued Charles Smith for injuries he incurred when he was struck by a car driven by Smith at the intersection of State and Main Streets. Johnson, the driver of a Ford sedan, was going northbound on State Street when he collided with Smith, the driver of a Chevy sedan that was going eastbound on Main Street. The accident happened on June 1, [-2]. Plaintiff claims that defendant Smith ran the red light.

At trial Kelly Jones, a plaintiff witness, testified on direct examination as follows:

Q.   Where were you standing?

A.   I was on the southeast corner of State and Main, waiting for the light to change so I could cross State Street.

Q.   What did you see next?

A.   I saw the northbound Ford go into the intersection just as the light turned yellow for State Street. The eastbound Chevy ran the red light.

You have the attached transcript of a deposition that Jones gave on June 1, one year ago.

1.   For the defendant, cross-examine Jones.

2.   For the plaintiff, conduct any necessary redirect examination.

3.   Assume that Jones will not admit giving the answers contained in the deposition transcript. Prove up any impeachment.

DEPOSITION OF KELLY JONES

Taken, under oath, on June 1, [-1], at office of
Wilbur Harrison, 800 Congress Ave., Suite 201

p. 18

1 Q. (by Wilbur Harrison, defendant's attorney) Did you
2   see the two cars involved before they actually
3   collided in the intersection?
4
5 A. Yes.
6
7 Q. What did the Ford do?
8
9 A. Well, it was going northbound on State, and got to
10   about five feet before the intersection when the
11   light for State turned yellow.
12
13 Q. What did the Chevy do?
14
15 A. It was going eastbound on Main Street. It slowed down
16   as it approached the corner. It was going about 20
17   mph when its light turned green. Then the Chevy went
18   into the intersection, and crashed into the Ford.

I have read the questions and answers contained in
this deposition and they accurately represent the
questions asked and answers given.

Kelly Jones
Kelly Jones

5.12   GRAND JURY TRANSCRIPT AND POLICE REPORT

This is a robbery prosecution. The defendant, William Hill, is charged with robbing a bank on May 2 of last year at about 9:00 A.M.

In the prosecution's case-in-chief a police investigator, Miley Byrne, testified as follows:

Q.   Did you eventually arrive at William Hill's apartment on May 2?

A.   Yes, sir.

Q.   When did you arrive there?

A.   It was about 11:30 in the morning.

Q.   When you arrived at the apartment, what happened?

A.   I knocked on the door. After a few seconds, Hill opened the door. He said, "What do you want?" I told him we were police officers and that he was under arrest. Then, before I had a chance to say anything else, he said, "I don't know anything about a robbery. I've been home with my brother all morning."

Q.   What happened next?

A.   I said, "Who said anything about this morning?" He just stared at us and didn't say anything else.

Q.   Then what happened?

A.   I put cuffs on him, gave him his *Miranda* rights, and took him to the station.

You have been provided with copies of the attached grand jury transcript and FBI report prior to trial.

1.   For the defense, cross-examine Miley Byrne.
2.   For the prosecution, conduct any necessary redirect examination.

IN RE: GRAND JURY INVESTIGATION GJ 867

MILEY BYRNE, having first been duly sworn,
testified on June 1, [-1], as follows:

p.11

1   Q. (by John O'Malley, Assistant District Attorney)
2   Later on, when you arrived at Hill's apartment, did
3   you have any conversation with him?
4
5   A. When he opened the door, I asked him his name, and
6   he said "William Hill." I told him he was under
7   arrest for armed robbery. He said: "Wait a minute,
8   you got the wrong guy. I've been home all morning."
9   He just kind of stared at me and wouldn't say
10   anything further.

FEDERAL BUREAU OF INVESTIGATION

Date of transcription: 5/2/[-1]

Investigator Miley Byrne was interviewed at the police headquarters and provided the following information:

After receiving the address of the car's registered owner, Byrne and his/her partner went to 6618 S. Sacramento, a three flat walk-up building, and went to the second floor. They knocked on the door and a man opened it. He was a white male, approximately 20-25, medium build. Byrne asked his name and he replied: "Billy Hill." He was advised he was under arrest for armed robbery. He replied: "You got the wrong guy. I've been here all morning with my brother." The other person having the same general description as Hill, was sitting on a sofa, but said nothing. Hill was then handcuffed, advised of his *Miranda rights*, and transported to police headquarters.

By _Gerald Anino_
Gerald Anino, FBI

5.13 POLICE REPORT

This is a murder and attempted armed robbery prosecution. Officer Terry O'Shea arrested the two defendants, Ernest Edwards and Frank Tucker. The case is now on trial.

On direct examination, O'Shea testified that s/he entered the apartment of Ernest Edwards and Frank Tucker at 405 W. Belmont Street in the late night hours of June 2 of last year. After giving *Miranda* warnings to both defendants and after receiving a statement from each defendant that he understood the warnings, O'Shea told them they were under arrest for the murder of Martha Talbert.

According to O'Shea, Tucker then said, "That dirty rat Ralston must have opened his big mouth." O'Shea then testified that s/he turned to Edwards and asked if he had anything to say. According to O'Shea, Edwards then said, "I ain't going to tell you a damned thing."

Attached is O'Shea's only police report concerning the arrests.

Assume there is no issue about the legality of the arrests, the adequacy of the *Miranda* warnings, or whether the defendants understood their rights.

1. For the defense, cross-examine Officer O'Shea.
2. For the prosecution, conduct any necessary redirect examination.

315

OFFENSE/INCIDENT REPORT

	Offense/Incident – Primary Classification						Secondary Primary Classification		Incident Code	Area of Occurrence
SCENE	Murder and Attempted Armed Robbery						Attempt Armed Robbery			12
	Address of Occurrence						Date of Occurrence (DD Month YY)		Time of Occurrence	
	117 Wilson Ave.						02 June [-1]		2200	
	Type of Location								Location Code	Unit Assigned
	☒ House/Townhome ☐ Apartment ☐ Business ☐ Other:									

All information, descriptions and statements in this entire report are approximations or summarizations unless indicated otherwise.

	Victims Name		Sex	Race		DOB	Occupation		Phone	E-Mail
VICTIM										
	Address						City		Other Contact Information	
	Parent/Guardian, if juvenile.								Phone	E-Mail

	Witness Name		Sex	Race		DOB	Occupation		Phone	E-Mail
WITNESS										
	Address						City		Other Contact Information	
	Parent/Guardian, if juvenile.								Phone	E-Mail

	Suspect #1 Name	Age	Sex	Race	Hgt	Wgt	Eyes	Hair	DOB	Phone	E-Mail
SUSPECT #1	Frank Tucker	19	M	W	5'2"	140	BR	BR	[-19]		
	Address							City		Alias or Gang Affiliation	
	405 Belmont									None	
	Parent/Guardian, if juvenile.									Phone	E-Mail

	Suspect #2 Name	Age	Sex	Race	Hgt	Wgt	Eyes	Hair	DOB	Phone	E-Mail
SUSPECT #2	Ernest Edwards	20	M	W	5'10"	200	BL	BR	[-20]		
	Address							City		Alias or Gang Affiliation	
	405 Belmont									None	
	Parent/Guardian, if juvenile.									Phone	E-Mail

	Owner of Involved Vehicle/Property	Year	Make	Style	VIN/Serial Number	Color	Lic. Plate
PROPERTY							
	Owner of Involved Vehicle/Property	Year	Make	Style	VIN/Serial Number	Color	Lic. Plate

NARRATIVE (Do not duplicate above information)

R/O learned through reliable informant that persons involved in murder and attempted armed robbery of Martha Talbert were Ernest Edwards and Frank Tucker, living at 405 W. Belmont. Officer O'Shea and other officers proceeded to location at 2330 hrs. Upon arriving at 405 W. Belmont the officers proceeded to the front entrance; Officer O'Shea knocked at the door and announced their presence. Upon no answer, hearing a radio in the background, the officers proceeded to force the apartment door open. Edwards and Tucker were found in their beds and were placed under arrest and given the Miranda warnings which were understood by the defendants. Upon entering the bedroom where the defendants were sleeping Officer O'Shea noticed a .38 caliber revolver serial no. 74969 in the open dresser drawer.

	First Officer on Scene		Date/Time Arrived	Time Departed	Area of Assignment
Police Personnel	O'Shea, Terry		02 June [-1]/2330		
	Officer Notifying Investigations		Date/Time Notified		Date/Time Investigations on Scene
	Same				
	Officer Notifying Supervisor		Date/Time Notified		Date/Time Supervisor on Scene
	Same				
	Reporting Officer's Name (PRINT)	Badge Number	Reporting Officer's Signature		
	Terry O'Shea	133	*Terry O'Sh #133*		
	Supervisor Approval Name (PRINT)	Badge Number	Supervisor Approval Signature		

FORM ID-10-T (3/[-2)

317

5.14 WRITTEN STATEMENTS

This is a personal injury and property damage action. On August 23, [-2], at about 4:00 P.M., a westbound Chevrolet driven by Sam Smith collided with a northbound Cadillac driven by George Gentry at the intersection of North Avenue, an east-west street, and Clark Street, a north-south street. Gentry sued Smith for $300,000 in damages, claiming it was Smith who went through the red light at a high rate of speed.

At the time of the collision, Jamie Taylor was waiting for a northbound bus on Clark Street. The bus stop is just off the southeast corner of the intersection. Taylor gave his/her name to the police officer who came to the scene.

The next day, Larry Long, an investigator for Smith's insurance company, went to Taylor's home, where Taylor gave the written statement that is attached. It is in Long's handwriting, except for those places where Taylor made initialed corrections and where s/he placed his/her signature.

The case is now on trial. Taylor is called as a witness by Gentry, the plaintiff. In summary, Taylor testifies that on August 23, two years ago, at about 4:00 P.M., s/he was standing at the southeast corner of North Avenue and Clark Street, waiting for a northbound Clark Street bus. S/he happened to look to the north when s/he saw a Chevrolet traveling in a westerly direction go through a red light at a high rate of speed. The Chevrolet collided with a Cadillac that was going north on Clark Street. The Cadillac had the green light.

Smith's lawyer has received credible information that two weeks before trial, Taylor and his/her fiancé were seen having dinner with Gentry's lawyer, Otto Oglesby, at LeBrech, the city's most expensive restaurant. Oglesby was seen paying for the dinner. Taylor, if asked, will admit that this information is accurate.

Smith's lawyer also knows that on August 28, two years ago, Taylor made another statement to Oglesby in the presence of a stenographer. That statement, which is also attached, is entirely consistent with Taylor's trial testimony.

1. For the defendant, cross-examine Taylor.
2. For the plaintiff, conduct any necessary redirect examination.

Statement of Jamie Taylor

I am My name is Jamie ~~A.~~ Taylor [N Jr]
I am 24 years old and single. I
work for General Electric as a
~~Maintenance clerk~~ [Jr] mechanic.

On August 23rd at ~~14~~ [about Jr] pm, I
was at the corner of North
and Clark waiting for a bus to
take me to the far North side.
At that time, I was looking
toward the South for my bus
when I heard the screeching
of brakes. I looked toward the
corner, when I saw a Westbound Chevrolet collide with a
North-bound Cadillac. At the
time of the collision, the
traffic light was green for the
West-bound traffic.

After the accident, I gave
my name and address to the
Police Officer. Signed _Jamie Taylor_

Witness: ~~Larry Long~~ _Larry Long_
Date: ~~August 24~~ [-2]

321

STATEMENT OF JAMIE TAYLOR

Dated: 8/28/[-2]

1 Q. Jamie, I'm here today, August 28, [-2], to ask you
2   about the accident on August 23, [-2], involving a
3   George Gentry and a Sam Smith at the intersection
4   of North and Clark Streets. Present in your living
5   room at 857 Park Street are myself, Otto Oglesby,
6   you, Jamie Taylor, and the stenographer, Sharon
7   Dodd. Is that correct?
8
9 A. Yes.
10
11 Q. You understand that the stenographer is taking down
       everything we say?
12
13 A. Yes.
14
15 Q. Jamie, please describe in your own words how the
16   accident happened.
17
18 A. Well, I was at North and Clark, on the southeast
19   corner, waiting for a bus. I was looking up Clark
20   Street when I noticed a Chevy, going west on North
21   Avenue, go into the intersection and ram into a
22   Cadillac going north on Clark.
23 Q. How fast was the Chevy going when it rammed into
24   the Cadillac?
25
26 A. The Chevy was going real fast, maybe 40 or 50 miles
27   per hour.
28
29 Q. Who had the green light when the collision
30   happened?
31 A. The Cadillac on Clark Street had the green light
32   when it happened.
33
34 Q. Jamie, is there anything you want to add to this
35   statement?
36 A. No, that's about the way it happened.

5.15 GRAND JURY TRANSCRIPT AND Q AND A SIGNED STATEMENT

This is a murder prosecution. The defendant, Ralph Tyler, is charged with the murder of a police officer on November 15, [-1].

The case is now on trial. Logan Richards is a prosecution witness. On direct examination, s/he testified that on the night of November 15, [-1], s/he was with the defendant, Ralph Tyler. Richards stated that at about 9:00 P.M. s/he and Tyler walked up to a marked police car parked on LaSalle Street, just south of Division Street, on the east side of the street. Richards stated that s/he, Richards, opened the passenger door of the squad car and that Tyler then pulled a .38 revolver from his jacket pocket, aimed it at the police officer sitting alone in the car, and fired, striking the officer in the head. Richards stated that all this was done pursuant to a conversation s/he had with Tyler about two hours before the shooting.

Richards became a state witness on December 15, one year ago, the day his/ her pending armed robbery trial was scheduled to begin. S/he had been arrested for the armed robbery of a liquor store on November 29, two years ago, as s/he was running out of the store with a gun in his/her hand.

On December 15, one year ago, Richards contacted Robert Bench, the prosecutor in the pending armed robbery case, and reached the following agreement:

(a) S/he will be a prosecution witness in the murder case against Ralph Tyler.

(b) S/he will not be prosecuted for any crime relating to the murder case, so long as s/he tells the truth.

(c) S/he will be allowed to plead guilty to the lesser included offense of plain robbery in the pending case involving the liquor store.

(d) The prosecution will not recommend any specific sentence in the liquor store robbery case.

You have the attached written statement and grand jury transcript of Logan Richards. All constitutional issues concerning admissibility of the statements have been resolved in favor of the prosecution.

The prosecution has informed the defense that Richards was convicted of burglary four years ago, for which s/he served one year in the state penitentiary.

The sentence for armed robbery is 6 to 30 years. For plain robbery it is 3 to 7 years.

1. For the defense, cross-examine Logan Richards.
2. For the prosecution, conduct any necessary redirect examination.

STATEMENT OF LOGAN RICHARDS TAKEN ON
NOVEMBER 29, [-1], AT MAIN POLICE STATION

QUESTIONS ASKED BY OFFICER FRANK KELLY:

1 Q. What is your name?
2
3 A. Logan Richards.

4 Q. How old are you?
5
6 A. Twenty-five.

7
8 Q. I am going to ask you some questions about the
9   killing of a police officer on LaSalle and Division
10   Streets on November 15 of this year.

11 A. I don't know anything about that.
12

13 Q. Were you anywhere near that corner on November 15
14   of this year at about 9:00 p.m.?
15
16 A. No. I think I was at a movie on the south side with
17   my friend.

18 Q. Do you have any information at all about the
19   killing of a police officer on that night?
20
21 A. I didn't even know a police officer was killed
22   until you told me about it a few minutes ago.
23
24 Q. Do you have anything to add?

25 A. No. I have told you the absolute truth.
26

27 Q. Will you sign this statement after reading it if it
28   is true and accurate?
29
30 A. Yes.

Logan Richards
Logan Richards

Witnessed by:

Frank Kelly
Officer Frank Kelly

GRAND JURY, DECEMBER TERM,

TRANSCRIPT OF TESTIMONY TAKEN DECEMBER 2, [-1]

(Reported by Claude Flynn,
Certified Shorthand Reporter)

LOGAN RICHARDS, having been first duly sworn,
testified as follows:

1 Q. (by Robert Bench, Assistant County Prosecutor) What
2   is your name?
3
4 A. Logan Richards.
5
   Q. Do you realize you are now under oath?
6
7 A. Yes, sir.
8
9 Q. I call your attention to November 15 of this year,
10   at around 9:00 p.m. Where were you at that time?
11
   A. I spent that entire evening on the south side.
12   I think I went to a movie with my friend.
13
14 Q. Were you anywhere near Division and LaSalle Streets
15   on that date?
16
17 A. No, sir. I was nowhere near that neighborhood any
18   time that day.
19
   Q. Do you have any information about the killing of a
20   police officer at Division and LaSalle Streets on
21   November 15 of this year, or any other day?
22
23 A. No. I don't know anything about it.
24
25 Q. Have you heard anything about the killing of a
26   police officer on November 15 of this year, at
27   around Division and LaSalle Streets?
28
   A. The first I heard of that was when the policeman
29   told me on the day I was arrested.
30
31 Q. Is there anything you wish to add?
32
33 A. No. I have told you the honest-to-God truth.

5.16   DEPOSITION TESTIMONY

This is a personal injury case. The defendant, Whitney Bell, is alleged to have struck nine-year-old Carl Heman with his car one year ago today, at 2:20 P.M., as the boy crossed Taylor Street from west to east at a point midway between Third and Fourth Avenues. The boy's mother, the named plaintiff, alleges Bell was driving his/her car at a speed well above the 25 mph speed limit on Taylor Street. Bell denies s/he was speeding and claims the accident happened because the boy ran out onto Taylor Street from between two parked cars.

At trial, on direct examination, Bell testified as follows:

Q. How many lanes of traffic are there on Taylor Street?

A. There is one parking lane and one traffic lane on each side, a total of four lanes.

Q. In what direction were you going?

A. I was going south, toward Fourth Avenue.

Q. Were there any cars in the parking lane on the west side of Taylor Street at the time of the accident?

A. Yes. Cars were parked all the way from Third to Fourth Avenue. That's a residential area.

Q. When did you first see the boy you struck?

A. When he ran in front of my car.

Q. How fast were you going when your car struck the boy?

A. I know I wasn't going more than 15 miles per hour.

Q. How do you know that?

A. Because I never go more than that on those residential streets during the day.

Q. Did you check your speedometer?

A. No, I don't like to take my eyes off the road in those neighborhoods.

Six months before he testified at trial, Bell's deposition was taken at the offices of plaintiff's lawyer, located at 100 South Clark Street. At the deposition, Bell testified as follows:

1   Q.   (by plaintiff's lawyer) Whitney Bell, as you traveled south on Taylor Street
2   toward Fourth Avenue, was anything located to your right?
3   A.   I don't remember.
4   Q.   How fast were you going when your car struck the boy?
5   A.   I was going the speed limit, 25 miles per hour. I know because I checked
6   my speedometer just after I passed Third Street.

1.   For the plaintiff, cross-examine Bell.
2.   For the defendant, conduct any necessary redirect examination.

5.17 DIAGRAM

This is a criminal prosecution. Arthur Martin, the defendant, is charged with the attempted murder of police officer Fran Blue.

One year ago today Officer Blue and his/her partner, Lou Redd, received a call on their police radio telling them to go to 6050 S. Woodlawn Avenue because the police had received a call that there was a man with a gun in the hallway of that building.

The officers entered the building and walked up the stairs to the second floor, where they eventually encountered Martin, who lived on that floor. Martin had a gun. There was an exchange of gunfire. Martin was shot in the shoulder. Blue was shot in the right arm just above the elbow, on the rear part of the arm. All three persons fired shots.

At the preliminary hearing, the following testimony was elicited:

Officer Blue

Q. Where was the defendant when you saw him for the first time?

A. He opened the door of his apartment. He had a gun in his hand and was aiming it at us. That's when the shooting began. Martin was right in his doorway. He never moved.

Q. How much time went by between the time you first saw the defendant and the time the shooting began?

A. Only a second or so.

Q. Where were you when the shooting began?

A. I was right in front of Martin's door, my left shoulder against the east wall, facing south and a little west, toward Martin.

Q. Where was Officer Redd at that time?

A. S/he was directly to my right, no more than two feet away.

Q. Were you two in the same place when the shooting stopped?

A. Yes, we were.

Q. Where was the defendant when you first saw him?

A. He had opened his apartment door. The door opens out into the hallway. He was just about in the doorway, toward the banister side of the hall. That's when I saw he was aiming at us. We all started firing.

Q. Did the defendant ever move from the time you first saw him until the shooting ended?

A. No.

Q. Where were you when the shooting began?

A. I was in the northeast corner of the hallway, opposite the defendant's door, facing the defendant.

Q. Where was Officer Blue?

A. S/he was directly to my right, with one foot on the first step and the other foot on the hallway floor.

Q. Did either of you two move from the time you first saw the defendant until the time the shooting stopped?

A. No.

The case is now on trial. The officers will testify on direct examination consistently with their preliminary hearing testimony. The attached diagram has already been admitted in evidence through the testimony of the police artist who prepared it.

1. For the defense, cross-examine Officers Blue and Redd, using the attached diagram to demonstrate the conflict between the two officers. (If no document camera is available in the courtroom, prepare an appropriate enlarged diagram for class.)

2. For the prosecution, conduct any necessary redirect examination of the officers.

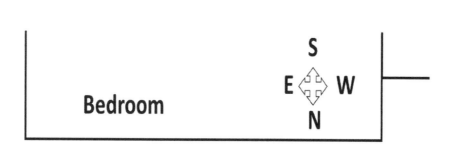

Hall

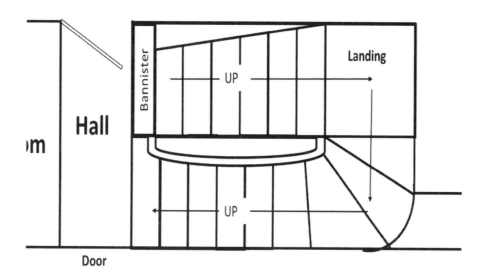

5.18   GRAND JURY TRANSCRIPT

This is a bank robbery prosecution. Haley Smith was the teller at the Maple Avenue Bank when it was robbed on May 18 of last year.

Four weeks later, on June 18, s/he testified before the grand jury. The transcript of the grand jury testimony is attached. At the time s/he testified before the grand jury, the defendant, Mark Bell, had not yet been arrested. Smith had been shown several police photographs, but none was of Bell.

Four days after the grand jury proceeding, Bell was arrested. That night, FBI Agent Sidney Goldstein called Smith. He asked him/her to appear in the preliminary hearing court the next morning. He told him/her someone had been arrested in connection with the bank robbery. The next morning, June 23, Smith and Agent Goldstein sat in the courtroom from about 9:00 A.M. until about 10:15 A.M. Five unrelated cases were called and disposed of during that time. At about 10:15 A.M., Smith heard Bell's name called by the clerk of the court and then s/he heard his/her name called. S/he looked up when his/her name was called and saw the uniformed deputy walk to a door at the side of the courtroom. When the door opened, the deputy brought Bell to the front of the judge's bench. Smith then said to Agent Goldstein, "That's the man." Then s/he and Agent Goldstein walked to the other side of the front of the judge's bench. Bell had not been shown to Smith, in person or by photograph, before his case was called. Smith will admit, if asked, that these facts are true.

Bell, the defendant, is a white male, 5′ 8″ tall, 31 years old, and weighs 178 pounds.

The case is now on trial. [**The instructor will provide the direct examination of Smith in class.**]

1.   For the defense, cross-examine Smith.
2.   For the prosecution, conduct any necessary redirect examination.

TRANSCRIPT OF TESTIMONY TAKEN JUNE 18, [-1]

(Reported by Genevieve Dodd,

Certified Shorthand Reporter)

HALEY SMITH, having been called as a witness and having been duly sworn, testified as follows:

1 Q. (by Gregory Jones, Assistant U.S. Attorney) Mr./Ms.
2   Smith, please describe what the man who handed you
3   the demand note looked like.
4
5 A. Well, he was a white man, maybe six feet tall, in
6   his late teens or early 20s, 180 pounds, dressed
7   in blue jeans.
8 Q. Did you notice anything unusual about his face or
9   appearance?
10
11 A. No, he didn't have any scars or really unusual
12   features that I noticed.
13
14 Q. Did you notice anything about his coat?
15
16 A. Well, he had his hand in his pocket and you could
17   tell he had something brown in his hand. I couldn't
18   really see what it was because his hand was over
19   it, but naturally I had to assume it was a gun.
20 Q. What happened next?
21
22 A. He told me to go to the back office, which I did,
23   and he told Mr. Jacobs, the branch manager, "This
24   is a stickup, don't move."
25 Q. Then what happened?
26
27 A. Well, he made us sit facing the wall, so we
28   couldn't see him. Mr. Jacobs kept asking him to
29   relax and not to do anything foolish.
30
31 Q. How long were you there?
32
33 A. It seemed like around five minutes or so.
34 Q. What happened next?
35
36 A. After a while we couldn't hear anything, so
37   I thought they had left. I then reached over to the
38   desk and triggered the alarm.

5.19 POLICE REPORT

The defendant, James Watts, is charged with the burglary of a store at the corner of LaSalle and Madison Streets. The case is now on trial. Other prosecution witnesses have testified that they saw two men run out of the burglarized store and jump into a black Chevrolet. They will say that the Chevrolet took off southbound on LaSalle at a high rate of speed, chased by a police car. They cannot identify the defendant as one of the burglars.

Officer Fran McCurry then testified on direct examination:

Q. On June 15 of last year, at about 3:30 P.M., what happened?

A. I was with my partner in our squad car. We were parked on LaSalle Street, facing south. I looked up and saw the two male whites running south on LaSalle Street, from Madison Street.

Q. What did you see the men do?

A. I saw them get into a black Chevrolet about halfway down the block, between Madison and Monroe. The car started going south.

Q. Could you see the license plate on the car?

A. Not at that time. All I could tell was that it was an Illinois plate. I did not see the plate until the arrest was made.

Q. What did you do when you saw all this?

A. We pulled up alongside the Chevrolet, and I motioned for the men to stop.

Q. Did they stop?

A. No, they sped up. We chased them in our squad car. My partner was driving. I was the passenger.

[The instructor will provide additional direct examination in class at this point.]

Q. When you left the area of 27th and State, what happened?

341

A. The chase continued, but we finally curbed the car at 31st and Parnell.

Q. Who was in the car at that time?

A. There was only one person in it, the defendant. We placed him under arrest.

Q. At any time during the chase were you able to see the faces of the men in the Chevrolet?

A. No, I didn't see either man's face during the chase. The first face I really saw was that of the defendant when I arrested him at 31st and Parnell.

You have Officer McCurry's signed report, which is attached. It is the only report McCurry made of the event.

1. For the defense, cross-examine Officer McCurry.
2. For the prosecution, conduct any necessary redirect examination.

ARREST REPORT

Name (Last)	(First)		(Middle)		Arrest Date		Arrest Time		Primary Arresting Officer Name / #	
Watts	James		-		15 June [-1]		1530		Fran McCurry / 1724	
Alias	Age	Sex	Race	Hgt	Wgt	Eyes	Hair	DOB	Phone	E-Mail
	19	M	W	508	140	BR	BR	15 June [-19]	Unknown	Unknown
Address of Arrest							City		SSN	
31st and Parnell							Chicago		278-43-6071	
Address							City		Gang Affiliation/Moniker	
Unknown									None	
Vehicle of Arrestee Held?		Year		Make		Style	VIN		Color	Lic. Plate
☒ Yes ☐ No		[-5]		Chevrolet		Car			Black	860-971

Victims Name	Sex	Race	DOB	Occupation	Phone	E-Mail
Marshall Co.						
Address				City	Other Contact Information	
La Salle & Madison						
Parent/Guardian, if juvenile.					Phone	E-Mail

Charges

Charge Number	Statute or Warrant Number	Title or Description

Narrative
Undersigned officers assigned to area 105 observed two M/W's running from Madison on La Salle southbound. Reporting officers observed suspects get into a [-5] Chevrolet, black sedan, State License #860-971. Officers then pulled up next to the car and motioned suspects to stop. Suspects then took off at a high rate of speed. Chase proceeded south and the Chevrolet was never lost sight of. Chase terminated at 31st and Parnell. Driver of the car was apprehended, but passenger was missing. Driver arrested, transported to station. Officer McCurry notified Jones, units 24, in the investigations unit of the incident.

Primary Arresting Officer Name / Badge #	Area Assignment
Fran McCurry / 1724	105
Secondary Arresting Officer Name / Badge #	Area Assignment
William Simon / 276	105
Arrestee Transported to:	Receiving Officer Name / Badge #
☐ County ☒ District ☐ Southern ☐ Temp:	Skyler Tonkanita / 1032

State Warrant Check		Federal Warrant Check		Medical Staff	
Called In	Received	Called In	Received	Notified	Intake Completed
(Clearly Print Your Initials and Badge Number in the appropriate block)					

FORM PD 11420 (7/[-2)

5.20   WRITTEN REPORT OF ORAL STATEMENT

This is an armed robbery prosecution. Ash Zamet was the only person in the store who saw the offender's face. Rudolph Jensen has been arrested and is on trial.

During direct examination, Zamet testified s/he was 45 years old, married, and had worked at the Schwartz Convenience Store for ten years. S/he told how a man walked into the shop, came up to the counter where s/he was standing, and pulled a revolver from his overcoat pocket. He aimed the gun at his/her stomach and said, "This is a stickup." Then he ordered him/her to open the cash register. S/he did. He told him/her to put the contents of the register in the paper bag he was carrying. S/he did. Then he turned and ran out of the store.

These questions were asked on direct examination:

Q.   From the time he entered until the time he left, how long was the man in the store?

A.   About two minutes. No less than that.

Q.   Can you describe the man who aimed the gun at you?

[The instructor will provide additional direct examination in class at this point.]

Q.   Do you see that man in court today?

A.   Yes, I do. He is right over there. (The witness points to the defendant, who fits the description just given.)

Zamet will also admit the following facts if asked: S/he met with the prosecutor in his office the day s/he testified and the day before s/he testified. Four weeks ago, the defense lawyer went to Zamet's house in the company of a court reporter. S/he identified himself/herself, told him/her why s/he was there, and asked him/her questions about the robbery, which s/he refused to answer. Zamet then ordered him/her out of the house.

1.   For the defense, cross-examine Zamet.

2.   For the prosecution, conduct any necessary redirect examination.

3.   Assume that Zamet denies or does not remember the conversation with the police officers. For the defense, call one of the officers to complete the impeachment.

OFFENSE/INCIDENT REPORT

<table>
<tr><td rowspan="4">SCENE</td><td colspan="2">Offense/Incident – Primary Classification</td><td colspan="2">Secondary Primary Classification</td><td>Incident Code</td><td>Area of Occurrence
2009</td></tr>
<tr><td colspan="2">Address of Occurrence
2436 West Devon</td><td colspan="2">Date of Occurrence (DD Month YY)
15 Jan [-1]</td><td colspan="2">Time of Occurrence
1550</td></tr>
<tr><td colspan="2">Type of Location</td><td colspan="2"></td><td>Location Code</td><td>Unit Assigned</td></tr>
<tr><td colspan="6">☐ House/Townhome ☐ Apartment ☐ Business ☐ Other:</td></tr>
</table>

All information, descriptions and statements in this entire report are approximations or summarizations unless indicated otherwise.

<table>
<tr><td rowspan="6">VICTIM</td><td>Victims Name</td><td>Sex</td><td>Race</td><td>DOB</td><td>Occupation</td><td>Phone</td><td>E-Mail</td></tr>
<tr><td>Schwartz Convenience Store</td><td></td><td></td><td></td><td></td><td>742-5313</td><td></td></tr>
<tr><td>Address</td><td colspan="3"></td><td>City</td><td colspan="2">Other Contact Information</td></tr>
<tr><td colspan="4"></td><td></td><td colspan="2"></td></tr>
<tr><td colspan="5">Parent/Guardian, if juvenile.</td><td>Phone</td><td>E-Mail</td></tr>
<tr><td colspan="5"></td><td></td><td></td></tr>
</table>

<table>
<tr><td rowspan="6">WITNESS</td><td colspan="2">Witness Name</td><td colspan="3">Home Address</td><td>Phone</td><td>E-Mail</td></tr>
<tr><td colspan="2">Ekter, Barbara</td><td colspan="3">7250 North Western</td><td>973-2762</td><td>(B) 742-5313</td></tr>
<tr><td colspan="2">Witness Name</td><td colspan="3">Home Address</td><td>Phone</td><td>E-Mail</td></tr>
<tr><td colspan="2">Schwartz, George</td><td colspan="3">5029 North Central Park</td><td>749-4419</td><td>(B) 742-5313</td></tr>
<tr><td colspan="2">Witness Name</td><td colspan="3">Home Address</td><td>Phone</td><td>E-Mail</td></tr>
<tr><td colspan="2">Zamet, Ash</td><td colspan="3">4250 North Marine Drive</td><td>525-9027</td><td>(B) 742-5313</td></tr>
</table>

<table>
<tr><td rowspan="6">SUSPECT #1</td><td>Suspect #1 Name</td><td>Age</td><td>Sex</td><td>Race</td><td>Hgt</td><td>Wgt</td><td>Eyes</td><td>Hair</td><td>DOB</td><td>Phone</td><td>E-Mail</td></tr>
<tr><td>Drk Overcoat - Blue & Green Shirt</td><td></td><td></td><td></td><td>600</td><td>165</td><td>Unk</td><td>Dr Brn</td><td></td><td></td><td></td></tr>
<tr><td>Address</td><td colspan="7"></td><td>City</td><td colspan="2">Alias or Gang Affiliation</td></tr>
<tr><td>Carrying brown paper bag</td><td colspan="7"></td><td>Slender Build</td><td colspan="2">Dk Brn Mustache</td></tr>
<tr><td colspan="9">Parent/Guardian, if juvenile.</td><td>Phone</td><td>E-Mail</td></tr>
<tr><td colspan="9">Displayed a gun</td><td></td><td></td></tr>
</table>

<table>
<tr><td rowspan="4">SUSPECT #2</td><td>Suspect #2 Name</td><td>Age</td><td>Sex</td><td>Race</td><td>Hgt</td><td>Wgt</td><td>Eyes</td><td>Hair</td><td>DOB</td><td>Phone</td><td>E-Mail</td></tr>
<tr><td></td><td></td><td></td><td></td><td></td><td></td><td></td><td></td><td></td><td></td><td></td></tr>
<tr><td>Address</td><td colspan="7"></td><td>City</td><td colspan="2">Alias or Gang Affiliation</td></tr>
<tr><td colspan="9">Parent/Guardian, if juvenile.</td><td>Phone</td><td>E-Mail</td></tr>
</table>

<table>
<tr><td rowspan="2">PROPERTY</td><td>Owner of Involved Vehicle/Property</td><td>Year</td><td>Make</td><td>Style</td><td>VIN/Serial Number</td><td>Color</td><td>Lic. Plate</td></tr>
<tr><td>Owner of Involved Vehicle/Property</td><td>Year</td><td>Make</td><td>Style</td><td>VIN/Serial Number</td><td>Color</td><td>Lic. Plate</td></tr>
</table>

<table>
<tr><td rowspan="2">NARRATIVE</td><td>Narrative (Do not duplicate above information)</td></tr>
<tr><td>P-205 sent by CC to 2435 W. Devon re: man with a gun. R/D's spoke to Schwartz, George J., the owner of Schwartz Convenience Store and two employee's #1) Ekter, Barbara and #2) Zamet, Ash. Zamet stated that the offender (description above) entered the store, walked over to Zamet, pointed a gun at Zamet's stomach and announced, "this is a stick up." The offender then ordered Zamet to open the cash register.</td></tr>
</table>

<table>
<tr><td rowspan="8">Police Personnel</td><td colspan="2">First Officer at Scene</td><td>Date/Time Arrived</td><td>Time Departed</td><td>Area of Assignment
2005</td></tr>
<tr><td colspan="2">Officer Notifying Investigations</td><td>Date/Time Notified</td><td colspan="2">Date/Time Investigations on Scene</td></tr>
<tr><td>Reporting Officer's Name (PRINT)</td><td>Badge Number</td><td colspan="2">Reporting Officer's Signature</td><td>Date/Time</td></tr>
<tr><td>D. Peterson</td><td>13441</td><td colspan="2"></td><td>15 Jan [-1] /1610</td></tr>
<tr><td>Reporting Officer's Name (PRINT)</td><td>Badge Number</td><td colspan="2">Reporting Officer's Signature</td><td>Date/Time</td></tr>
<tr><td>D. Shehn</td><td>5709</td><td colspan="2"></td><td>15 Jan [-1] /1610</td></tr>
<tr><td>Supervisor Approval Name (PRINT)</td><td>Badge Number</td><td colspan="2">Supervisor Approval Signature</td><td>Date/Time</td></tr>
<tr><td>Gallager</td><td>5201</td><td colspan="2"></td><td>15 Jan [-1] /1800</td></tr>
</table>

FORM CDP 1113 (3/[-2)

5.21 DEPOSITION

This is a civil suit for damages arising out of allegedly negligent medical treatment rendered to 11-month-old Jonathan McKinley at the East Suburban Medical Center on March 22, [-2]. The plaintiff, Jonathan's mother, claims failure of the emergency room physician, Dr. Eric Dutton, to recognize and treat symptoms of congestive heart failure, resulting in Jonathan's death. Dr. Dutton had diagnosed Jonathan as having a "touch of pneumonia." He prescribed antibiotics and sent Jonathan home, where he died of a heart attack the next morning.

Experts on both sides agree that if Jonathan had been timely and properly treated he would have lived a normal life expectancy, without disability.

Dr. Dutton brings a third-party action against Dr. Selwyn Cook, the Medical Center radiologist. Dr. Dutton claims Dr. Cook's conduct was the sole proximate cause of Jonathan's death because s/he failed to notify the emergency room staff that X-rays taken of Jonathan on March 22, [-2], showed findings of interstitial infiltrates, cardiomegaly, mild air trappings, and pleural effusion, all of which are consistent with congestive heart failure.

Dr. Cook's deposition, taken November 15, [-1], at the plaintiff's lawyer's office at 300 N. Clark Street, contains the following:

1 Q. Did you examine Jonathan's X-rays taken on March 22?

2 A. Of course.

3 Q. Didn't you see findings that were consistent with congestive heart failure?

4 A. They were consistent with congestive heart failure, but that is a condition
5   we rarely see in a child of Jonathan's age. It was my opinion that the X-ray
6   findings indicated viral pneumonia, although I could not rule out congestive
7   heart failure. That's what I said in my report.

8 Q. Why didn't you call Dr. Dutton to report your findings?

9   A.   I tried to call Dutton, twice in ten minutes, but I couldn't get through

10   to the emergency room. That's when I put a copy of my report in the

11   interdepartmental mail, which usually gets delivered within an hour.

12   Q.   Did it get delivered within the hour?

13   A.   I don't know. My shift was over by then, so I went home. I never saw the

14   report again. It must have been lost. We can't find it.

At trial, Dr. Cook is called as an adverse witness by Dr. Dutton's lawyer, and testifies as follows:

1   Q.   Dr. Cook, you examined Jonathan's X-rays, didn't you?

2   A.   Yes.

3   Q.   You found interstitial infiltrates, cardiomegaly, mild air trappings, and

4   pleural effusion?

5   A.   Yes.

[The instructor will provide additional adverse examination in class at this point.]

1.   For Dr. Dutton, continue the adverse examination.

2.   For Dr. Cook, conduct any necessary examination.

5.22 ARMED ROBBERY IDENTIFICATION

This is a criminal prosecution. Melvin Simpson is charged with the armed robbery of Campbell Burke.

As Burke walked past the alley at 6140 S. Park Street at 9:45 P.M. on February 1, [-1], a man stepped out of the alley and pointed a gun at his/her head. The man said, "Give me your wallet or I will blow your head off." Burke reached into [his back pocket]/[her purse], pulled out his/her wallet, and handed it to the man. The man took the wallet, turned, and ran into the dark alley. Burke ran to a nearby liquor store, where s/he called the police.

Detective O'Brien met Burke at the liquor store at 10:15 P.M. O'Brien interviewed Burke. The results of that interview are contained in O'Brien's report, which states, in part, the following:

> Victim related that the light from a streetlight about ten feet away allowed him/her to see the offender's face for three or four seconds. R/O asked victim for a complete description of the man who robbed him. Victim responded that offender was 5′ 6″ tall and weighed about 140 pounds. Victim described the gun as an automatic with a short, black barrel.

A preliminary hearing in the case was held on May 5, [-1]. Campbell Burke testified, and on cross-examination testified as follows:

1 Q. You saw the face of the man who robbed you for about three or four seconds?
2
3 A. Yes. He is sitting down right over there, at the table.
4 Q. For the record, Your Honor, the witness has pointed to the defendant, Melvin
5   Simpson. Mr./Ms. Burke, how would you describe Mr. Simpson?
6
7
8 A. He is about 6′ tall, heavy, maybe 200 pounds, and he has a thick mustache—
9   the same way he looked when he robbed me.
10
11 Q. What is your height and weight?

12	A. I'm 5′ 7″, and I weigh about 145 pounds.
13 14	Q. Before today, were you ever asked to look at any photographs or persons to
15 16	attempt to identify the man who robbed you?
17	A. Yes. About a month after I was robbed, Detective O'Brien came to my
18 19	house and showed me a photograph. It was the guy who robbed me.
20 21	Q. How many photographs did he show you?
22	A. Just the one of the guy who robbed me.
23 24	Q. Did the man in the photograph have a thick mustache?
25 26	A. Yeah. Same as now.

The case is now on trial. On direct examination Burke was asked to look around the courtroom to determine if the man who robbed him was present. Burke pointed to the defendant, Melvin Simpson, who was sitting next to his lawyer at counsel table. Simpson is 6′ 1″ tall and weighs 210 pounds. He has a thick mustache. The prosecutor then asked:

Q. When did you first identify the defendant as the man who robbed you?

A. In early April of last year, when Detective O'Brien came to my home and showed me some photographs.

Q. How many photographs did the detective show you?

A. He showed me six or seven photographs of different men. I picked out the defendant right away. He was the only one with a mustache.

1. For the defendant, cross-examine Burke.

2. For the prosecution, conduct any necessary redirect examination.

VI

EXPERTS

INTRODUCTION

The problems in this chapter represent basic situations involving experts who frequently appear at trial. The problems cover expert qualifications, basic direct and cross-examination situations, impeachment with treatises, and more complex expert situations.

In addition to these problems, three of the trials in Chapter 9 contain expert witnesses who can be the bases for separate problems. Trial 9.2 has contractors, Trial 9.4 has product design experts, and Trial 9.14(C) has police use of force experts. These trials also feature opposing experts, so you will have an opportunity to see how the examinations of these experts are interrelated.

Your instructor may modify the assignments and make specific additional assignments for these exercises.

The suggested background reading is Mauet & Easton, *Trial Techniques and Trials*, Chapter 8.

6.1 MEDICAL EXPERT QUALIFICATION

This is a contested civil commitment proceeding brought by the children of Sadie Thompson, in which the children allege that their mother, because of increasing senility, is no longer able to care for either herself or her property.

Pursuant to court order, petitioners retained Dr. Robin Schultz to conduct a psychiatric evaluation of Thompson. Along with his/her report, Dr. Schultz submits a curriculum vitae.

At the hearing on the petition, the petitioners call Dr. Schultz as a witness.

1. For the petitioner, conduct a direct examination of Dr. Schultz.
2. For the respondent, cross-examine Dr. Schultz.

Robin Schultz, M.D.
100 Main Street

November 15, [-1]

Robert Kelly, Attorney at Law
42 W. Madison

Re: Sadie Thompson
     Clinical Evaluation Report

Dear Mr. Kelly:

I have examined Sadie Thompson per your request.
The examination took place November 1, [-1], in my
offices. It lasted 30 minutes, and consisted of examination and interview. I conducted the usual psychiatric
and neurological tests.

It is my opinion that Mrs. Thompson suffers from
senile dementia, moderate stage. This diagnosis reflects
a chronic organic brain syndrome associated with gener-
alized atrophy of the brain due to aging. I found elements of self centeredness and childish emotionality.

In my opinion, Sadie Thompson is unable to care for
herself or her property, which, as you informed me, is
quite extensive and varied.

My fee for services to date is $3,000. I will bill
you for any required court time at my usual rate of $800
per hour.

My curriculum vitae is enclosed.

Very truly yours,

Robin Schultz

Robin Schultz, M.D.

CURRICULUM VITAE
Robin Schultz, M.D.

Occupation: Physician, specializing in forensic
    psychiatry.

Present practice: Elgin Mental Health Center (assistant
    director), private practice, Chicago, specializing
    in evaluation of psychotic conditions, particularly
    in criminal cases.

Teaching positions: Associate clinical professor of
    psychiatry, Loyola University Medical School.

College: University of Chicago, B.A. degree, [-29].

Medical School: Northwestern University, M.D. degree, [-25].

Internship: Cook County Hospital, [-24] to [-23].

Residency: In psychiatry, at Bellevue Hospital, New York,
    [-23] to [-19].

Present Hospital Staff Positions: Northwestern University
    Hospital (since [-16]); Loyola University Hospital
    (since [-19]).

Licenses: Illinois, [-24].

Professional Associations: American Medical Association;
    American Psychiatric Association; American Academy
    of Forensic Psychiatrists (chairman, [-6] to [-3]).

Publications:

    "The Folly of the Insanity Defense in Criminal
        Cases," *American Psychiatric Journal*, Spring,
        [-6], Vol. 14, pp. 122-140.
    "Hoodwinking the Psychiatrist: The Malingering
        Defendant in Criminal Cases," *Psychiatry
        Quarterly*, Vol. 20, [-2], pp. 16-40.
    "The Myth of the Insanity Defense," *Clinical
        Psychiatry*, Winter, [-1], Vol. 13 pp. 111-140.

Board Certification: American Board of Psychiatry
    and Neurology (Diplomate, [-10]); Committee on
    Certification of Mental Health Administrators
    (certified, [-6]).

6.2 FINGERPRINT EXPERT QUALIFICATION

This is a burglary prosecution. The case is now on trial. As part of the prosecution's case-in-chief, you intend to call Charlie Henderson, a fingerprint expert, who will testify that s/he made a comparison of a latent fingerprint found at the burglarized premises with the known fingerprints of the defendant. According to Henderson, the latent fingerprint was made by the defendant.

Henderson has previously told you that s/he graduated from high school ten years ago, attended the local community college for two years, and then joined the local police department, where s/he was assigned to the crime laboratory. S/he has been assigned to the fingerprint unit for seven years. During the first three years, s/he was assigned to the classification section (where s/he classified approximately 50 sets of fingerprints each day so that the fingerprints could be indexed in a master filing system), and thereafter began work in the identification section (where s/he compares latent fingerprints with known fingerprint cards, approximately 10 to 30 each day). S/he remains there to this day.

Henderson says s/he is a member of the American Academy of Forensic Sciences and has read the major professional literature in the field. S/he says that his/her specialty is a "learn-by-doing field, where you learn by working as an apprentice in each section for at least two years under established experts. Only then can you begin doing your work independently."

Henderson says s/he now trains new personnel at the crime lab as well as lectures on the basics of fingerprint identifications at the crime laboratory. S/he has two articles (on the iodine vapor method of raising latent fingerprints on papers and documents) published by the American Academy of Forensic Scientists in its quarterly publication. S/he was promoted to the rank of sergeant one year ago. S/he has testified for the prosecution in criminal cases about five times per year since being assigned to the identification section.

1. For the prosecution, conduct a direct examination of Henderson, limited to qualifying him/her as an expert in the appropriate field.

2. For the defense, cross-examine Henderson on his/her qualifications.

6.3 TREATING PHYSICIAN AND DIAGRAMS OF SPINE

This is a personal injury case arising out of an automobile accident. Since the date of the accident the plaintiff has been complaining of pains in his back and periodic shooting pains down his legs.

Plaintiff's treating physician, Dr. Dakota Baird, an orthopedist, has testified that as a result of his/her examinations and tests s/he determined that the plaintiff suffered a herniated disc at the L3-L4 level, which is pushing against the plaintiff's spinal cord, causing pain.

Dr. Baird has already described the basic anatomy of the back, including a description of the intervertebral discs. S/he has brought the attached anatomical charts to court.

1. For the plaintiff, continue Dr. Baird's direct examination, using the charts to illustrate the basic components of a typical lumbar vertebra and how a herniated disc can produce painful pressure on the spinal cord. (You may use any other available anatomical chart.)

2. For the defendant, oppose the introduction of the charts.

Lumbar Vertebra

(Horizontal Cross Section)

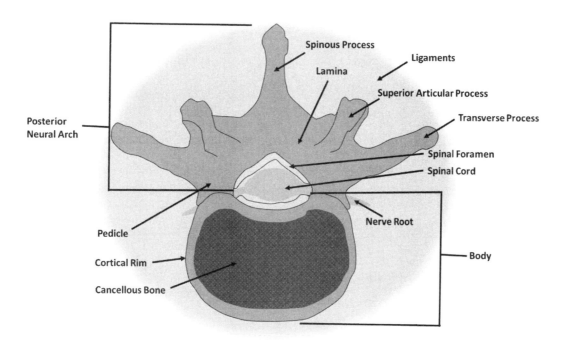

Spinous Process

Ligaments

Lamina

Superior Articular Process

Posterior
Neural Arch

Transverse Process

Spinal Foramen

Spinal Cord

Pedicle

Nerve Root

Cortical Rim

Body

Cancellous Bone

Lumbar Vertebrae

(Vertical Cross Section)

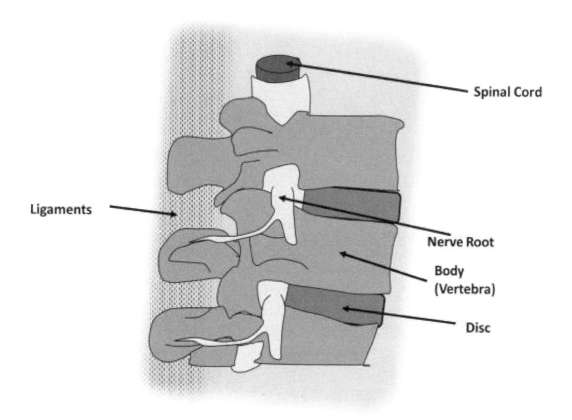

Spinal Cord

Ligaments

Nerve Root

Body
(Vertebra)

Disc

6.4　TREATING PHYSICIAN

This is a negligence action arising out of an automobile accident. Both liability and damages are in issue. The case is now on trial.

As part of her case-in-chief, plaintiff Helen Griggs calls Dr. Reilly Worthington, an orthopedist who treated her at the St. Mary's Hospital emergency room and continued treating her throughout her confinement at the hospital and as an outpatient afterward. At the conclusion of his/her services, Dr. Worthington submitted his/her bill to the plaintiff, which was paid.

Attached are the St. Mary's Hospital emergency room report and doctor's progress notes, as well as Dr. Worthington's patient history card and final bill.

Assume that Dr. Worthington has been qualified as an expert in the appropriate field.

1.　For the plaintiff, conduct a direct examination of Dr. Worthington, using the attached records as you see fit.

2.　For the defendant, cross-examine Dr. Worthington.

ST. MARY'S HOSPITAL
EMERGENCY ROOM / URGENT CARE

Rapid Assessment

Date/Time of Arrival	Pain Scale	Triage Category
1-15-[-1] / 3:18 P.M.	☐1 ☐2 ☐3 ☐4 ☐5 ☐6 ☐7 ☐8 ☐9 ☐10	☐I ☐II ☐III ☐IV ☐V

Patient Name	Address	Phone
Helen Griggs	1843 E. Broadway	

Chief Complaint (Subjective)

	Pt. states she was in car accident caused when other driver ran red light and crashed into the front of her car. Force of collision crushed her against steering column. Pt. wearing seatbelt at time. Pt. thinks left leg is broken.

Vitals

Temperature	Pulse	RESP/MIN	Blood Pressure
99	88	18	130 / 85

Objective Assessment

	Pallor noted, organ systems (HEENT, h/l) within normal limits. Marked tenderness and palpable swelling in distal third left lower leg with apparent subcutaneous venous oozing and crepitation of bone.

Diagnostic Workup

☐Blood Glucose	☐Creatinine test	☒X-Ray: Left lower leg lateral
☐BUN	☒EKG	☒X-Ray: A-P x-rays
☒CBC	☒Electrolytes	☐X-Ray:
☐CEA	☒SMA-12	☐X-Ray:
☒Chest X-ray	☒U/A	☐X-Ray:

Problems

Apparent fx left tibia / fibula; possible shock.

Plan

Admit, to OR.

Worthington

Physicians Signature

373

Patient Name	
Helen Griggs	

Date	Notes
1/15/ [-1]	Report of Operation: Surgeon: Worthington Assisted by: T. Karnes Anesthesia: Sodium-pentothal Pre-op diagnosis: Fracture of left tibia/fibula Post-op diagnosis: Compound fracture, distal 1/3 left tibia, simple fracture distal 1/3 left fibula with displacement. Procedure: Patient in usual position, anesthesia given intravenously. Patient left leg x-rayed with portable unit (patient pain prevented x-ray while conscious). X-rays disclosed fracture noted. Patient left tibia and fibula manually manipulated until bones in apparent alignment (tibial fragment not sufficiently large or structural to require pins, etc.). X-ray showed alignment within normal limits. Left leg casted in plaster from toes to upper thigh in usual fashion. Patient tolerated procedure well. Vital signs stable. EBL=none. Rx 5% saline IV, Tylenol 10 mg as needed, morphine at bedtime. In: 4:30 P.M., out 5:17 P.M. Patient to postop in good condition. *Worthington*

Patient Name	
Helen Griggs	
Date	Notes
1/16/[-1] 9 A.M.	Patient complains of pain radiating up left leg and throbbing at fracture site. Temperature 101.8 Increased swelling. Rx Tylenol 10 mg four times a day, leg elevation, morphine at bedtime. 5% saline discontinued. *Worthington*
1/17/[-1]	Patient complains of pain. Temperature 101 Swelling stabilized. Maintain same orders, morphine discontinued. *Worthington*
1/18/[-1]	Patient complains of pain, but intermittent. Temperature 99 Pressure sensation less. Same Orders. *Worthington*
1/19/[-1]	Patient pain periodic, controlled with Tylenol. Afebrile. Swelling gone. Patient instructed to keep leg elevated as much as possible – crutches only when necessary. Will discharge with Tylenol, to return to office in 1 week. *Worthington*

REILLY WORTHINGTON, M.D.
PATIENT HISTORY CARD

Patient Name: Helen Griggs	
Address: 1843 E. Broadway	
Date	Notes
1/30/[-1]	Patient still complains of periodic pain, states swelling worse when leg not elevated – instructed to keep leg up whenever possible. Rx Tylenol only if needed. Return in 1 month.
3/3/[-1]	Cast removed, left leg x-rayed and examined. Good callus formation at fracture sites. Normal atrophy. Patient states pain gone, except for occasional throbbing or twinges at end of day. No longer uses Tylenol or aspirin. Leg re-casted, to knee. Patient instructed to exercise knee, without weight on leg, to restore full motion. Return 8 weeks.
5/1/[-1]	Cast removed, leg x-rayed and examined. Callus formation excellent. No complaints of pain. Atrophy normal. Leg wrapped in elastic bandage. Patient instructed to soak ankle and leg in hot water, twice daily, exercise ankle to restore full motion, walk without crutches, gradually putting increasing weight on leg. Return 1 month, earlier if problems.
6/3/[-1]	Patient examined. Full motion in knee, essentially full motion in ankle. Some residual swelling and puffiness in ankle. Calf and thigh still moderately atrophied. Patient walks with slight limp – should disappear in a few weeks as muscles restored to full strength. No pain, even on palpation. Patient instructed to continue physical therapy as described in booklet until recovery complete. Return only if problems.
6/30/[-1]	Bill for $12,000.00 sent – all services during course of treatment 1/15/[-1] to 6/3/[-1]
7/20/[-1]	Bill paid in full.

STATEMENT OF PHYSICIAN SERVICES

REILLY WORTHINGTON, M.D.

STATEMENT DATE	June 30, [-1]
PAY THIS AMOUNT	$12000.00

FORWARDING SERVICE REQUESTED

FOR BILLING INQUIRIES, CALL (555) 555-5555
MON-FRI 8:30 AM—4:30 PM

PATIENT: HELEN GRIGGS

DATE	CODE	DESCRIPTION	CHARGE	BALANCE DUE
1/15/[-1] TO 6/3/[-1]	44	PROFESSIONAL SERVICE RENDERED	12000.00	12000.00

- ✂

PATIENT: HELEN GRIGGS

If paying by credit card, fill out below:

MAY CHECKS PAYABLE TO:

REILLY WORTHINGTON, M.D.

FORWARDING SERVICE REQUESTED

FOR BILLING INQUIRIES, CALL (555) 555-5555
MON-FRI 8:30 AM—4:30 PM

CARD NUMBER	AMOUNT
SIGNATURE	EXP. DATE / CVV CODE

STATEMENT DATE	June 30, [-1]
PAY THIS AMOUNT	$12000.00

6.5 TREATING PHYSICIAN

Martha Hiller is suing Thomas Randolph for personal injuries suffered in an auto accident on February 10, [-3]. Her suit asks for substantial damages. Her claim is based primarily on the pain and suffering she says have resulted from the accident.

The case is now on trial. Hiller will testify that her neck and head pains are as severe today as they were when she initially saw Dr. Pat Flanagan after the accident. She will say that she stopped going to the doctor because s/he was not helping her, and she did not want to incur additional expense.

Hiller was not employed at the time of the accident, having retired one year earlier after 30 years of employment at Western Electric.

Aside from Dr. Flanagan's bill, her actual expenses were as follows:

St. Joseph's Hospital emergency treatment	$4,250.00
X-rays	1,300.00
Prescriptions	725.00

Dr. Flanagan is now called as a witness for the plaintiff. His/Her report and the hospital X-rays are attached. Assume that there is a stipulation that Dr. Flanagan is a qualified physician, specializing in the field of orthopedics.

1. For the plaintiff, conduct a direct examination of Dr. Flanagan.
2. For the defendant, cross-examine Dr. Flanagan.

Pat Flanagan, M.D.
30 North Michigan Avenue

July 18, [-1]

Samuel Levin
Attorney at Law
221 N. La Salle Street

Re: Martha Hiller

Dear Mr. Levin:

I have written this report pursuant to your request for information concerning my patient, and your client, Martha Hiller, of 5770 N. Washtenaw. Ms. Hiller has signed the appropriate consent form for release of this information.

Martha Hiller is a 62-year-old white female. She is five feet, three inches in height and weighs 120 pounds. I first saw her in the emergency room at St. Joseph's Hospital on February 10, [-3]. She had been brought there by a Fire Department ambulance after an auto accident that took place at the intersection of Sheridan Road and Surf Street.

The patient told me she was proceeding north on Sheridan Road when a westbound car went through a red light on Surf Street and struck her vehicle at about the right front door. She described the impact as "heavy." She said that on impact her body was "thrown to the left and back again." She felt stunned and just sat behind the wheel for a few minutes. When the police came to the scene she asked to be transported to the hospital. She said she never before had suffered any injuries in an accident. She reported no prior injuries to, or difficulties with, her neck, back, or head.

In the emergency room Ms. Hiller complained of soreness in her neck and shoulders. A visual examination was made and no sign of trauma was found. X-rays were taken and were negative. The patient was released with the suggestion she rest at home for the balance of the day and take aspirin as needed.

I next saw Ms. Hiller on Feb. 14, [-3], at my office. She had called for an appointment that morning.

The patient reported that the pain in her neck and shoulders had been steadily increasing. In addition, she complained of severe headaches for the past two days.

A thorough physical examination was conducted, including the usual sensory, motor, and radiographic tests. All tests were negative for objective findings, although I noted a slight limitation in head movement. I could find no objective explanation for the pain she described, although she obviously was in discomfort.

I suggested she use an electric heating pad, take hot baths, and use aspirin as required. I asked her to see me again if the pain continued.

I saw Ms. Hiller again on Feb. 21, [-3]. She told me the pain in her shoulders had diminished, but that the neck pain and the headaches had not diminished, and had, in fact, become worse.

Again, I conducted a complete physical examination, although I did not order radiographic tests. I made no objective findings. I gave her a prescription for the analgesic Emperin Compound No. 3, with codeine, and I recommended bed rest and the taking of hot baths.

I next saw Ms. Hiller on March 10, [-3]. She again described continuous pain in her neck, at the base of the skull, along with severe headaches, at least once a day. I told her to continue taking the Emperin Compound, and I recommended she restrict herself to light activity and as much bed rest as possible.

The next and final time I saw Ms. Hiller was April 10, [-3]. She again complained of neck pain. She said the headaches now occurred every two to three days. I renewed the prescription for the Emperin Compound, and told her to refrain from any exertion.

I have not seen or heard from Ms. Hiller since that last visit.

I find it difficult to make an exact diagnosis. I believe the pain is real and that she is not malingering. Since she told me she never experienced neck or shoulder pain or anything other than an occasional mild headache before the accident, it is my opinion that Ms. Hiller's condition was caused by the accident of February 10, [-3]. I would classify her condition as cervical sprain.

Since I have not seen the patient for more than two years, I have no opinion concerning her present condition.

My fee for services to Ms. Hiller, in the hospital and at my office, was a total of $3,300. Those bills were paid. My fee for preparing this report is an additional $2,000. If I am called upon to testify in this case, I, of course, expect to be paid for my time.

Very truly yours,

Pat Flanagan, M.D.

CURRICULUM VITAE

Pat Flanagan, M.D.

30 N. Michigan Avenue

Occupation

Physician, private practice limited to orthopedics
since [-8]

Education, Training & Licenses

B.A., Northwestern University, [-20]

M.D., Johns Hopkins, [-16]

Internship, Bellevue Hosp., New York City, [-16] - [-15]

Medical licenses, NY [-16], IL [-15]

Residency in orthopedics, Loyola University Hospital,
    Chicago, [-15] - [-11]

Board certified, [-8], American College of Orthopedic
    Surgeons

Employment

Northwestern University Hospital, Chicago, staff
    physician, [-11] - [-8]

Chicago Orthopedic Surgeons, member of group practice,
    since [-8]

Professional Associations

American Medical Association, since [-16]

Illinois State Medical Society, since [-15]

Cook County Medical Society, since [-15]

Publications

"Whiplash," *American Medical Association Journal*,
    June, [-10]

"Cervical Trauma," *Journal of Orthopedics*, January, [-5]

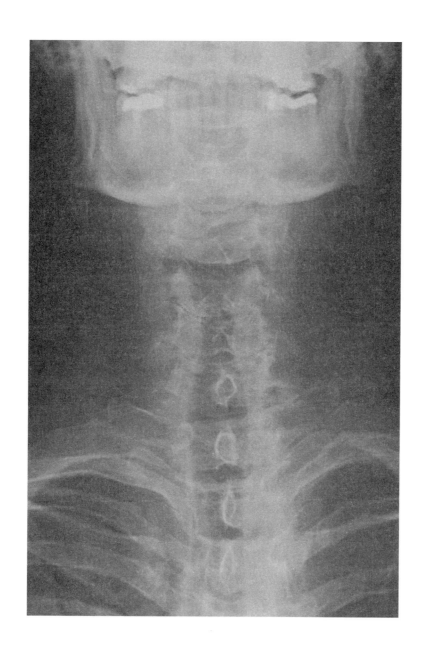

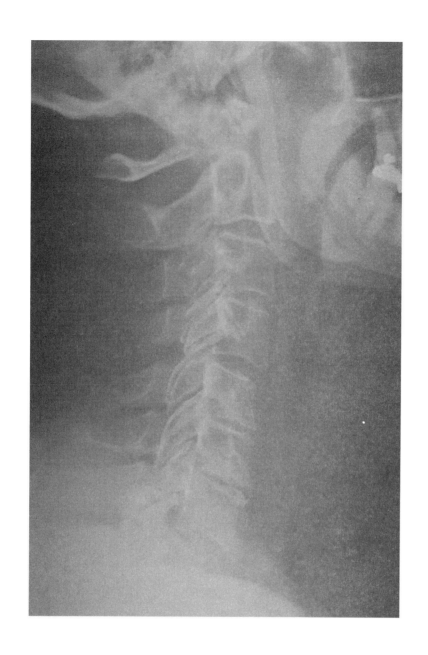

6.6 ECONOMIST

Two years ago today Richard Schiller was killed while working for the U.S. Steel Corporation. A steam boiler manufactured by the Gorp Corporation exploded, killing Schiller instantly. The explosion was caused by a faulty weld in the boiler. Pretrial investigation has developed the following information:

Richard Schiller

Schiller was born on January 1, [-36]. Until his death he was in good health. He weighed 185 pounds and was six feet tall. He played basketball for his high school team but turned down an athletic scholarship at Notre Dame to enter the Marine Corps. He served in the Marines for three years, two of them in the Middle East, where he won the Distinguished Service Medal. He was never injured and received an honorable discharge.

Following his discharge in January [-15], Schiller went to work for U.S. Steel. He began as a steam boiler mechanic and kept that job until he was killed. His starting wage was $44,000 a year. He received wage increases of 5 percent each year until the year of his fatal accident. He had no other income.

Schiller was active in church affairs. He was a deacon at the First Activist Church. At the church he taught basketball to teenage children, including his son Mickey.

Harriet Schiller

Harriet was Richard's wife at the time of his death. She was born on January 1, [-33]. She has never worked outside the home before or since the accident. Harriet has spent these past two years following Richard's death raising Mickey and being active in the Ladies' Auxiliary at the church.

Harriet and Richard went steady throughout high school and kept in constant communication during the three years he was in military service. They were married the day after he was discharged from the Marines. Mickey was born ten months later.

Harriet and Richard were very close. When he was not working or at the church, he was at home with her. He would help with the needed repairs on their house and with the yard and house work.

Harriet has not remarried, nor has she dated anyone since Richard's death.

Mickey Schiller

Mickey was born on January 1, [-14]. He and his father were very close and did many things together, such as playing checkers and going to sporting events. Mickey is the star center on the church basketball team and learned everything he knows about basketball from his father. Mickey hopes to go to college on an athletic scholarship. He is now six feet tall and weighs 150 pounds.

Additional Information

1. Under Schiller's union contract the mandatory retirement age is 62. Pensions vest after 20 years. There is no ceiling on a permissible rate of wage increases. After 30 years of employment, the full pension is 50 percent of the employee's highest annual wage prior to retirement.

2. Schiller smoked one-half pack of cigarettes each day. He drank beer socially but not hard liquor.

3. Schiller drove the only family car, a six-year-old Kia, to work each day. He bought the house his widow still lives in for $200,000 in January [-14]. The amount of $110,000 was owed on the mortgage at the time of this trial.

4. Schiller bought a new suit each spring, as well as a few pants, shirts, and other usual clothing items each year. He spent about $125 each week on personal items such as food and other incidentals.

The administrator of the estate of Richard Schiller has brought a wrongful death action against Gorp Corporation. The complaint is based on a strict liability theory. The defendant in its answer admitted liability, so the only issue remaining is damages. The case is being tried in your state, and your jurisdiction's tort law applies. Assume that the plaintiff has presented evidence in his case-in-chief that proves the facts stated above.

Plaintiff now calls Morgan Mason, an economist, as his last witness. Mason's résumé is attached.

1. For the plaintiff, conduct a direct examination of Mason to prove the economic loss to the survivors caused by Schiller's death. Assume that you are in federal court.

2. Use the same information as in No. 1, but assume that you are in a state jurisdiction that requires the use of a hypothetical question.

3. For the defense, cross-examine Mason.

Résumé
Morgan Mason, Ph.D.

200 Maple Lane

Occupation:

Economist, self-employed consultant.

Education:

1)   University of Wisconsin, B.A. in economics, [-15].
2)   University of Wisconsin, M.A. in economics, [-13].
3)   Purdue University, Ph.D. in economics, [-10].

Employment:

1)   Metropolitan Insurance Co., [-9] to [-6], actuary and risk analyst.
2)   Allstate Insurance Co., [-6] to [-4], actuary.
3)   Self-employed economist since [-4], specializing in actuarial and economic loss analysis in personal injury cases. I have done economic loss analysis in about 200 cases, including approximately 40 death cases. In about 80 percent of them I was retained by the plaintiff's lawyer. I have testified at trials as an economic expert eight times, six for plaintiffs and two for defendants. I charge $400 an hour for deposition and court time, and $300 an hour for review, preparation, and consultation.

Publications:

1)   Ph.D. thesis: "The Effect of Taxes and Inflation in Present Cash Value Analysis."
2)   "Loss of Future Income in Wrongful Death Cases," [-4], *The Economist*.
3)   "Predicting Future Income," [-2], *Economics Review*.

Teaching:

1)   Teaching Assistant, Purdue University, [-13] to [-10].

2)   Assistant Professor, Purdue University, [-10] to [-9].

Professional Association:

American Economics Association, since [-13].

6.7 IMPEACHMENT WITH TREATISE: FINGERPRINT EXPERT

This is a burglary prosecution of James Evens. The case is now on trial. Previous witnesses have testified to locating and removing a latent print at the crime scene and taking the defendant's fingerprints on a standard fingerprint card following his arrest. These witnesses have also testified that they personally delivered the latent print and the fingerprint card to Freddy Bolger, a fingerprint expert employed by the police department. No computer analysis was available due to equipment malfunction.

The prosecution then calls Bolger as a witness. After being qualified as an expert in fingerprint comparisons, s/he testifies that s/he personally received the latent print and the fingerprint card and that s/he made a comparison between them.

Bolger testifies that s/he found seven identical friction ridge characteristics in the latent print and one of the fingerprints on the card, and on that quantitative basis only concluded that the latent print was made by the same person whose fingerprints are on the card.

You have the attached excerpt from Moenssens, Starrs, Henderson, and Inbau, *Scientific Evidence in Civil and Criminal Cases* (4th ed. 1995), pp. 513-516, one of the standard works in the field.

1. For the defense, cross-examine Bolger.
2. For the prosecution, conduct any necessary redirect examination.

§8.08 Fingerprint Identification

To compare an unknown latent impression with an inked impression of known origin with the aim of determining whether both were made by the same finger, the technician looks for four different elements: The likeness of the general pattern type (or, if the type cannot be determined because the questioned pattern is incomplete, for a general similarity in flow of the ridges); the qualitative likeness of the friction ridge characteristics; the quantitative likeness of the friction ridge characteristics; and the likeness of location of the characteristics.

Many latent impressions developed at crime scenes are badly blurred or smudged, or consist of partially superimposed impressions of different fingers. As long as a sufficiently large area of friction skin is available which is not blurred, smudged, or rendered useless through superimposition, identity can be established. . . . The size of area required varies according to the number of individual ridge characteristics discovered and the frequency of their appearance in a given area. This relates to the element of quantitative likeness in that it requires that a sufficient number of characteristics be found to match in both prints, without unexplained dissimilarities. By tradition, though not by empirical studies, latent print examiners in the United States have required a matching of at least eight characteristics in both prints for identity, though most experts prefer at least 10-12 concordances. In England, 14 to 16 matches are required for court testimony. The qualitative comparison of the friction ridge characteristics refers to whether or not the characteristics (bifurcations, ridge endings, enclosures, ridge dots, etc.) are the same in both prints. The likeness of location of the friction ridge characteristics refers to the relationship with one another within the contours of the pattern. In other words, identity can be established if the ridge characteristics are in the same relative position to one another in both prints, with the same number of intervening ridges in both.

403

Because of criticism that had been leveled against the fingerprint examiners for failing to agree on a rule setting the minimum number of ridge characteristics that must establish a match between two prints before they can be said to be from the same digit, the International Association for Identification, a professional body composed primarily of fingerprint identification specialists, created in 1970 a Standardization Committee. The Committee consisted of 11 members whose aggregate experience in the identification field amounted to roughly 250 years. The group was charged with several mandates, one of which was to recommend adoption of a minimum standard for matching characteristics, if feasible. After a concentrated study of nearly three years' duration, the committee concluded that there exists no valid basis, at this time, for requiring a predetermined minimum number of friction ridge characteristics in two impressions in order to establish positive identification. The decision on whether two prints under examination are made by the same digit is one that must be made, the committee concluded, on the basis of the expert's experience and background, taking into account, along with the number of matching characteristics, other factors such as clarity of the impressions, types of characteristics found, location of the characteristics in relation to the core or delta, etc. The committee's formal report was unanimously approved by the association's general membership at the 58th annual conference of the IAI in 1973.

In extensive testing and research with tens of thousands of "similar," though not identical prints, experts have been unable to find more than four *clearly defined* characteristics that are quantitatively and qualitatively the same in two prints known to be from different fingers. By adhering to the old-time tradition in the profession that at least eight matching characteristics be found in both the known and the unknown print before identity is established, a degree of certainty of identification is introduced which accounts for the fact that there is very seldom a "battle of opposing experts" in fingerprint cases. Yet, in a great number of criminal cases an expert or consultant on fingerprints for the defense has been instrumental in seriously undermining the state's case by demonstrating faulty procedures used by the state's witnesses or by simply showing human errors in the use of fingerprint evidence.

6.8　IMPEACHMENT WITH TREATISE: MICROANALYST

This is a sexual assault prosecution. You represent the defendant, John Finley. The defendant has denied having any contact with the victim. His defense is based on a claim of mistaken identification.

The prosecution calls Dr. Riley Jones, a microanalyst for the police department crime laboratory.

On direct examination, Dr. Jones testifies that s/he received from the Lutheran-General Hospital a year ago today a slide prepared by means of a swab of the victim's vaginal pool. The slide was prepared one hour after the rape. With it was a request by investigating police officer Martin Casey, who asked the laboratory to determine whether human spermatozoa were present.

Dr. Jones testifies that s/he performed the appropriate microbiological analysis on the slide. In his/her opinion, human spermatozoa were present. No DNA test was performed due to lack of funding.

You have the attached excerpt from Moenssens, Inbau, and Starrs, *Scientific Evidence in Criminal Cases* (3d ed. 1986), pp. 342-347.

1.　For the defense, cross-examine Dr. Jones.
2.　For the prosecution, conduct any necessary redirect examination.

§6.11 Identification of Human Blood Types

After determining that the blood is of human origin, the blood is further classified as to blood group. Blood analysis and group determination is based on antigen antibody reactions or by enzyme system tests. The most frequently used antigen systems are the *ABO*, the *M*, *N*, *mn*, *Rh*, and *Gm* systems.

It is beyond the scope of this chapter to explain, in detail, each and every blood grouping system. By way of example, the basic and oldest blood grouping method—the *ABO* system—is explained here as representative of the antigen systems.

Blood grouping into types, *A*, *B*, *AB,* and *O* (really meaning zero) may be used as positive or negative evidence in a criminal prosecution. A person's blood group remains constant throughout life notwithstanding age, disease, or medication. The types are named according to the presence or absence of the *A* or *B* agglutinogen in the red blood cell. Roughly 40 percent of the population in the United States is type *A*, 43 percent is type *O*, 14 percent is type *B*, and 3 percent is type *AB*.

In 1900 Landsteiner established that the serum of one individual would clump (agglutinate) the red blood cells of another individual. The explanation for this was that red blood cells contain a substance known as an antigen and the serum of the blood contains antibodies. The two antigens in the *ABO* blood system are the antigens *A* and *B*; the two antibodies in the *ABO* blood system are anti *A* (alpha) and anti *B* (beta). In the red blood cells of a human being there will be either the *A* antigen, the *B* antigen, both the *A* and *B* antigens, or neither *A* nor *B* antigens.

These antigens may also be referred to as blood group factors; therefore, a person having *A* antigen in his red blood cells has group *A* blood, a person having *B* antigen has group *B* blood, a person having both *A* and *B* has group *AB* blood, and a person who has neither *A* nor *B* antigens in his red blood cells has group *O* blood. If a person has *A* antigen in his red blood cells he cannot have an anti *A* antibody in his serum, for this would agglutinate (clump) his own cells. The same is true of an individual having *B* antigen in his blood cells; he cannot have anti *B* antibody in his serum. It follows that a person with both *A* and *B* antigens in his blood cells can have neither anti *A* nor anti *B* antibodies in his serum. However, a person who has neither antigen *A* nor *B* in his red blood cells (Group *O*) has both antibodies, anti *A* and anti *B* in his serum.

In addition to the *ABO* system of grouping blood, there are also other systems which can be used, such as *MN* blood groups, *Rh* blood groups, and others.

Blood group substances are not only present in blood. Approximately 80-85 percent of the population, known as secretors, have blood group substances in their saliva, tears, perspiration, semen, vaginal fluids, mucus, gastric contents, etc. The ability to secrete is an inherited dominant trait; the genes responsible for it are not linked to the *ABO* genes. If a person carries the secretor gene (*Se*), the *H* substances genes are identifiable by the use of anti *H* sera. If a person carries the nonsecretor gene (*se*), the *H* substance does not react to any antigen. In essence, a nonsecretor is a person with no secretor gene in his body fluid, his *H* substance is alcohol soluble, so does not mix with body fluids. By contrast, in a secretor the *H* substance is water soluble and therefore extracted in the body fluids so that the antigens are subject to detection by the use of anti sera.

6.9 IMPEACHMENT WITH TREATISE: PHYSICIAN

This is a medical malpractice action. The defendant, Dale Rosen, M.D., an obstetrician, delivered an infant, Michael Healy, at St. Mary's Hospital. Michael's parents have brought this action, alleging that Michael's retardation was caused when he experienced respiratory distress immediately following delivery and the doctor and attending nurses failed to use all the necessary standard procedures and techniques to properly ventilate and oxygenate the infant after birth.

At trial Dr. Rosen testified on direct examination that after an uneventful delivery, the infant, who was born full-term, immediately experienced respiratory distress. He was not breathing regularly or adequately, and his hands and feet were pale and blue, indicating oxygen deprivation—that is, central cyanosis.

Dr. Rosen stated that s/he immediately had the nurses suction the infant's airway while s/he stimulated his feet. When this failed to induce normal breathing, the doctor inserted a 3.5-mm endotracheal tube into the infant's trachea to ensure an airway. The infant was given an oxygen mask that was connected to pure oxygen, but no positive pressure ventilation was provided.

Dr. Rosen stated that the infant's cardiac output and acid-base status appeared normal. Accordingly, the infant was thoroughly dried and wrapped in blankets and was taken to the infant nursery about 20 minutes after delivery. The infant's extremities turned pink within 30 minutes following delivery, so the doctor removed the endotracheal tube but kept the oxygen going for approximately two more hours.

You have *The Merck Manual of Diagnosis and Therapy* (13th ed. 1977). Pages 985 to 988, which are attached, are taken from chapter 10 (Pediatrics), section 2 (The Newborn).

The *Merck Manual* is a standard reference text for nurses and hospital staffs. It deals with the diagnosis and treatment of common, recurring medical problems. Dr. Rosen will acknowledge that it is a standard authority, insofar as it describes the standard prevailing procedures for treating common medical situations.

1. For the plaintiff, cross-examine Dr. Rosen.

2. For the defendant, conduct any necessary redirect examination.

DISTURBANCES OF THE NEWBORN
ASPHYXIA AND RESUSCITATION
(Asphyxia Neonatorum)

An infant who does not breathe spontaneously at birth, or who has acute blood loss, requires resuscitation to minimize the possibility of brain damage, as well as to prevent death. Although instituting adequate ventilation usually is the main concern in newborn resuscitation, the rapid replacement of blood lost by hemorrhage during delivery is equally critical.

Treatment

Step 1. Airway: The airway should first be quickly cleared of secretions, fluid, or blood by suctioning the pharynx and nostrils with a soft catheter. Suctioning must be gentle and limited to 5 to 10 seconds, since prolonged vigorous suctioning may cause apnea or bradycardia through the vagal reflex.

The infant depressed by anesthetic agents may be stimulated repeatedly for as long as 2 min. by a method such as slapping the feet, before other efforts at resuscitation are begun. However, if central cyanosis or bradycardia develops, positive pressure ventilation (see Ventilation, below) must begin immediately. For an infant meconium-covered and depressed at birth, it is essential to visualize the vocal cords directly using a laryngoscope and to perform endotracheal suction

411

repeatedly until the airway is clear of aspirated meconium. Instilling small amounts of saline into the trachea may help to loosen the meconium and to make aspiration easier. An endotracheal tube with the largest possible diameter should be used: a 3.5 mm tube can usually be used for full-term infants, a 3 mm tube for infants under 1.5 kg, and a 2.5 mm tube for infants of 1 kg or less. The trachea may be effectively suctioned by a mouth-to-tube technique (with intervening face mask). These procedures must be performed quickly and followed by positive pressure ventilation with O_2 in order to prevent severe anoxia.

Step 2. Ventilation: Positive pressure ventilation is effectively provided by mouth-to-mouth or bag and mask resuscitation with the infant's head in the neutral position and the jaw raised slightly to ensure a clear airway. Endotracheal intubation should be used only by experienced personnel who are comfortable at rapid intubation. Ventilation should be instituted at a rate of about 40/min.; the effectiveness is judged by upper chest movement, since hearing-transmitted breath sound is not always a reliable indicator of adequate ventilation in the new born.

. . .

Step 6. Temperature: Maintaining the infant's temperature during resuscitation is essential and is often overlooked. Cooling increases the infant's metabolic rate 2 or 3 times above the basal rate, increasing O_2 requirements. In the face of O_2 lack, the infant more rapidly develops severe O_2 debt, which can result in neurologic damage or death. After the baby is dried thoroughly, use of a radiant heater is recommended, rather than blankets, since it permits continuous observation of the infant's color and activity during resuscitation.

6.10 MEDICAL EXAMINER IN MURDER CASE

The defendant, Horace Johnson, is charged with the murder of Alma Lee Bradshaw. During discovery, the defendant stated that his defense will be that Bradshaw might have died as a result of the alcohol consumed on the day of her death and not as a result of any act he performed.

An autopsy and blood-alcohol test were performed on Bradshaw at the County Morgue.

The file contains Dr. Keegan Tapp's pathological report, the toxicological report, and statements of witnesses. It also contains a report to the defense from Dr. Ralph Schultz, a forensic pathologist. The State has a copy of the report.

Both sides have stipulated that the Cozy Tavern is located six blocks from Rose Prince's apartment.

1. For the State, conduct a direct examination of Dr. Tapp.
2. For the defense, cross-examine Dr. Tapp.

PATHOLOGICAL REPORT AND PROTOCOL

County Medical Examiner's Office
Edward Tapp

#25 of August, [-1]

Name Alma Bradshaw   Date of Death August 4th, [-1]

Address 515 W. 63rd Street   Exam. at County Morgue

Identification   Date Examined August 5th, [-1]

Address   Examined by Keegan Tapp, M.D.

External Examination:

Race_____   Sex Female   Age 37   Length 5'2"

Weight 80 lbs Hair____   Iris____ Sclera_____

Musculature   Skeleton: Slender
Pigmentation   Medium
Edema   Powerful
Docubitus   Deformed
                                        Amputations

Signs of Death:

Cornea Cloudy-Turbid   Decomposition: Skin-Slip
        Dry   Shrunk   Tissue Gas
Body Heat   Discoloration
Lividity   Dehydration
Rigor Mortis   Putrefaction

History of Cause of Death

    Place removed from: 6136 S. Princeton. The character
of this place is an apartment. Pronounced dead at
Provident Hospital on August 4th, [-1], at 4:15 p.m.
The diagnosis is supposed assault. The body was
brought to the morgue August 4th, [-1] at 5:00 p.m. by
police.

External Examination

The body was that of a well developed undernourished female
who measured 5'2" and weighed about 80 lbs. The scalp is
covered with black hair. In the left lateral forehead over

the posterior 3rd of the left eyebrow there is an oblique laceration measuring 2 cm. The margins are red brown abraded. The laceration is 2 cm. in depth and tore the aponeurosis covering the inferior border of the left roof of the brain. Below the inferior border of this laceration there is a pale brown abrasion measuring 1 cm. There is greenish discoloration of the external angle of the left eye. There is a faint violaceous red discoloration of the left eyelid. There is swelling associated with no abrasion and swelling of the right eyelid which are discolored dark vidlaceous red. There are eggs of maggots present in the mouth. There is ecchymosis of the sclera and conjunctiva of the right eye. The irises are brown. Pupils equal 0.3 cm. in diameter. The lower gum is dentate. The upper gum sustained a frontal partial denture. There are 2 linear abrasions of the inferior aspect of the right side of the face. One is located midway below the right side of the body of the mandible and measured 0.5 cm. The other extends into the left of the inferior aspect of the chin located 0.5 cm. in front of the neck. It is interrupted and measured 4-1/2 cm. There is an old scar linear of the anterior aspect of the neck located in the thyroid cartilage and it measured 6 cm. It is located 3 cm. above the superior end of the sternum. This scar is 1 cm. to the right of the midline and extends into the left side of the neck. The chest is symmetrical. The breasts are unremarkable. The abdomen is scaphoid. The external genitalia are those of a normal female. Extending from the left inguinal region into the lateral aspect of the left thigh down to the lower 3rd including the upper half of the posterior aspect of the left thigh and extending into the external portion of the left buttock there is an area of diffuse contusion consisting of violaceous red discoloration. There is swelling of the left knee and violaceous red discoloration of both knees. There are multiple dark red abrasions of the anterior aspect of the knees measuring up to 3 cm. There are 2 dark red brown abrasions of the medial aspect of the right ankle measuring up to 1-1/2 cm. Seven dark red brown abrasions varying from 0.3 cm. to 2 cm. in longest diameter are noted in the anterior aspect of the left ankle and dorsum of the left foot. Rigor mortis is moderately present. Extending from the left interscapular dorso-vertebral region there is an old surgical scar for a left thoracotomy which measured 23-1/2 cm. and ends in a point located 7 cm. below the left nipple and 3 cm. to the left of this nipple. Dependent lividity is present in the back. There is a contusion of the dorsum of the right hand associated with multiple dark red abrasions. There is violaceous red discoloration of the dorsum of the right hand. These abrasions measure up to 1 cm. The right side of the right thigh showed diffuse contusions, swelling and violaceous red discoloration. There are multiple red brown abrasions in number of 5 of the lumbar region measuring up to 1 cm.

INTERNAL EXAMINATION

HEAD: The scalp was reflected and the soft tissue covering the inferior portion of the right occipital region
showed minimal hemorrhage in a patch measuring 3 cm. There
is minimal hemorrhage of the inferior 3rd of the latero-
anterior aspect of the right forehead. There is also
minimal hemorrhage of the soft tissue covering the left
superior orbital bridge. There are about a few cc of bright
clotted blood in the subdural space of the left occipital
lobe which is associated with contusion 0.4 cm. in length,
dark red of the inferior medial surface of the left occipital lobe. There were no fractures of the skull. The brain
was edematous. The vessels of the surface of the brain were
engorged. The brain weighed 1085 grams. There was diffuse
congestion of the inner area of the cerebral cortex.
Petechial hemorrhages were seen in the white matter. The
ventricular system contained clear fluid. There were no contusions or lacerations of the spinal cord or inter-vertebra
discs of the cervical vertebral column nor in the remainder
of the vertebral column; however, the cervical vertebral
column was supple.

BODY: The body was opened with a Y incision to reveal the
subcutaneous tissue in the midline to measure 2 cm. The left
lung was missing and replaced by dense fibrous adhesions.
There were old sutures in the left hilar region. The right
lung was attached to the chest wall by multiple fibrous
adhesions. The amount of blood in the body was reduced.
There was scoliosis of the dorsal vertebral column with the
concavity pointing toward the left. The left leaf of the
diaphragm was at the left 6th intercostal space while
the right leaf was at the 12th intercostal space. Both were
in the posterior portion. The internal genitalia were unremarkable.

RESPIRATORY SYSTEM: The right lung weighed 400 grams. The
right lung showed obstructive emphysema and the traceo-
bronchial tree contained tenacious mucous tinged with blood.
There was a bleb formation of the areas of the lung. The
exterior was reddish gray mottled with black. The cut surface was pale red brown and oozed frothy fluid. The lung was
partly hypercrepitant and partly hypocrepitant.

CARDIOVASCULAR SYSTEM: The heart weighed 220 grams. The apex
was formed by both ventricles. The epicardium was smooth.
The myocardium was pale brown and showed a slight infiltra-
tion of the right anterior ventricle. The endocardium was
smooth. The mitral valve showed thickening of the free edge.
The coronary arteries and aorta showed minimal arterio-
sclerotic changes. The spleen weighed 55 grams. The edges
were sharp. The capsule was wrinkled and gray. The cut
surface was pale red brown. The architecture was intact.

417

GASTROINTESTINAL SYSTEM: The liver weighed 1075 grams. The leading edge was blunt. The capsule was transparent. The cut surface was diffusely yellow and showed occasional patches measuring up to 1 cm. of hemorrhage. The liver was markedly pliable and the superior and inferior aspect could be placed together. The remainder of this tract was unremarkable. The stomach contained mucous in an amount of 25 cc.

GENITOURINARY SYSTEM: The kidneys together weighed 250 grams. The capsule stripped with ease to reveal a smooth pale brown external surface. The cortex and medulla were in their normal ratio. The cortico medullary markings were distinct. The exterior of the kidneys was noted with spiders. The urinary bladder was empty. The remainder of this tract was unremarkable.

ANATOMICAL DIAGNOSIS

1. Edema of brain
2. Multiple internal injuries and fatty liver
3. Contusion laceration and abrasion of the left eyebrow
4. Minimal contusion of brain
5. Minimal left subdural hemorrhage
6. Contusions of thighs
7. Contusions of eyelids

TOXICOLOGIST'S REPORT

Analysis of the blood showed the presence of three-hundred seventy-eight (378) mg. percent alcohol.

IN MY OPINION THE SAID _____Alma Lee Bradshaw_____ death was

Part I - Death was caused by (enter only one cause per line for (a), (b), and (c))

Immediate Cause (a) ___Edema of brain_____

due to (b) ___multiple internal injuries_____

due to (c) _____

Part II - Other significant conditions contributing to death but not related to the terminal condition given in Part I (a).

_____fatty liver_____

_____

Date ___8/11/[-1]___   Signed   *Keegan Tapp*
                                       Keegan Tapp, M.D.

Résumé

Keegan Tapp, M.D.

100 Elm Street

Occupation:

Physician, specializing in pathology.

Education:

University of Florida, B.S. in chemistry, [-10]
Loyola University, M.D. [-7]

Training:

Internship, Cook County Hospital, Chicago, [-6] to [-5]
Residency in pathology, Loyola University Hospital,
Chicago, [-5] to [-2]

Employment:

County Medical Examiner's Office [-2] to present. I perform
autopsies to determine the causes of death. Over the
past two years, I have performed approximately 500 such
autopsies. I testify regularly in homicide cases on causes
of death, and have done so in over 25 cases to date.

Licenses:

Illinois, [-6]; this state, [-2]; board certified,
American College of Pathology, [-1]

Publications:

"Coup-Contre-Coup: Death on the Streets," *Journal of the
American Medical Association*, Fall, [-2]

Professional Associations:

American Medical Association
American College of Pathology
American Association of Forensic Pathologists

County Medical Examiner's Office

Phillip Smith, M.D.

TOXICOLOGIST'S REPORT

Your case No. 25 of Aug., [-1] Date Material received Aug. 5, [-1]

Toxicology case No.   835   Date of this report Aug. 9, [-1]

To Dr. _Tapp_____ Deputy _____

    Analysis of the specimens submitted and recorded by you as pertaining to the dead body of __Alma Lee Bradshaw__, and on which you requested an analysis by the Toxicologist for __alcohol__.

Analysis of the blood showed the presence of three-hundred seventy-eight (378) mg. percent alcohol. ****

                                          Joseph E. Ksiazek, Chemist

Typed and questioned by Inv. Frank Schmidt at police
headquarters. Also present is Inv. Sam Caldwell.
Statement taken August 4, [-1], at 8:15 P.M.

1 Q. What is your name, address, and occupation?
2
3 A. Rose Prince. I live at 6136 S. Princeton in a third-
4   floor walkup apartment. I am not presently employed.
5
6 Q. With whom do you live at 6136 S. Princeton?
7
8 A. I live alone.
9
10 Q. What is your education?
11
12 A. I graduated from high school.
13
14 Q. Do you know Horace Johnson?
15
16 A. No. But I know Alma lived with him on 63rd Street.
17
18 Q. How well did you know Alma Bradshaw?
19
20 A. She was my cousin. We grew up together.
21
22 Q. Did you see Alma Bradshaw earlier today?
23
24 A. Yes. At about 3:00 P.M. She knocked on my door.
25
26 Q. Tell us in your own words what happened when she
27   knocked on your door.
28
29 A. Well, I opened the door and she kind of stumbled into
30   the apartment. Her eyes looked funny and she smelled
31   like she had been drinking. She looked terrible. She
32   kind of staggered around for a couple of minutes.
33   I asked her what the matter was, but I could not
34   understand her when she answered. She just mumbled.
35   I couldn't make out the words. Then she just collapsed
36   on the floor. That's when I called the police.
37
38 Q. When is the last time before today that you had
39   seen Alma?

40 A. I hadn't seen her for about six months. She sure
41   looked different when I saw her today. She had lost
42   a lot of weight and her knees looked all scraped
43   up. She kept holding her head with her hands.
44
45 Q. Are there any questions about this incident that
46   I may have failed to ask you?
47
48 A. Not to my knowledge.
49
50 Q. After reading this statement, if you find the statement
51   correct as typed, will you sign the statement?
52
53 A. Yes.
54

SIGNED *Rose Prince*
      Rose Prince

Typed and Questioned by Inv. Frank Schmidt at police
headquarters. Also present is Inv. Sam Caldwell.
Statement taken August 4, [-1], at 8:54 P.M.

```
 1   Q. What is your name, address, and occupation?
 2
 3
 4   A. I am Arthur Kent. I live at 515 W. 63rd Street, in
 5      Apartment 203. I am presently unemployed.
 6
 7   Q. How long have you lived in that apartment?
 8
 9   A. About three years.
10
11   Q. Do you know Horace Johnson and Alma Bradshaw?
12
13   A. Sure. They lived next door to me for a year now.
14
15   Q. Did you see either one of them today?
16
17   A. I saw them both. But first I heard them.
18
19   Q. What time did you hear something?
20
21   A. It was about 10:00 or 10:30 this morning.
22
23   Q. What did you hear?
24
25   A. Well, the walls are thin. I heard both their
26      voices. They were loud. It sounded like an
27      argument. It must have gone on about 15 minutes.
28
29   Q. Could you hear what was being said?
30
31   A. Well, I heard Alma crying. Then I heard Horace
32      say: "I've had enough of you. You're finished.
33      I don't care how sick you are." At least it was
34      something like that. Horace sounded real mad.
35      That's all I remember hearing.
36
37   Q. What happened next?
38
39   A. Well, I heard their apartment door open, and then
40      I heard running sounds in the hall. And they both
41      were yelling. I went to my door and opened it.
42
43   Q. What did you see?
```

44	A.	I saw Johnson chasing Alma down the hall. He was
45		swinging a board at her and they both were yelling.
46		
47	Q.	How big was the board?
48		
49	A.	It looked real big, about three feet long. He was
50		holding it in one hand, like a club.
51		
52	Q.	Did he hit her with the board?
53		
54	A.	He sure did.
55		
56	Q.	How many times did he hit her?
57		
58	A.	I would say twice, maybe three times.
59		
60	Q.	What part of her body did he hit?
61		
62	A.	I know he hit her on the head at least once.
63		I can't say what part of her head.
64		
65	Q.	What happened next?
66		
67	A.	Well, she ran down the stairs, but he didn't go
68		after her. He went back into the apartment.
69		
70	Q.	Did you see what he did with the board?
71		
72	A.	He took it back into the apartment with him.
73		
74	Q.	Did you see either one of them again?
75		
76	A.	Yes. Right after that I went to the Cozy Tavern
77		to get some cigarettes. Alma was in there. She
78		was sitting at a table and she had a glass and a
79		bottle of gin in front of her. She was alone.
80		
81	Q.	Did you see her again?
82		
83	A.	Well, I walked past the tavern about two hours
84		later. When I looked in I saw she was still there
85		at the same table. That was about 1:00. She was
86		sitting with her head in her arms.
87		
88	Q.	Do you have anything else to add?
89		
90	A.	No, except that they were always arguing and
91		carrying on.

```
92 Q.  Are there any questions about this incident that
93     I may have failed to ask you?
94
95 A.  I don't think so.
96
97 Q.  After reading this statement, if you find the
98     statement is correct as typed, will you sign the
99     statement?
100
101 A.  Yes.
```

Signed: *Arthur Kent*
Arthur Kent

STATEMENT OF HORACE JOHNSON

Typed and questioned by Inv. Frank Schmidt at police
headquarters. Also present is Inv. Sam Caldwell.
Statement taken August 4, [-1], at 9:15 P.M.

1   Q. What is your name, address, and occupation?
2
3   A. Horace Johnson. I live at 515 W. 63rd Street,
4   Apartment 202. I work at United States Steel.
5
6   Q. Do you understand that you are being charged with
7   the murder of Alma Bradshaw?
8
9   A. Yes, I do.
10
11 Q. You have been told that you do not have to say
12   anything without a lawyer being present, and that
13   if you do say anything it will be used against you
14   in a court of law. If you can't afford a lawyer,
15   one will be appointed for you. Do you understand
16   your rights?
17
18 A. Yes. I don't want a lawyer. I want to tell you
19   what happened.
20
21 Q. Do you know Alma Bradshaw?
22
23 A. Of course. Alma and I lived together for the past
24   year. We were going to get married.
25
26 Q. How did you get along with her?
27
28 A. We had our differences, like anyone else. But we
29   always made up.
30
31 Q. What happened between you and Alma earlier today?
32
33 A. It was about 10:00 or so. I was dressing to go to
34   work at U.S. Steel. I was going to work from noon
35   to five. Alma was putting her clothes on. I asked
36   her where she was going. She said she was going
37   to the Cozy Tavern on the corner for something
38   to drink. I told her it was too early to start
39   drinking. She started yelling at me and swearing
40   at me. We argued back and forth for a while. Then
41   she opened the door and said she was going to the
42   Cozy and I could go to hell. I got mad and picked
43   up a board that we use to prop the door closed.

431

44   It's about two feet long and three inches wide,
45   maybe an inch thick.
46
47 Q. What happened next?
48
49 A. She ran out the door and I ran after her.
50
51 Q. Did you hit her with the board?
52
53 A. I think I touched her lightly on the rear end, but
54   that's all.
55
56 Q. Did you hit her on the head?
57
58 A. Absolutely not. I didn't want to hurt her.
59
60 Q. Go ahead.
61
62 A. She ran to the landing and down the stairs.
63   I stopped at the head of the stairs. I knew
64   I had to get to work and I didn't want to fight
65   anymore. So I went back to the apartment, finished
66   dressing, and went to work.
67
68 Q. What did you do with the board?
69
70 A. I must have thrown it down the hallway. I know
71   I didn't take it back to the apartment. I don't
72   know where it is.
73
74 Q. Did you see Alma again?
75
76 A. No. The next thing I know is that I saw you in the
77   hallway outside my door.
78
79 Q. Have you ever been convicted of a crime?
80
81 A. Yes. I was convicted of aggravated assault five
82   years ago. They told me it was a felony, but
83   I received three years' probation. It was just a
84   fight in a bar. I had to use a bottle.
85
86 Q. Is there anything else you want to say?
87
88 A. No, only that I loved Alma. I would never hurt her.
89
90 Q. After reading this statement, if you find the
91   statement correct as typed, will you sign the
92   statement?

                                   Horace Johnson
93   Horace Johnson
94 A. Yes

Memorandum to Defense Counsel

Re: Death of Alma Bradshaw

   As you requested, I have examined Dr. Tapp's report
and the toxicologist's report. I do not understand
how Dr. Tapp could have concluded Bradshaw died
of a trauma-induced edema of the brain. Given the
deceased's height, weight, and physical condition it
seems obvious to me that it is just as likely that she
died of acute alcoholic poisoning. Her liver was in
terrible shape. She had ingested an enormous amount of
alcohol. Evidence concerning trauma indicates she did
not receive any severe blows. In addition, the amount
of time and distance between the receiving of the blows
and Bradshaw's collapse leads me to believe the trauma
had very little to do with her death. As you know, an
extremely high dose of alcohol taken by a person with
one lung can cause asphyxiation, and thus a resulting
edema of the brain. You should also understand that
alcoholics bruise easily, and they are known to walk
into objects and to fall frequently when intoxicated.
These possibilities should be explored in this case.
The bruises Dr. Tapp found could have been caused when
Bradshaw collapsed in Mrs. Prince's apartment.
Please call me if you would like further details
concerning my findings and opinions.

                              Ralph Schultz, M.D.

Curriculum Vitae

Ralph Schultz, M.D.
100 Franklin Street

Occupation:

M.D., forensic pathologist

Education:

Harvard University, B.S. in biology, [-30]
John Hopkins University, M.D., [-26]

Training:

Internship, Massachusetts General Hospital, Boston, [-26]
to [-25]
Residency in pathology, Harvard University Hospital,
Cambridge, [-25] to [-22]

Employment:

New York County (Manhattan) Medical Examiner's Office,
deputy coroner, [-22] to [-16]
University Hospital, clinical assistant professor of
pathology, [-16] to [-10]
Private practice in pathology, [-16] to [-10]
University Hospital, professor of forensic pathology, [-
10] to present. I have been the pathology department head
since [-3].

Licenses:

New York, [-22]; this state, [-16]; board certified,
American College of Pathology, [-14]

Publications:

I have published 12 articles to date, all dealing with
various aspects of forensic pathology, in the *AMA
Journal, New England Journal of Medicine,* and pathology
journals.

<u>Professional Associations:</u>

American Medical Association
American College of Pathology
American Association of Forensic Pathologists

I have testified more than 100 times as an expert in forensic pathology. I testified on behalf of the defense about half the time. My fee for writing a report is $3,000. My fee for a court appearance is $5,000, plus expenses.

6.11 PSYCHIATRIST TESTIMONY IN MURDER CASE

The defendant, Ronald Wasserman, is charged with murder. He does not deny committing the acts that resulted in his mother's death. He asserts the affirmative defense of insanity (or not guilty by reason of mental disease or defect, if that is the terminology used in your jurisdiction).

You have in the file a psychologist's report and the report of the witness, Dr. Reese Hopkins, who conducted an independent, court-ordered examination. In addition, you have a summary of the statements of various witnesses to relevant events. That summary was made available to Dr. Hopkins after s/he filed his/her report.

Dr. Hopkins is called as a witness for the defense.

Your state's substantive law concerning the insanity (or mental disease or defect) defense will apply. Among the references to be used is the *Diagnostic and Statistical Manual of Mental Disorders*, American Psychiatric Association.

1. For the defendant, conduct a direct examination of Dr. Hopkins.
2. For the State, cross-examine Dr. Hopkins.

Ronald Wasserman was 23 years old when he shot and killed his mother on August 8, [-1].

Wasserman was born and raised in this city. During last year he was in his final year at the State University Circle Campus. Throughout grade school, high school, and college he was very affectionate with his mother. His love and affection toward her became even greater during the time that he was 20, 21, 22, and 23.

Until sometime in May of last year, Wasserman was described by people who knew him well as very outgoing, friendly, and interested in other people. Wasserman would ask questions and make jokes and was always smiling. He would always answer when spoken to and he was communicative with others. He appeared to be a young man normal in every way. Before May of last year, Wasserman would take part with his father in such activities as hunting, fishing, and going to parks and zoos. Wasserman was congenial, friendly, and easy to communicate with in his relations with other young men and women of his own age group, as well as with members of his family and friends of his parents.

In the last days of May, last year, Wasserman was informed by his father, Arthur, that his mother was in the final stage of a terminal disease, namely, leukemia, and that there was no hope that she would survive. When Wasserman was informed of his mother's condition, he began to cry in the company of his father and when he was alone. From that time on a change in Wasserman's personality and demeanor began to take place.

Wasserman became withdrawn, melancholy, moody, dejected, and uncommunicative. He would stare at the floor constantly. He would not take part in conversations in the presence of others, and when asked questions at times he would not respond and other times his responses were brief.

Wasserman's speech was forced, in phrases, but was not gibberish. He would stare off into space and at times put his hands to his eyes after staring into space.

Wasserman, with his father, was at his mother's Southeast Memorial Hospital bedside on June 3, last year, when his mother told a family friend, Estelle London, that she had leukemia and that she felt horrible. Then his mother said, "If this is the way I have to feel the rest of my life, I would rather be dead; I am not going to make it." At the time Wasserman appeared to be in a complete fog, he just stood and did not move. When a family friend who had known him since his birth tried to talk to him in the hospital room, he would not say a word.

On the following day at his mother's hospital bedside, he was present, with his father, when his mother said, "I feel miserable—I would rather be dead," and he was present when his father told the family friend who asked about his mother's condition,

439

"There is no hope." At that time, Wasserman said nothing and is described by his father as looking like the whole world had come to an end for him.

In early June, last year, Wasserman was seen by his father looking at books connected with his university work, and in the early days of June, last year, he took his final examinations. Wasserman took four courses: One he did not finish, and in the other three his grades were two Cs and one D. He thereafter enrolled in summer school to complete one course needed for graduation. Before last year, Wasserman had a B+ grade average at the university.

In late June, at the Wasserman home and in his and his father's presence, his mother told a family friend, Irene Doss, that she was "much worse," that "the pain is unbearable." Wasserman and his father were present when the friend asked his mother if she had told the doctor, and his mother answered, "There is nothing he can do. If I have to go back to the hospital, I will kill myself." The family friend described Wasserman at that time as sitting still, like a stone, with no visible reaction.

On June 30, Wasserman purchased a .22 caliber automatic pistol at the Stein gun shop, and he furnished his correct name, date of birth, and his address, etc. In early July, in Wasserman's presence, his father asked his mother how she felt, and she said, "If it is possible to be in more pain, this is it. If I have to come back here again, I will kill myself." His father described Wasserman as quiet, staring down to the floor, then up to his mother and back to the floor, and as not answering when his father tried to talk to him.

During early July, last year, at the Southeast Memorial Hospital where Wasserman's mother again was hospitalized, she told Wasserman and his father that she was "getting worse. There is great pain, I don't think I will live to come out of it." On another occasion at that hospital, in Wasserman's presence, she said to his father she felt "very bad; if I have to come back to the hospital I will kill myself." At that time Wasserman walked out of the room and when his father tried to talk to him, he would not respond. He is described by his father at that time as a completely different person, one who was becoming more dejected. On another occasion, in early July, last year, at the family home, his father told him that his mother was despondent and that she had asked his father "to kill her, to get her out of her misery." At that time Wasserman cried and said he wished he could have the pain instead of her.

In late July, at the family home and in his presence and in his father's presence, his mother said she was in pain and then said, "Please won't one of you kill me and put me out of my misery?" At that time Wasserman said nothing and walked out of the room.

During the months of June and July, last year, Wasserman's mother underwent physical outward changes—that is to say her face was distorted and had a flattened appearance, there appeared on her extremities an open rash, her feet were swollen, and she had open sores on her hands.

In early August, last year, at the family home at a time when his mother was weak, with her face swollen and the rash all over her body, she said to Wasserman and his father that she was in great pain and she said, "Please won't you kill me and put me out of my misery?" At that time Wasserman lowered his head, stood still for a moment, and walked out of the room. He was in tears. When his father tried to talk to him he would not talk.

Mrs. Wasserman was readmitted to the hospital on August 4.

On August 5, Wasserman was visiting the home of a young woman, Irene Doss, whom he had known since grade school days and with whom he had visited two or three times a month prior to May of last year. During June and July, after learning of his mother's illness at the end of May, Wasserman visited her home once a week. Wasserman told the young woman that his mother was slipping fast and that she was pleading with him to put her out of her misery. At that time he stared off into space and put his hands to his eyes. His eyes seemed blank. He would not look at her.

On August 7, Wasserman visited briefly with his mother at the hospital. Her condition was unchanged.

On the next day, August 8, Wasserman entered his mother's room. Only he and his mother were in the room. His father had brought him to the hospital, but sat in the visitor's waiting room when Ronald went to see his mother.

Mrs. Wasserman was sleeping. Ronald took the .22 automatic out of his pocket. He fired three shots into his mother's head. After a few seconds, he turned and walked out of the room. He walked to where the attending nurse, Harriett Stone, was sitting.

Miss Stone had been the attending nurse when Wasserman visited his mother on the earlier occasions. She is 34 years old, single, and lives two blocks from the hospital. She had been a registered nurse for eight years. For the first two years she moved through various departments at Southeast Memorial, but has spent the past six years on the floor where Mrs. Wasserman's room is located. That floor is set aside for terminally ill patients, many of them suffering from cancer.

During the time Mrs. Wasserman was in the hospital, Nurse Stone came to know Ronald, mostly through informal conversations, either while Ronald was waiting to get into his mother's room or after he had paid a visit to his mother. They talked about Mrs. Wasserman and about other things, such as sports and his school classes.

When Ronald came to the floor on August 8, she greeted him, but his only response was a nod. Nurse Stone sat at her desk, opposite Mrs. Wasserman's room, when Ronald went inside. She noticed nothing unusual about him. She was working at the desk when she heard three shots. She immediately looked up and saw Ronald standing next to his mother's bed. He was pointing the gun at his mother's head. He then turned, came out of the room, and walked the few feet to the desk where Nurse Stone was sitting.

She saw Wasserman remove the clip from the gun. He placed the clip and the gun on Nurse Stone's desk.

Wasserman said to the nurse: "Please see if my mother is dead." The nurse went into the hospital room, where she determined that Mrs. Wasserman was dead. There were three bullet wounds in her head.

The nurse then came back to the desk, where Ronald was standing. Nurse Stone said: "She is dead. Why did you do it?" Ronald answered: "She begged me to do it."

Ronald then lit a cigarette and said he wanted to go out and tell his father what he had done. He walked into the visitor waiting room, where his father sat. He told his father: "Mother won't have to suffer anymore. I put her out of her misery. I just shot her."

Police officers, answering Nurse Stone's call, arrived a few minutes later and placed Ronald under arrest. He was charged with murder. Pursuant to court orders, Ronald was examined by Dr. Arturo Guzman, a psychologist, on August 13, and by Dr. Reese Hopkins, a psychiatrist, on September 14, [-1].

Nurse Stone told the police that shortly before Ronald arrived, she had made her rounds and had given Mrs. Wasserman a sedative to allow her to sleep. In her opinion, Ronald was sane on the day he shot his mother. She told police Ronald obviously was grieving over his mother's condition, but that was not an unusual occurrence among family members of patients suffering from cancer.

Psychologist's Report

Subject: Ronald Wasserman
Date: August 13, [-1]
Location: Interview and Testing Room, County Jail

Findings:

Subject was friendly and cooperative on a superficial level.

In the field of intelligence Subject's performance was adequate and his intellectual level was in the bright-normal range. The test for personality functioning suggested that in the area of reality orientation Subject's ability to perceive reality adequately was sufficient and adequate under essentially neutral conditions, but under stress his reality contact tended to become tenuous, that is, impaired. His emotional functioning at the time was labile, that is, unstable, vulnerable.

He did not maintain adequate emotional control over his intellectual and social functioning in the testing situation.

His emotions showed signs of immaturity and impulsivity. That is, he did not have his emotions under good control.

His fantasy life was not particularly good and it showed signs of vulnerability, and under stress showed signs of some bizarre and some emotionally unstable functioning.

The Rorschach, T.A.T., and draw-a-person tests also showed Subject's intellectual control over his emotional function was not adequate under stress; that on the surface without the situation of stress, an emotional response would come to the surface, along with some confusion. Underlying confusional reasoning may come to the fore.

Under situations without stress, Subject maintains adequate controls and could function in situations where there was not great emotional stress and upheaval put upon him.

There were no major signs of organic brain damage.

Although it is not unusual for people to have some impairment of reality perception under stress, the degree of impairment in this case was very considerable.

Although it is not unusual within limits for persons to lose some emotional stability under stress, the test showed Subject's loss of emotional stability was beyond the usual limits.

Arturo Guzman Ph.D.

Arturo Guzman, PhD
30 N. Michigan

Reese Hopkins, M.D.
112 N. State Street

September 16, [-1]

The Honorable _____

Court Center

RE: RONALD WASSERMAN

Dear Judge _____

The following psychiatric report is subsequent to your order requesting psychiatric evaluation of the defendant Ronald Wasserman. The evaluation was requested concerning criminal responsibility at the time of the alleged offense.

SUMMARY:

Mr. Ronald Wasserman is a 23-year-old single white male who is presently in confinement at the County Jail House of Corrections. His charge is murder, based on an incident which occurred on August 8, [-1].

CURRENT CHARGE:

In his interview with this examiner, the defendant was extremely reluctant to discuss the events leading up to and including his mother's death. He stated that his memory of the event was somewhat foggy and confused, and that only a few incidents were clear to him during this period of time. He recalled that he first learned of his mother's illness from his father in May and stated that he reacted with shock, because his mother had seemed perfectly healthy to him. He had thought that his mother had never been ill before, as far as he knew. While at first he visited his mother in the hospital voluntarily, he soon found himself finding the visits very troubling, so that he tended to avoid visiting her whenever possible. Sometime in early June, according to the defendant, he began experiencing difficulty falling asleep at night; this progressed to the point where he was unable to fall asleep before 3:00 or 5:00 in the morning. He was also awakened by recurrent frightening dreams about animal corpses, to which he gave little thought. He did not, however, feel tired during the daytime, and did not attempt to nap; but he did experience a change in his activity and interest pattern. He visited his friends and girlfriend much less frequently, stopped playing tennis, and did not — during the entire summer of these events — go swimming or to the beach or participate in dances or parties of any kind. He felt himself somewhat cut off from other people, experienced things as somewhat dream-like or unreal, although he could not clarify this further. Regarding schoolwork, he found himself rereading pages or paragraphs and then not recalling what he had just read; after some time he gave up trying to read completely. He did believe that he was doing well in school nevertheless, and expected to receive good grades. He was baffled by the Cs and Ds he reportedly achieved in his examinations. He also recalled having been late to class several times, or even walking into a wrong classroom before realizing he had done so. He recalled having difficulty making decisions and, for example, wore the same clothes repeatedly on different days because of this inability to make decisions. His personal grooming and dressing habits deteriorated, and he had to be reminded to shower and shave. He also reported having difficulty driving his car, in that he frequently was honked at by other drivers because he was driving too slowly. On one occasion, he had a minor car accident by rear-ending another car, but no injuries resulted. He also reported mild confusion in his thinking processes, which he described as "being slowed." He experienced difficulty starting to talk and found himself talking a lot less than usual. He experienced subjectively a lack of energy, difficulty getting out of bed in the morning, as well as a marked decrease in appetite, so that he lost 20 pounds from his already thin body. In general, he described his feeling as being "numbed" or "I lost my feelings entirely," but there is no distinct depressive mood noted or reported. There were also small fluctuations from day to day or within the day, as to his mood. During this period of time, he denied suicidal ideation, anxiety symptoms, somatic symptoms, unusual use of alcohol or drugs, experiences of thought broadcasting or thought insertion, or frank hallucinations. He recalled experiencing some persistent rumbling noises and sometimes wondered if, somehow, his thoughts had been withdrawn from his head because his mind seemed so blank much of the time. He stated that it did not occur to him to seek professional help at any time, nor did he think that anything was wrong with him during that period. When he was asked in particular why he had purchased the handgun on June 30, he was unable to account for this. He stated that he did not, however, carry this gun around with him until the day on which he used it. He was also unable to account for why he shot his mother, although he commented somewhat vaguely that he was unable to tolerate his mother's suffering.

PAST RELEVANT HISTORY:

The defendant did not have a previous psychiatric history of any kind. He has not been in psychiatric treatment, and on review of systems, denied notable psychiatric or psychological dysfunction. There was also no previous involvement with alcohol or drugs, and no involvement in the Criminal Justice system. He was never involved in gang activities, and had only a very rare boyhood fistfight. He tended to describe himself as efficient, independent, contented, and likable — but also gave some indication of being a loner.

Personal history indicates that he was an only child to his parents, with whom he lived until he was 20 years of age, when he entered college. At age 20 he moved into an apartment with a roommate, with whom he has continued to live over the last three years. Even though he left his parents' home, he continued to see his parents on a regular, almost weekly basis. He described his mother as loving and generous; he described his father as somewhat distant and hardworking. There are no family disruptions of any kind, and no reported family history of mental disorder, substance abuse, or sociopathy. The defendant has always been in good medical health, and has never had a hospitalization for any reason.

CURRENT MENTAL STATUS:

The undersigned psychiatrist performed a psychiatric interview on the defendant on September 14. The interview lasted for two hours and was conducted at the undersigned's office. The defendant was initially informed of the non-confidentiality of the interview.

The defendant appeared as a very thin, pale, college-age young man, who appeared somewhat younger than his stated age. He was groomed somewhat sloppily, and shook the examiner's hand somewhat limply. He immediately gave an impression of being troubled by something without being able to understand or explain it very well. His speech was slow and generally coherent. There were no neologisms and no formal thought disorder, but his speech tended to be vague, sparse, and metaphorical at times, making precise understanding difficult. His speech was not spontaneous, and he responded only when spoken to. No clear-cut delusional thought content was observed. No signs of hallucinations were observed, and no hallucinations were admitted. Throughout the interview he appeared withdrawn, with a distinctly saddened affect which was, however, sometimes labile. His eyes became

447

wet on several occasions, but he was unaware of this, he claimed, until it had been pointed out to him. He never smiled or laughed during the interview. As noted above, it was difficult to get him to talk about the events leading up to the current charge. No clear-cut guilt or remorse was identified. There was moderate psycho-motor retardation, but without mutism, posturing, waxy-flexibility, or negativism. Suicidal ideation was denied. He was oriented to place, but was off by three days on the day of the week, and four dates on the place in the month. He could state the name of the U.S. president and our state's governor. He was only able to recite four digits forward and three digits in reverse. He made several mistakes on Serial Seven Subtractions before abandoning the task prematurely. When asked to interpret the proverb, "Don't count your chickens. . . " he responded, "A cat has nine lives", but was unable to explain what he meant by this.

DIAGNOSIS:

According to the most recent edition of the *Diagnostic Manual* published by the American Psychiatric Association, the patient can be diagnosed as Major Depressive Disorder.

CONCLUSION:

Criminal Responsibility: This young man had no prior psychiatric disturbance of any kind prior to his current episode of a major depressive disorder, which has been characterized by: distinct and persistent mood change, loss of interest and pleasure in activities, withdrawal, loss of appetite and weight, initial insomnia, nightmares, difficulty thinking and concentrating, difficulty making decisions, and subjective loss of energy. No signs of catatonia were noted. The defendant became apparently preoccupied with the issues surrounding his mother's severe illness and was unable to attend to his other activities and responsibilities during this interim. While there were no gross, florid psychotic symptoms (such as frank delusions or hallucinations), the patient reported derealization, memory loss, subjective experiences of confusion, thought withdrawal, vague rumbling noises or sounds. Additionally, on interview, I observed moderate but subtle alterations in speech and thinking — all of which suggest some definite impairment in his reality testing processes — which persists even unto the present, about five weeks after the admitted homicide. In my opinion, Ronald Wasserman was suffering from mental disease or defect at the time he killed his mother. Further, it is my opinion that as a result of that mental disease or defect Ronald Wasserman lacked the substantial capacity to conform his conduct to the requirements of the law.

Very truly yours,

Reese Hopkins, M.D.

Reese Hopkins, M.D.

<u>Curriculum Vitae :</u>

Reese Hopkins, M.D.   Office Address:
                                       112 N. State

<u>Education:</u>
  University of Illinois, Urbana-Champaign:
     B.S. Psychology, [-14]
     M.D. Medicine, [-11]
  Rotating Internship, Cook County Hospital, [-11 to -10]
  Residency in Psychiatry, Cook County Hospital, [-10 to -9]
  Post-Doctorate Fellowship, University of Chicago,
     Research in Major Depression, [-8]

<u>Specialization of Practice:</u>
  General Practice of Psychiatry, [-8 to present]
  Adjunct Clinical Professor of Psychiatry, University of
     Illinois-Chicago Circle, [-8 to present]

<u>Licensure:</u>
  State of Illinois Board of Physicians, [-11]
  Illinois Board of Psychiatry, [-7]
  Board Certified by American Board of Psychiatry and
     Neurology, [-7]
  Certified, American Board of Forensic Psychiatry, [-5]

<u>Professional Organizations:</u>
  Member American Psychiatric Association, [-7 to present]
  Member of A.P.A. National Psychiatric Trauma Task Force,
     [-7 to present]
  American Medical Association, [-9 to present]

<u>Articles Published:</u>
  Post Traumatic Stress Disorder - Distinguishing the Myth
     from Reality, 74 *A.M.A. Journal of Psychiatry* 36, 7/
     15/[-7]
  Bereavement from the Loss of a Loved One in a Traumatic
     Accident, 83 *A.M.A. Journal of Psychiatry* 129, 7/15/
     [-5]
  Co-Author, [-5] A.P.A. National Psychiatric Trauma Task
     Force Guidelines for Treatment of Trauma Victims
  The Insanity Defense in Criminal Cases, 87 *A.M.A.
     Journal of Psychiatry* 72, 9/15/[-5]

6.12   PSYCHIATRIST TESTIMONY IN CIVIL CASE

This is a personal injury case. On January 9, [-3], the plaintiff, Rachel Tyson, was a passenger on the City Transit Authority (CTA) elevated subway system, which is owned by the city. The subway car in which Tyson was sitting was stopped when it was hit from the rear by another subway train. Several persons were killed in the crash. Tyson was pinned in the subway car. She was eventually removed by rescue workers and taken to a nearby hospital. At the hospital Tyson was treated by Dr. Ramon Suarez and later released.

In February [-2], Tyson was seen by a psychiatrist, Dr. Arthur Shapiro. Dr. Shapiro died three weeks before this trial takes place. Each side immediately hired a psychiatrist to examine the Suarez and Shapiro reports and reach an opinion based on the facts and findings in those reports. Neither expert has personally examined the plaintiff, and neither expert prepared a written report of his opinion.

The plaintiff's expert, Dr. Leslie Horvath, has said s/he believes that Tyson is suffering from post-traumatic stress disorder. S/he believes that the disorder and the symptoms described in Dr. Shapiro's report were caused by the accident. The defendant's expert, Dr. Damien Fuller, has reached a diagnosis of compensation neurosis and/ or complicated bereavement and/or malingering. The defense has also located a man named Timothy Swenson. At one time he was a social friend of Tyson. His deposition was taken last year.

Since the accident, Tyson has not returned to her job at the City Electric Company. Her gross salary at the time of the accident was $1,500 per week. Tyson's medical expenses, including the hospital bill of $16,000, Dr. Suarez's bill of $3,000, and Dr. Shapiro's bill of $5,500, have not been paid.

Tyson is suing the CTA for negligently causing the collision. The CTA has admitted liability. The only issue is the amount of damages that will reasonably and fairly compensate the plaintiff for her injuries. The case is being tried in your state and your jurisdiction's tort law applies.

You have in the file the reports of Dr. Suarez and Dr. Shapiro, Tyson's deposition, Swenson's deposition, and the résumés of the plaintiff's expert, Dr. Leslie Horvath, and the defendant's expert, Dr. Damien Fuller.

The parties have already stipulated to the admissibility of Tyson's medical expenses. The plaintiff now calls Dr. Horvath. (You should consult the *Diagnostic and Statistical Manual of Mental Disorders*, American Psychiatric Association, and other relevant sources, to prepare for the examinations.)

1.   For the plaintiff, conduct a direct examination of Dr. Horvath.
2.   For the defendant, cross-examine Dr. Horvath.

DR. RAMON SUAREZ
111 West Washington

MEDICAL REPORT — January 12, [-3]

NAME OF PATIENT: Rachel Tyson

HISTORY: Patient was seen for first time on January 9, [-3], in emergency room of the Northwestern Memorial Hospital. She was brought there by Fire Department ambulance from scene of CTA elevated train crash. She complained of pain in chest and head and of dizziness. There were mild bruises on the mid-sternal areas of the chest. She said she was struck on the head and suffered momentary loss of consciousness, with amnesia two or three minutes after impact. Patient was hospitalized for three days.

SUBJECTIVE SYMPTOMS: In addition to above, patient complained of headaches, nausea, and dizziness.

OBJECTIVE FINDINGS: X-rays were negative. Electroencephalogram was negative. No sign of internal injuries. With exception of mild bruises on the mid-sternal areas of the chest, no objective symptoms were observed.

TREATMENT: During hospitalization, patient was observed. Bed rest. Analgesics prescribed. Cervical collar prescribed.

DIAGNOSIS: Post-concussion syndrome. Severe whiplash of cervical spine.

PROGNOSIS: Uncertain. Patient still complains of headaches, nausea, and dizziness. Discharged from hospital this date with instructions to wear a cervical collar for one month and take analgesics as needed.

Ramon Suarez, M.D.

455

ARTHUR SHAPIRO, M.D.
500 N. Michigan

REPORT CONCERNING RACHEL TYSON, Re: Tyson v. CTA

The plaintiff is a 50-year-old white female who was in good physical and emotional health prior to the January 9, [-3], CTA elevated train crash that occurred in the downtown area of the city. The plaintiff, who had no previous psychiatric history of any kind, and whose past medical history included removal of a benign breast mass in [-18], and a partial thyroidectomy for hyper-thyroidism in [-6], was facing forward in the last car of a four-car CTA subway train, which was heading east aboveground. The train in which the plaintiff was riding was at a complete stop when it was hit by another CTA train from the rear, moving at about 25-30 miles per hour. The plaintiff was pinned in her seat, wedged between it and the metal railing in front of her surrounding the middle exit of the CTA car.

She sustained mild contusions of the mid-sternal areas of the chest and a blow to the head, which resulted in momentary loss of consciousness with amnesia two to three minutes after impact. Immediate medical evaluation, including hospitalization for three days, included negative X-rays, negative electroencephalogram, and no signs of internal injuries. Post-concussion syndrome was diagnosed as the patient presented with headaches, nausea, and dizziness.

She was discharged with instructions to wear a cervical collar for one month and take analgesics as needed. It was also noted that plaintiff had a severe whiplash injury during the accident. Her headaches, nausea, dizziness, and periods of irritability persisted through about four months following the injury, during which she was not able to return to work. Her employer offered to assign her to a less stressful job, but she refused this. She has not yet returned to any type of work. She said she is living on the proceeds of her mother's $250,000 life insurance policy.

Approximately seven months after the accident, she began to have feelings of depression, unexplainable startle reactions, tearing whenever she heard of accidents of any kind in the city, and nightmares in which she would relive aspects of the above-described accident. She continued her inability to return to work, suffered a decreased interest in dating and sexual activity, and had less contact with her close friends.

Approximately one year after the accident her attorney, who represents her in her case against the CTA, referred her to the undersigned for psychiatric assessment because of her continuing dreams, crying spells, and symptoms of anxiety and depression. It should also be noted that three passengers of the CTA car, seated within 15 feet of her, were killed in that train crash. She watched them die. Apparently it was a gory scene. Injured people in the car were screaming and crying, and there was much blood. I saw her for the first time on Feb. 5, [-2].

Prior to the injury, the plaintiff was socially active and had a number of mature heterosexual relationships, none of which eventuated in marriage. She described herself as outgoing, popular, and an active dancer and bowler. She had an outstanding job record with the City Electric Company, though on several occasions had turned down promotions to the supervisory level. She was her parents' only child, her father having died of carcinoma 20 years before the accident. The plaintiff was the sole provider for her elderly mother until her mother's death, which occurred approximately three months prior to the accident. The patient had lived with her mother all of her life until her mother's death.

When I asked her how she felt about her mother's death, she said she loved her mother very much, but that it wasn't until after the accident that she really felt the loss. It wasn't until then that she was able to cry about the death of her mother. She said she didn't really "feel depressed" about her mother's death until after the accident.

There is no history of prior psychiatric difficulties or psychiatric treatment for the patient or her family. At age 25, she had been involved in an automobile accident in which she was rear-ended. She suffered a mild whiplash injury, without neurological or orthopedic sequelae. An out-of-court settlement awarding her $5,000 was reached.

My physical evaluation in February [-2] demonstrated a completely normal physical examination. Neurological examination was similarly without evidence of organic dysfunction. Skull X-rays, cervical neck X-rays, and an EEG were again reported to be within normal limits. Mental status examination revealed a moderately depressed 50-year-old white female, who was preoccupied with the impact of the aforementioned injury on her subsequent life. She blames the injury for every event in her life,

458

including her inability to date, inability to return to work, her inability to "enjoy life," and the recurrent physical discomforts described above. She reported a disturbed sleep pattern; more frequent dreams of the accident; tearing easily when describing the events, both during and after the accident; and expressed considerable anger at her physicians, her employer, and her attorney, whom she felt was not acting rapidly enough with the resolution of her physical problems or her legal case against the CTA.

She clearly understood the personal injury lawsuit pending against the CTA, and stated that she sought damages both for physical injuries and "emotional trauma."

The undersigned recommended to patient that she begin a course of psychiatric treatment. Her attendance was extremely erratic and, after a few months, she stopped completely.

SIGNED: _Arthur Shapiro_____
             ARTHUR SHAPIRO, M.D.

DATE OF REPORT: NOV. 1, [-1]

1   RACHEL TYSON, having been first duly sworn,
2   testified as follows:
3
4 Q. (by defendant's attorney) What is your name?
5
6 A. Rachel Tyson.
7
8 Q. Are you currently employed?
9
10 A. No. I have not been able to work since the crash.
11
12 Q. Have you read the report Dr. Shapiro wrote to your
13   lawyer?
14
15 A. Yes, I have. Several times.
16
17 Q. Does that report accurately reflect the things you
18   said to Dr. Shapiro?
19
20 A. Yes. It is very accurate.
21
22 Q. Does that report leave out anything you told
23   Dr. Shapiro?
24
25 A. Not that I can remember at this time.
26
27 Q. Why did you stop the course of psychiatric
28   treatment Dr. Shapiro prescribed?
29
30 A. I just couldn't stand talking about the crash.
31   That's all they wanted to talk about.
32
33 Q. Why haven't you returned to work?
34
35 A. Everything I do reminds me of the crash. I can't
36   stand the loud noises when I go outside. I can't
37   travel. It was so difficult for me to get here
38   today.
39
40 Q. What is your educational level?
41
42 A. I graduated from high school. I never went to
43   college, but I have educated myself. I read a lot
44   of everything.

```
1  Q. Why did you bring this lawsuit?
2
3  A. My life has been destroyed. Someone has to pay for
4     that.
```

This is to certify that I have read the transcript of my deposition taken on the 20th day of December, [-1], and that the transcript accurately states the questions asked and the answers given.

Rachel Tyson
Rachel Tyson

Subscribed and sworn to before
me this 20th day of December, [-1]

Felix Jasmer
Notary Public

TIMOTHY SWENS3ON, having been first duly sworn,
testified as follows:

1 Q. (by plaintiff's attorney) Please state your name.
2
3 A. Timothy Swenson.
4
5 Q. Where are you now employed?
6
7 A. I am a teller at the First Mutual Bank. I have been
8   there for about ten years.
9
10 Q. How old are you?
11
12 A. I'll be 55 on my next birthday.
13
14 Q. Are you married?
15
16 A. No. Never married.
17
18 Q. Do you know a woman named Rachel Tyson?
19
20 A. Ycs.
21
22 Q. When did you first meet her?
23
24 A. It was just before Christmas of [-3]. We met at a
25   party given by some mutual friends.
26
27 Q. Would you mind describing your relationship with
28   Miss Tyson?
29
30 A. Well, we went out seven or eight times, dinner,
31   bowling, movies, things like that.
32
33 Q. You were social friends?
34
35 A. Yeah. But she would never let it be more than
36   just friends. I mean she wouldn't invite me to her
37   apartment. And she wouldn't come to mine. We just
38   went out.
39
40 Q. For how long a period of time did you go out with
41   her?
42
43 A. It was over a period of about three months.

44 Q. During that time, did you notice anything unusual
45   about her?
46
47 A. What do you mean?
48
49 Q. Well, did she ever complain of headaches or any
50   kind of pain?
51
52 A. No. Not that I can recall.
53
54 Q. Did she ever seem depressed, or sad?
55
56 A. No, every time I was with her she seemed happy. She
57   was always smiling and making little jokes. And she
58   laughed at my jokes. I can't remember a time when
59   she seemed sad.
60
61 Q. Did she ever cry in your presence?
62
63 A. Never. I would remember that.
64
65 Q. What kind of things would you do on your dates with
66   Miss Tyson?
67
68 A. Well, we would have dinner, maybe go dancing. She
69   loved to dance. She also liked to go bowling. We
70   went once, but I wasn't much good at it.
71
72 Q. Did she ever talk about her mother?
73
74 A. No, the subject never came up.
75
76 Q. Did you know she had been in a CTA accident the
77   January before you met?
78
79 A. No. The first I heard of it was when the train
80   company's lawyer called me. She never mentioned it.
81
82 Q. Was there a reason why you stopped seeing Miss Tyson?
83
84 A. Well, we had kind of a difference of opinion about
85   where our relationship was going. She started hinting
86   about marriage and I wasn't interested in that.
87   I told her I just wanted to have a good time. We
88   agreed to disagree, if you know what I mean. I just
89   didn't call her again. She didn't call me either.

This is to certify that I have read the transcript of my deposition taken on the 15th day of December, [-1], and that the transcript accurately states the questions asked and the answers given.

Timothy Swenson

Subscribed and sworn to before
me this 20th day of December, [-1]

Notary Public

CURRICULUM VITAE

LESLIE HORVATH, M.D.

Education:

Northwestern School of Medicine
- degree M.D. [-15]
- residency in psychiatry [-15] - [-13]
- fellowship: stress related disorders [-13] - [-11]

Professional:

- Rush Hospital
* attending physician [-11] - present
* associate professor, Rush University College of
  Medicine, Department of Psychiary [-10] - present
- Private Practice
* office located at 444 N. Michigan Avenue

Publications:

- *Malingering*, New England Journal of Medicine, Vol.
  10, [-5]
- *Post Traumatic Stress Disorder: Fact or Fiction*,
  University of Chicago Press, [-3]

Memberships:

* American College of Psychiatrists member - Committee
  on Stress Related Disorders
* American Medical Association

Licenses:

* Illinois [-15]
* Michigan [-10]
* Board eligible

CURRICULUM VITAE

DAMIEN FULLER, M.D.

EMPLOYMENT

- Private Practice [-13] - present. Provide direct patient care to private patients.
- Teaching [-7] - present. Psychiatry and Medicine, University of Chicago. Course includes a general overview of topics of current interest on the relationship between physical and mental health.

EDUCATION

- B.S. University of Wisconsin, Madison, [-24]
- M.S. University of Chicago, [-23]
- M.D. University of Chicago, [-20]
- Residency, University of Chicago, Billings Hospital, [-19]
- Post-Doctorate Fellowship, University of Chicago, Billings Hospital. Providing direct patient care to students and staff of the University. Research in depression.

LICENSES

- Illinois Board of Physicians, [-20]
- Illinois Board of Psychiatrists, [-19]
- Board Certified in Depressive Disorders by the American Board of Psychiatry and Neurology, [-18]

ORGANIZATIONS

- American Psychiatric Association

PUBLICATIONS

- The Etiology of Affective Disorders, *American Journal of Psychiatry*, Fall, [-7]
- Situational Depression: Sadness Is Not a Disease, *American Journal of Psychiatry*, Spring, [-5]

6.13 HEARING REGARDING ADMISSIBILITY OF EXPERT OPINION

Rose Kowalski has filed a products liability complaint against Nuevas Pharmaceuticals, Inc., manufacturer of a drug called Parlux. The drug is prescribed for prevention of postpartum physiological lactation following childbirth. Mrs. Kowalski contends the drug caused her to suffer an intracerebral hemorrhage (stroke) on day 13 of a 14-day course of Parlux following the birth of her child. Nuevas denies that its product can cause or did cause the stroke.

The plaintiff's proposed expert witness is Dr. Alexis Salkov. The defendant has moved to bar Dr. Salkov's testimony, citing FRE 702, *Daubert v. Merrell Dow Pharmaceuticals*, 509 U.S. 579 (1993), and *General Electric v. Joiner*, 522 U.S. 136 (1997). The trial court has agreed to conduct a FRE 104(a) hearing into the admissibility of the expert testimony.

The trial court has announced the hearing will be confined to Dr. Salkov's testimony. The court has ruled that Dr. Salkov is qualified to render opinions in medicine and vascular neurology, in general, but has not determined whether the proposed testimony will be allowed in the case at hand.

You have Dr. Salkov's deposition, which is consistent with the doctor's FRCP Rule 26(b) report, and you have Dr. Salkov's Curriculum Vitae. The case is being tried in a jurisdiction that has adopted the Federal Rules of Evidence that relate to expert testimony.

(1) For the plaintiff, conduct a direct examination of Dr. Salkov at the pretrial hearing and argue for admission of his/her proposed testimony.

(2) For the defendant, conduct a cross-examination of Dr. Salkov at the pretrial hearing and argue against admission of his/her proposed testimony.

(3) Be prepared to address the following questions:
   (a) Which side has the burden of production regarding the admissibility of Dr. Salkov's testimony (i.e., the burden of presenting evidence to raise an issue for the court's consideration)?
   (b) Which side has the burden of persuasion regarding whether Dr. Salkov's testimony is admissible or inadmissible?

(4) Would the procedure be any different if the case were being tried in a *Frye* jurisdiction?

DEPOSITION OF ALEXIS SALKOV
On February 14, [-1]
at the offices of defendant's attorney

ALEXIS SALKOV, having been first duly sworn, testified as follows:

1 Q. Please state your name and spell it for the
2   record?
3
4 A. Yes. I am Dr. Alexis Salkov, A-L-E-X-I-S, S-A-L-K-
5   O-V.
6
7 Q. Thank you. Dr. Salkov, I have here your Curriculum
8   Vitae. Is this a true and accurate account of your
9   qualifications?
10 A. Yes.
11
12 Q. Turning to the events surrounding Mrs. Kowalski's
13   stroke, what medication was Mrs. Kowalski using
14   postpartum?
15 A. Mrs. Kowalski was given Parlux, a Nuevas
16   Pharmaceuticals product, to prevent lactation
17   postpartum. She took it orally for 13 days
18   following delivery by Caesarian section.
19
20 Q. Please describe what happened while she was taking
21   Parlux.
22
23 A. On day 13 of her 14-day course of Parlux, she
24   presented at the hospital complaining of an
25   excruciating headache. A CT scan revealed an
26   intracerebral hemorrhage — blood in the brain
27   tissue. Although surgery was performed immediately
28   to evacuate the blood and to repair the damaged
29   artery, the ICH caused permanent motor paralysis
30   and speech difficulty.
31 Q. Do you believe that Parlux can cause intracerebral
32   hemorrhage, or ICH?
33
34 A. Yes, I do.
35
36 Q. How do you determine whether a drug can cause an
      adverse reaction?

473

37 A. Researchers and physicians use several methods.
38   You can do a differential diagnosis and look at
39   case reports. You also learn about the drug in
40   question — for example, you can find out about
41   known side effects of the drug and the drug
42   family from textbooks and articles. You look at
43   dechallenge/rechallenge reports, which are often
44   found in case reports. Epidemiological studies,
45   if they exist, are important. Clinical trials and
46   animal studies are also important.

47
48 Q. Do you believe Parlux caused Mrs. Kowalski's ICH?

49 A. Yes, I do. I have concluded that she suffered from
50   a bleeding-type stroke caused by her ingestion of
51   Parlux.
52

53 Q. Please explain what you mean by a bleeding-type
54   stroke?
55

56 A. Yes. A CT scan revealed blood in the brain tissue.
57   Surgery later revealed that an artery had burst.
58   So this was a bleeding-type stroke, as opposed
59   to a "dry stroke" or ischemic-type stroke, in
60   which blood flow is stopped due to a clot that has
61   formed elsewhere in the body and has traveled to
62   the brain, but the clot does not cause blood to
63   enter the brain tissue.

64 Q. What methodology did you use to identify Parlux as
65   the cause of Mrs. Kowalski's ICH?
66

67 A. I used the differential diagnosis method.
68   Differential diagnosis is a patient-specific
69   process of elimination that medical practitioners
70   use to identify the most likely cause of a set
71   of signs and symptoms from a list of possible
72   causes. Basically, you learn what you can about
73   the patient, then you learn what you can about
74   the drug in question, and then you put all that
75   information together and ask the question: Was
76   the drug in question the cause of an adverse drug
77   reaction?

78
79 Q. Is this a common method of analysis?

80 A. This is basically the scientific method for
81   analyzing adverse drug reactions in a particular
82   person. It does not address causation as a general
83   matter.
84

85 Q. Where did you learn this method?

474

86 A. I've talked to many people. I've heard many
87   lectures on the subject. I've read textbooks on
88   this. And I've used it hundreds of times in my own
89   practice.
90
91 Q. Is this method reliable and widely used?
92
93 A. This is what is done on a daily basis by
94   physicians, scientists, regulatory agencies, and
95   drug manufacturers, and I believe that this is
96   the approach that was used by Nuevas itself in
97   analyzing cases of possible adverse drug reactions
98   reported to it at their Drug Monitoring Center in
99   Basel, Switzerland.
100 Q. How did you apply it to Mrs. Kowalski's case?
101
102 A. I looked at possible other causes of her ICH. To
103   begin, I reviewed her medical records. Normally,
104   if you have the patient in front of you, you would
105   do a history and physical, or an H and P. And
106   you would ask many questions about their past
107   history, what drugs they've been on in the past,
108   what drugs they're on now. Are there any risk
109   factors for stroke? If it's a stroke patient, was
110   there a family history of stroke? Do they have
111   hypertension? Et cetera. In this case I wasn't
112   able to interview the patient because the stroke
113   had affected her ability to speak, but her medical
114   records showed that she had none of these factors.
115   The CT scan, an angiogram, her blood work, and
116   other tests showed she had no other condition
117   that would lead to a stroke — no head injury, no
118   anatomical defect in the brain, no blood clotting
119   disorder, no heart abnormalities. No brain tumor,
120   no evidence of treatment for hypertension. She
121   was overweight, but not clinically obese. Her
122   cholesterol was only minimally elevated. She did
123   have a history of smoking, about a pack a day, but
124   at the end of the differential diagnosis process
125   it doesn't change the result.
126 Q. Why not?
127
128 A. Although she had a pretty heavy habit, and I think
129   nicotine can cause some vasoconstriction, her
130   smoking history is short — only six years. I think
131   it did not cause her stroke because there was no
132   evidence for atherosclerosis, or hardening of the
133   arteries, on her angiogram, which is one of the
134   reasons smoking may be associated with stroke to
135   begin with. Her blood vessels were clean. There is a
136   distinct difference between risk factor and cause.

137 Q. Isn't advanced maternal age also a risk factor for
138   intracerebral hemorrhage?
139
140 A. Barely, in this case — she was only 36.
141 Q. Mrs. Kowalski also had a history of headaches.
142
143 A. She does have a five-year history of intermit-
144   tent vertex throbbing headaches. However, migraine
145   headaches do not cause bleeding-type strokes.
146   There is evidence that migraine headaches can
147   cause ischemic strokes where blood vessels can
148   clamp down so that brain tissues no longer receive
149   blood, but that is different than hemorrhagic
150   stroke.
151
152 Q. Can differential diagnosis establish general
153   causation of a disease by a drug?
154 A. Well, it's not designed to do that. Differential
155   diagnosis is designed to be used for a specific
156   patient, which is not what general causation
157   concerns.
158
159 Q. You mentioned other case reports.
160
161 A. Yes. These are important. The two cases that I am
162   aware of are the basis for an article I published
163   on the relationship between Parlux and headaches
164   attributable to vasospasm.
165 Q. Tell me about the first case.
166
167 A. The first woman I saw was a postpartum patient
168   taking Parlux for lactation suppression. She
169   developed a very bad headache while taking
170   the drug. The hospital gave her Midrin, which
171   is a common headache medication, and released
172   her. She returned in critical condition, in
173   ventricular tachycardia. She apparently did not
174   suffer a myocardial infarction, but she was in
175   preinfarction condition.
176
177 Q. And the second case?
178 A. The neurologist who was involved in treating
179   the first woman related a second case history
180   to me. The second woman was also taking Parlux
181   for lactation suppression when she developed a
182   headache. She was also given headache medication.
183   The second patient actually suffered a stroke.
184   The day after her stroke, she had an angiogram,
185   which showed widespread diffuse vasospasm on the
186   angiogram. A repeat angiogram performed several
187   months later was normal.

476

188 Q. Is there evidence that Parlux causes vasospasm?
189
190 A. There is some evidence to indicate that it does.
191   It was my belief that Parlux, with or without
192   the other drug, was clearly causing spasm and the
193   subsequent stroke.
194 Q. Do these case reports establish causation—that
195   Parlux can cause an intracerebral hemorrhage?
196
197 A. No, case reports by themselves do not prove
198   causation and I would never attempt to do so.
199   Case reports are traditionally viewed as the
200   least vigorous form of proof of a hypothesis or
201   validation of a theory, particularly single case
202   reports, which are not controlled. You can't
203   establish relative risk factors from a single
204   case.
205
206 Q. What evidence leads you to believe that Parlux
207   causes vasospasm?
208 A. Looking at the family of drugs from which the
209   drug originated is important. If you know the
210   side effect of aspirin, for example, and there's
211   a drug that is an aspirin derivative, one might
212   conclude that you would expect the side effects
213   of that derivative to be like aspirin. It may or
214   may not be true, but it's a good place to start.
215   That doesn't tell you automatically that the drug
216   must act like other family members, but it gives
217   you an idea of what the expected side effects
218   might be. Parlux shares some common properties
219   with pergolide and with the parent family of ergot
220   compounds. Ergots can cause digital vasospasm;
221   Parlux itself is on the differential diagnosis for
222   myocardial infarction. It contains bromocriptine,
223   the active ingredient in Parlux.
224
225 Q. So because Parlux is an ergot alkaloid it causes
226   vasoconstriction?
227
228 A. Not necessarily. However, because there is clear
229   myocardial infarction, it appears that Parlux
230   possibly could cause stroke as well because the
231   physiologic mechanism is identified. You would
232   have to have some evidence, as well, but again,
233   you're looking at a toxicologic syndrome of
234   ergotism where these things happen together from
       the same drug.

235 Q. Do you have an opinion as to the specific
236   biological or pathological mechanism by which
237   Parlux causes the vasoconstriction in humans?
238
239 A. I've given multiple possibilities as to what the
240   cellular pharmacologic receptor mechanism could
241   be for that vasoconstriction, but I am not able to
242   say that there is one that is more likely than not
243   the mechanism. But if one ergot alkaloid can be
244   proven to a reasonable degree of medical certainty
245   to cause a vasoconstriction, for example, by
246   one mechanism, I think that is likely to be the
247   mechanism of the others as well, but that is not
248   necessarily the case.

249 Q. So you cannot testify to the mechanism to a
250   reasonable degree of medical probability?
251
252 A. No, I cannot.
253
254 Q. Are you aware of Dr. Ellenhorn's treatise, in
255   which he reported that the vasoconstrictive
256   property for Parlux is zero?

257 A. Yes, I am aware of it, but I disagree with that
258   conclusion.
259
260 Q. Have any animal studies shown that Parlux can
261   cause intracerebral hemorrhage?
262
263 A. There have been hundreds of animal studies
264   on Parlux relating to humans. These studies,
265   particularly the "hindlimb" study, show
266   that Parlux can cause vasoconstriction and
267   hypertension.

268 Q. Did any of the studies on animal models show a
269   relationship with Parlux causing intracerebral
270   hemorrhage?
271
272 A. No. They weren't designed to do so. I am not aware
273   of any studies involving intact animals showing
274   that Parlux causes high blood pressure or any
275   other injury secondary to cerebral vasospasm.
276   I think we would be able to say that the animal
277   study shows Parlux is a vasoconstrictor.

278 Q. Is there a preferred animal model to rely upon
279   to study potential effects of the blood pressure
280   system in man?

281 A. I believe that most primates metabolize drugs
282   similarly, but what happens isn't entirely known.
283   Humans may metabolize Parlux differently from
284   other primates. With respect to the "hindlimb"
285   study, comparing a mongrel ten-kilogram dog to a
286   pregnant woman I would say is a stretch.
287
288 Q. So what happens in animal studies generally with
289   regard to animals would not necessarily happen to
290   humans.
291
292 A. Correct.
293 Q. On a more general level, can a cause-and-
294   effect relationship be established for a common
295   disease without showing an association through a
296   controlled epidemiological study?
297
298 A. It can be difficult, but not impossible.
299   A controlled study alone is not enough. Clinical
300   trials are just one component of the entire list of
301   evidence that I would consider — clinical trials
302   in isolation don't necessarily prove anything.
303
304 Q. How would the scientific method be applied in a
305   clinical study?
306 A. Scientific methodology today is based on
307   generating hypotheses and testing them to see if
308   they can be falsified. For example, double-blind
309   randomized placebo controlled studies are the way
310   to use the scientific method to determine whether
311   substance A causes effect B.
312
313 Q. Are there any studies that show that Parlux can
314   cause intracerebral hemorrhage in postpartum
315   women?
316 A. There are no such studies where the authors
317   state that Parlux probably caused intracerebral
318   hemorrhage in postpartum women, but it's important
319   to keep in mind that when a drug comes to market,
320   there may have only been a few hundred or at most
321   a few thousand patients who have received that
322   drug in clinical trials, meaning premarket trials
323   where the drug is being tested to see if it's
324   effective and if it's safe. If the adverse effect
325   in question is very rare, if it only occurs in one
326   in 5,000 patients, it would be unusual to see it
327   in the clinical trials.

328 Q. Is it fair to say, to say to a reasonable degree
329   of medical probability, that drugs that cause
330   vasospasm or vasoconstriction are also drugs that
331   cause stroke?
332
333 A. I try not to be that general. That's language
334   I would not want to use.
335 Q. You mentioned rechallenge/dechallenge as being
336   another significant form of medical evidence. What
337   are "rechallenges" and "dechallenges"?
338
339 A. Dechallenge is removing the drug exposure to
340   determine if an adverse event abates while
341   rechallenge involves re-exposing a patient to the
342   drug in order to ascertain whether the adverse
343   event reappears. If you have a given case where
344   the patient develops an adverse drug reaction,
345   they get better when the drug is withdrawn, and
346   they're rechallenged with the same drug and they
347   develop the exact same phenomenon that can be
348   objectively measured, that's critical to the
349   thinking that the drug was the cause of the
350   reaction in that particular patient.
351
352 Q. Have dechallenges/rechallenges been used to
353   examine Parlux?
354 A. There have been three human dechallenge/
355   rechallenge studies involving Parlux that show
356   evidence of coronary artery spasm and myocardial
357   infarction.
358
359 Q. Any involving ICH?
360
361 A. No.
362 Q. Are rechallenges and dechallenges "experiments" in
363   the strict sense of the word?
364
365 A. They are more like case studies, not experiments,
366   strictly speaking, because they aren't controlled
367   for other factors. It's not proof necessarily,
368   but it's powerful evidence, and regulatory
369   agencies, as well as manufacturers, place a very
370   heavy emphasis on rechallenge information. These
371   cases tend to indicate that Parlux possesses the
372   vasoconstrictive processes of ergot derivatives.
373
374 Q. You also mentioned epidemiology. Are you familiar
375   with the Kittner study, published in the New
376   England Journal of Medicine in 1996?

480

377 A. Yes. The authors reported that the relative risk
378   of intracerebral hemorrhage at a point during the
379   six-week period after delivery was more than 28
380   times the risk for a woman not in the postpartum
381   period. The paper concluded that a causal role for
382   a preeclampsia and eclampsia, seizures associated
383   with hypertension, could not fully explain the
384   much stronger associations with stroke found for
385   the postpartum state than for pregnancy itself.
386
387 Q. Does Parlux cause preeclampsia or eclampsia?
388
389 A. Parlux does not cause preeclampsia or eclampsia or
390   eclampsia stroke or eclampsia seizure.
391 Q. Is there any epidemiology for Parlux?
392
393 A. Not with respect to postpartum stroke. It's
394   unusual for there to be epidemiology involving
395   adverse drug reactions. One must examine that
396   scientifically to determine if it's valid
397   epidemiology and if the conclusions are supported
398   by the data presented. I don't recall any
399   statistically significant studies demonstrating an
400   association between ergot and stroke. Epidemiology
401   is generally helpful, but because stroke in the
402   postpartum period is not a common event, the small
403   sample sizes of these studies makes it difficult
404   to draw conclusions. A much larger sample size
405   is really needed to tell us more. Of course,
406   I recognize that pregnancy and delivery can be
407   risk factors for development of a stroke, but
408   I don't believe that is what happened to Mrs.
409   Kowalski.
410 Q. Do you have any other support for your opinion
411   that Parlux caused Mrs. Kowalski's stroke?
412
413 A. There is one thing. The FDA has published a
414   finding that bromocriptin — the major ingredient
415   in Parlux — has been related to some serious
416   adverse experiences, like hypertension, seizures,
417   and CVAs when the drug is used to prevent
418   lactation in new mothers.
419
420 Q. Did the FDA say Parlux caused those adverse
        reactions?

421 A. No, just that bromocriptine seems to be a risk
422   factor, but the FDA no longer approves of using
423   Parlux to prevent lactation, although Parlux
424   still is approved for other conditions, such as
425   Parkinson's therapy and some cases of female
426   infertility.
427
428 Q. How do you evaluate all the various forms of
429   medical evidence when you are drawing a conclusion
430   about cause and effect?

431 A. You attribute an appropriate weight to the
432   various components of the medical evidence. The
433   medical evidence could include, involving the
434   drug Parlux, is Parlux a vasoconstrictor? Does
435   Parlux cause vasospasm? Has Parlux been associated
436   with stroke in human beings? Is there animal
437   evidence that Parlux is a vasospastic agent? Do
438   the pharmacokinetics of the drug lend themselves
439   to saying it makes sense, that it's plausible the
440   drug was the cause? And again, I'm not saying that
441   any of these components individually leads one to
442   draw that conclusion, but in compilation of all of
443   the evidence involving all of these components,
444   one should be able to reach such a conclusion.

This is to certify that I have read the transcript of
my deposition taken on the 14th day of February, [-1],
and that the transcript accurately states the questions
asked and the answers given.

_____
                    Alexis Salkav
                    February 24, [-1]

482

CURRICULUM VITAE

Alexis Salkov, M.D.
800 North Michigan Avenue

Education

[-12]	Post-Doctorate Fellowship in Vascular Neurology, Milton S. Hershey Medical Center
[-13]	Residency in Neurology, Northwestern University Feinberg School of Medicine
[-14]	Residency in Internal Medicine, Northwestern University Feinberg School of Medicine
[-16]	Rotating Internship, University of Chicago Hospitals
[-17]	M.D. in Medicine, Harvard Medical School
[-21]	B.S. in Chemistry, Cornell University

Licensing and Board Certification

[-13 to present]	Licensed to practice medicine in the State of Pennsylvania
[-16 to present]	Licensed to practice medicine in the State of Illinois
[-7 to present]	Diplomate in Neurology, Subspecialty Vascular Neurology, American Board of Psychiatry and Neurology
[-8 to present]	Diplomate in Neurology, American Board of Psychiatry and Neurology

Employment

| [-12 to present] | Private practice in neurology, specializing in vascular neurology |
| [-12 to present] | Adjunct Clinical Professor of Neurology, Northwestern University, Feinberg School of Medicine |

Professional Organizations

| [-12 to present] | American Medical Association American College of Neurology |

<u>Publications</u>

[-3]   Case Notes on Intracerebral Hemorrhage Associated with Pregnancy, 87 *New England Journal of Medicine* 140

[-12]   Causes of Ischemic Stroke Revisited, 87 *A.M.A. Journal of Neurology* 223

VII

ADVANCED DIRECT AND CROSS-EXAMINATION

Introduction

485

INTRODUCTION

The cases in the resources section of this book on CasebookConnect represent a bridge between Chapter 3, involving discrete, self-contained witness problems, and Chapter 9, involving full trials. The chapter consists of twelve cases, five civil and seven criminal. Each case in this chapter has two witnesses, one for the plaintiff or prosecutor, the other for the defendant.

These cases, of varying levels of sophistication and complexity, require more case analysis, since the direct examination of one witness must be coordinated with the cross-examination of the other. The direct and cross-examinations must serve your overall theory of the case, be consistent with your themes, and carry out your trial strategy.

You should prepare your specific assignments as though the case were actually on trial. Accordingly, you should determine whether any admissibility issues exist and anticipate objections and arguments your opponent is likely to make. In addition, you should plan and execute your direct and cross-examinations so that you will effectively present the witnesses' testimony to the jury in a way that supports your theory of the case and your trial strategy.

To keep this book from becoming overly large, the problem files themselves are included in the resources section of this book on CasebookConnect, and this chapter contains only brief overviews. You should use the exhibits in the case files found in the resources section of this book on CasebookConnect. You may also prepare additional appropriate exhibits, such as enlargements of diagrams or anatomical drawings, or obtain suitable objects shown in photographs, such as weapons or clothing.

NOTE: The parties must stipulate to the authenticity of all reports, transcripts, records, memos, letters, and other documents in the files. The documents may be admitted, in whole or in part, where relevant and admissible according to the rules of evidence.

Some of the witnesses do not have background information. Be prepared to develop realistic, credible backgrounds for them.

Your instructor may modify the assignments and make specific additional assignments for these cases.

The suggested background reading is Mauet & Easton, *Trial Techniques and Trials*, Chapters 5, 6, and 7.

7.1 VEHICLE COLLISION CASE

JORDAN GABLE
v.
DYLAN CANNON

This case involves an accident that occurred on June 6, [-2], at the intersection of Main and Elm Streets in this city. Jordan Gable, the plaintiff, was driving southbound on Main, at its intersection with Elm. Dylan Cannon, the defendant, had been driving northbound on Main and was in the process of turning left onto Elm when the collision took place.

Gable suffered a broken collarbone in the collision. S/he is suing for money damages. The jury is being asked to decide only the issue of liability.

Both Main and Elm Streets are two-way streets, with one moving lane in each direction and one parking lane on each side. The traffic signals show green, yellow, and red, but no turn signal. The parties agree that the traffic signal has a three-second yellow light.

It is the law of this jurisdiction that the driver of a vehicle intending to turn to the left within an intersection shall yield the right-of-way to any vehicle approaching from the opposite direction when that oncoming vehicle is so close as to constitute an immediate hazard. Further, a car may enter an intersection when the light is yellow for that car if the driver reasonably believes s/he can do so with safety.

You have the partial depositions of Gable and Cannon, a police report by the investigating officer, a photograph of Cannon's car (Pl. Ex. 1), a photograph of Gable's car (Pl. Ex. 2), and a non-scale drawing of the intersection.

1. For the plaintiff, conduct a direct examination of Gable and cross-examine Cannon.

2. For the defendant, conduct a direct examination of Cannon and cross-examine Gable.

7.2 CIVIL RIGHTS CASE

ESTATE OF JOSE GARCIA
v.
PAT RICHARDS

The mother of Jose Garcia brings this 42 U.S.C. § 1983 action against City Police Officer Pat Richards. She claims that Officer Richards, while on duty, intentionally shot and killed Jose Garcia on May 2, [-2]. The shooting took place in the parking lot of Jack's Restaurant. Richards was there because Stacey Major informed him/her that s/he had received a call from a man who said he would sell back Major's stolen Cadillac.

The Court has held this action is appropriately brought under plaintiff's claim that the defendant violated her son's Fourth Amendment right not to be subjected to unreasonable or excessive force while being arrested. The law also provides that in making a lawful arrest an officer has the right to use such force as is necessary under the circumstances to effect the arrest. [For additional discussion of the law, including restrictions on the use of deadly force, see City Police Department General Order No. 24.] Whether the force used in making the arrest in this case was unreasonable or excessive is a question for the finder of fact. A seizure occurs when there is a termination of freedom through means intentionally applied.

The case is on trial. You have portions of the discovery depositions of Stacey Major and Officer Richards, police department General Order 24, Richards's Firearms Discharge Report, and Plaintiff's Interrogatory Number 7.

The parties have reached the following stipulations:

(a) The Chief Medical Examiner of the County believes that the decedent was shot from a distance of less than five feet but probably not closer than two feet. The fatal bullet entered the decedent's back 16 inches below the top of the head in about the middle of the back. The path was slightly upward.

(b) The fatal bullet was fired from Officer Richards's .357 magnum caliber Smith & Wesson revolver.

1. For the plaintiff, conduct a direct examination of Major and cross-examine Officer Richards.

2. For the defendant, conduct a direct examination of Officer Richards and cross-examine Major.

7.3 THEFT OF TRADE SECRETS CASE

MID-CONTINENT, INC.

v.

C.W. BLOCK AND TRACK OIL COMPANY, INC.

This is a civil theft of trade secrets case brought by Mid-Continent, Inc., against C.W. Block and Track Oil Company, Inc. Mid-Continent sells a gas additive, "STP," and Track Oil sells a competing gas additive, "PSSST." The case is brought in federal district court.

Mid-Continent claims that Block, a former employee, stole the formula for the gasoline additive that Mid-Continent had developed and sold the formula to his/her new employer, Track Oil, in violation of Block's written agreement not to disclose Mid-Continent's trade secrets to a competitor. Mid-Continent further claims that Track Oil conspired with Block to steal the formula.

Both defendants deny that Block stole the formula for the gasoline additive or sold it to Track Oil.

A trade secret consists of any valuable formula, process, or other information that is held in secret, is used in a business, and gives the owner of the secret a competitive advantage over others who do not know the secret.

A theft of a trade secret occurred if Mid-Continent possessed a trade secret, a confidential relationship existed between Mid-Continent and Block, Block acquired the trade secret and gave it to Track Oil, Track Oil used the trade secret in violation of the confidential relationship, and Track Oil's use of the trade secret caused damage to Mid-Continent.

The federal district court has bifurcated the issues of liability and damages. Consequently, the present trial is on the issue of liability only.

You have the depositions and affidavit of the parties and other employees of the parties. You also have documents that were obtained during discovery.

1. For the plaintiff, conduct a direct examination of Block (as an adverse witness) and cross-examine Robbie McCoy of Track Oil.

2. For the defendant, conduct whatever further examination of Block you deem appropriate and a direct examination of McCoy.

7.4 HOME PURCHASE CONTRACT CASE

ROBIN JOHNSON
v.
SUPERIOR HOMES, INC.

This case is a contract dispute involving the sale of a house. Robin Johnson, the plaintiff, bought the house from Superior Homes, Inc., the defendant. The house was part of a new subdivision that Superior Homes was building in town. Jerry Williams was the sales representative employed by Superior Homes who entered into the sales contract with Johnson.

After Johnson bought the house and moved in, s/he noticed that the concrete floor in the house was developing cracks. Superior Homes denied any responsibility for the cracks, and Johnson brought this lawsuit alleging breach of implied warranty of habitability and fraud. Johnson asks for all proper damages, including punitive damages.

A breach of the implied warranty of habitability occurs when a builder constructs a new house containing a substantial latent defect. A latent defect is a defect in the house that cannot be discovered by ordinary and reasonable care.

A fraud occurs when a person makes a false statement of a material fact, the person making the statement knows it is false, the statement is made with the intent to induce another person to act, the other person acts in justifiable reliance on the truth of the statement, and the relying party suffers damage as a result of the reliance. Mere puffing or expressions of opinion are not statements of material fact.

You have the depositions of Johnson, the plaintiff, and Williams, the defendant's sales representative. You also have the attached documents that were obtained during discovery.

1. For the plaintiff, conduct a direct examination of Johnson and cross-examine Williams.

2. For the defendant, conduct a direct examination of Williams and cross-examine Johnson.

7.5 AGE DISCRIMINATION EMPLOYMENT CASE

FRAN BOYLE

v.

HOME MART, INC.

Fran Boyle brings this civil action in the U.S. District Court against Home Mart, Inc. S/he alleges s/he was discharged from his/her job on September 1, [-2], because of his/her age, in violation of the Age Discrimination in Employment Act (ADEA), 29 U.S.C. § 621 et seq. The ADEA prohibits employers from discriminating against employees at least 40 years old based on their age.

Boyle alleges s/he was within the protected age group, that s/he performed his/her job satisfactorily, that s/he was fired because of his/her age, and that s/he was replaced by a substantially younger employee who was otherwise similarly situated. Boyle has received a 29 U.S.C. § 626 "right to sue" letter from the Equal Employment Opportunity Commission.

Home Mart denies any age discrimination. In its affirmative defense, Home Mart alleges Boyle was fired as part of a company reorganization. It further alleges Boyle was fired because his/her job performance was not satisfactory, s/he had a negative attitude, and employee morale in the department s/he headed was so low that sales were affected. The company's answer was signed by Pat Seaborg, vice president for sales at Home Mart and general manager of the store where Boyle had been employed.

This is the liability stage of the trial. You have the depositions of Boyle and Seaborg, affidavits from two Home Mart employees, Boyle's last job evaluation, a corporate memo to Seaborg, and the termination letter sent to Boyle by Seaborg.

1. For the plaintiff, conduct a direct examination of Boyle and cross-examine Seaborg.

2. For the defendant, conduct a direct examination of Seaborg and cross-examine Boyle.

7.6 MURDER CASE

STATE

v.

DARLENE LINZY

This is a murder case brought against the defendant, Darlene Linzy. Linzy is charged with the murder of Linda Goodrom on January 1 of last year.

A police officer, Avery Jordan, will testify for the prosecution. You have his/her grand jury testimony and Officer Jordan's report of his/her post-arrest interview with the defendant.

Darlene Linzy will testify on her own behalf. **[The defense attorney should ask the instructor for a copy of the former defense lawyer's memo. The prosecution will not have access to that memo.]**

1. For the prosecution, conduct a direct examination of Officer Jordan and cross-examine Linzy.

2. For the defense, conduct a direct examination of Linzy and cross-examine Officer Jordan.

7.7 DRUG ENTRAPMENT CASE

STATE

v.

MICKEY DRANE

The defendant, Mickey Drane, is charged with Unlawful Delivery of a Controlled Substance, i.e., cocaine. S/he admits making the delivery, but asserts the affirmative defense of entrapment.

In this state, "A person is not guilty of an offense if his conduct is incited or induced by a public officer or employee, or Agent of either, for the purpose of obtaining evidence for the prosecution of such person. However, this section does not apply if a public officer or employee, or agent of either, merely affords to such person the opportunity or facility for committing an offense in furtherance of a criminal purpose which such person has originated."

This case was tried once before, one year ago today. The defendant was found guilty by a jury, but the conviction was reversed on appeal because of faulty jury instructions. It is being retried. You have the partial trial transcripts of the key prosecution witness, Leigh Schindler, and the defendant, Mickey Drane. You also have an excerpt from the report of Detective Martha Arnold of the State Police Narcotics Task Force.

Assume that Detective Martha Arnold is a 20-year law enforcement veteran. After she was hired in [-20], she worked for ten years as a patrol officer before being promoted to detective. She was assigned to the Narcotics Task Force in [-5]. Before joining the Task Force, she was assigned to investigate burglaries and other felonies. **[Note: The defense attorney should ask the instructor for a memo to the file written by the defense attorney's private investigator.]**

1. For the prosecution, conduct a direct examination of Schindler and cross-examine Drane.

2. For the defense, conduct a direct examination of Drane and cross-examine Schindler.

501

7.8 CRIMINAL FRAUD CASE

UNITED STATES

v.

ROBIN JONES

This is a federal criminal case. The defendant, Robin Jones, is charged in a federal mail fraud indictment with defrauding the victim, Dr. Kelly Gibson, of $50,000. The indictment charges that Jones fraudulently induced Gibson to invest the money into a new company that Jones was starting. Jones denies that s/he obtained the money from Gibson fraudulently.

You have the reports of the FBI agent who investigated the case, the Grand Jury testimony of both Gibson and the Jones, and the attached documents.

1. For the prosecution, conduct a direct examination of Gibson and cross-examine Jones.

2. For the defense, conduct a direct examination of Jones and cross-examine Gibson.

7.9 ARMED ROBBERY CASE

STATE

v.

LARRY RILEY

This is an armed robbery case. Larry Riley is charged with the armed robbery of Val Potempa. The indictment charges that on December 15, [-1], Larry Riley, while armed with a handgun, took approximately $400 in U.S. currency from the person and presence of Val Potempa by the use of force or by threatening the imminent use of force.

You have police reports concerning the Potempa robbery and the Grandhoff robbery and the arrest of Riley, a court-reported statement Riley gave to a prosecutor on the night of his arrest, and the preliminary hearing testimony of Potempa. The Grandhoff robbery has not been formally charged against Riley. **[Note: The defense attorney should ask the instructor for the memo to file written by Riley's former attorney, an assistant public defender. This memo will be available only to defense counsel.]**

1. For the prosecution, conduct a direct examination of Potempa and cross-examine Riley.
2. For the defense, conduct a direct examination of Riley and cross-examine Potempa.

7.10   BRIBERY CASE

UNITED STATES
v.
HARLEY WIGGINS

This is a federal criminal case. Harley Wiggins is charged with bribery in violation of 18 U.S.C. § 666. The indictment charges that Wiggins received a $9,500 bribe from Pat Hanson, a real estate developer, on February 15, [-1], in return for Wiggins's promise to promote passage of a zoning change proposal brought before the County Board. Wiggins is a member of the Board and chair of its Zoning Committee.

You have the report of the FBI agent who investigated the case, an excerpt from the County Board Proceedings where the zoning change was voted on, certain bank records, and the grand jury testimony of Hanson and Wiggins.

1. For the prosecution, conduct a direct examination of Hanson and cross-examine Wiggins.

2. For the defense, conduct a direct examination of Wiggins and cross-examine Hanson.

7.11 INSIDER TRADING CASE

UNITED STATES

v.

RYLEE SANBORN

This is a federal criminal case. Rylee Sanborn is charged with insider trading in violation of 15 U.S.C. §§ 78j and 78ff, and making a false statement to the Securities and Exchange Commission (SEC) investigators in violation of 18 U.S.C. § 1001. The indictment charges that Sanborn used inside information to earn a profit on corporate stock s/he bought and sold, and then lied about it to the SEC.

You have the indictment against Sanborn and the depositions of Devyn Martin, chief financial officer for the corporation, and Sanborn. You also have two e-mails written by Martin and one e-mail written by Sanborn.

1. For the prosecution, conduct a direct examination of Martin and cross-examine Sanborn.

2. For the defense, conduct a direct examination of Sanborn and cross-examine Martin.

7.12 CELL PHONE FROM SEARCH INCIDENT TO ARREST CASE

STATE

v.

DUSTIN SCOTT

This is a criminal case against Dustin Scott for possession of cocaine with intent to distribute, i.e., drug dealing, on January 10, [-0]. On that date, Police Officer Kelly Anderson arrested Scott outside the local basketball arena, shortly before a Thankful Cadavers rock concert at the arena. The Thankful Cadavers are a tribute band honoring the Grateful Dead.

After Officer Anderson arrested Scott, s/he conducted a search incident to arrest. During that search, Anderson found fourteen fifty-dollar bills, twelve twenty-dollar bills, three ten-dollar bills, six one-dollar bills, and 78 cents in coins. S/he also found four "8-ball"-sized packages containing a powdery substance, plus a cell phone. Immediately after taking possession of the cell phone, s/he removed its battery, then gave it to a fellow officer who placed the cell phone in a bag designed to block signals sent by another cell phone or other device.

On January 11, [-0], Officer Anderson drafted and signed, in the presence of the Police Department's Notary Public, an affidavit, then filed it with the court. Before the magistrate could decide whether to grant the search warrant, Scott appeared at an arraignment on January 11, [-0]. He was represented by private counsel at the arraignment. Pursuant to his attorney's instructions, he entered a "not guilty" plea.

At the arraignment, defense counsel stated, "Your Honor, I would like to put the court on notice that I will be filing a motion to suppress all of the items the officer found when s/he conducted an illegal search of my client—the money, the small bags, and the cell phone. I plan to file this motion within the next two days. Also, based upon my experience in these cases, I assume that the police will seek a search warrant to allow them to examine the contents of the cell phone. While we understand that the court usually decides whether to issue search warrants in ex parte proceedings, we request the right to be heard before the court reaches a decision on the search warrant request. After all, we will be raising the same issues if the court does grant the search warrant, in yet another motion to suppress."

The magistrate responded by saying, "I think you raise a good point. I will schedule one hearing where I will consider your motion to suppress the fruits of the search and consider the police department's request, if any, for a search warrant authorizing examination of the contents of the cell phone."

You are now appearing at that hearing. At the hearing, the state will call Officer Anderson. The defendant will call Dakota Sorensen, a friend of the defendant.

The defendant has filed a motion to suppress all items found in the search incident to Officer Anderson's arrest of Dustin Scott, on the grounds that Officer Anderson did not have probable cause to make a warrantless arrest. The state has responded to this motion by arguing that Officer Anderson had sufficient information, including information provided by a confidential informant, to constitute probable cause that Scott was selling cocaine.

The state had filed Officer Anderson's affidavit with the court at the same time as Scott was being arraigned. The state is seeking a search warrant to examine the contents of the cell phone and to chemically test the powder inside the four small packages to determine if it is cocaine.

You have Officer Anderson's affidavit, which s/he wrote with the expectation that, as in most cases, the court would consider the request for a search warrant in an ex parte proceeding.

You also have an e-mail that Dakota Sorensen sent to the Police Department. The prosecutor sent a copy of this e-mail to defense counsel, under its *Brady v. Maryland*, 373 U.S. 83 (1963), and Model Rule 3.8(d) duty to provide potentially exculpatory information to the defendant. You also have a copy of the arrest records for Dustin Scott and Dakota Sorensen.

You should assume that a state statute makes it an infraction to "sell a ticket to any entertainment event for more than the face value of the ticket." As a narcotics officer, Officer Anderson has never arrested or ticketed anyone for violation of this anti-scalping statute.

1. For the prosecution, conduct a direct examination of Officer Anderson and cross-examine Sorensen.

2. For the defense, conduct a direct examination of Sorensen and cross-examine Anderson.

VIII

CLOSING ARGUMENTS

Introduction

INTRODUCTION

The cases in Chapter 9, prepared as full trials, may also be used in this chapter as representative civil and criminal cases on which to base separate closing argument assignments. In addition, the two-witness cases in Chapter 7 may be used for additional closing argument assignments. This chapter contains six problems that involve commonly encountered situations in which effective closing arguments may be particularly important. For each problem assigned, you should be prepared to present an effectively organized and persuasively delivered closing argument to the jury.

In preparing your closing arguments, be prepared to tell the jury not only what the evidence is, but what the evidence means and why it should compel the jury to decide the case your way. Use jury instructions, analogies, and other techniques to construct a persuasive argument.

Your instructor may modify the assignments and make specific additional assignments for these exercises.

The suggested background reading is Mauet & Easton, *Trial Techniques and Trials*, Chapter 9.

8.1 LIABILITY ARGUMENT IN CONTRACT ACTION

This is a suit for breach of contract. Kane Construction Company entered into an agreement with the Glen County Highway Department to build a road extending five miles from River Bend to Tall Trees. The contract price was $7,500,000 and the contract was awarded to Kane as low bidder among ten construction companies. The other bids ranged from $8,000,000 to $10,000,000.

The contract provided for partial progress payments for "work actually completed." Kane contends that the phrase "work actually completed" includes any work done, such as excavating and grading, but the department contends that the phrase applies only to the actually completed paved road. Since the contract is ambiguous on that point, the jury will determine what the parties intended when they used that phrase.

At the end of the first 30 days, Kane submitted a bill for partial payment. At that point, only preliminary excavating and grading work had been done. No paved portion of the highway had been completed. The department refused to pay.

When the department refused to make the progress payment, Kane walked off the job, notifying the department that it would not continue the work because the contract had been breached. Kane then filed this suit for breach of contract.

The judge will instruct the jury that if it finds that the phrase "work actually completed" means any work, and not just actual road completed, that would mean that the department breached the contract and Kane would be entitled to recover the amount of profit it would have earned under the contract, which Kane says is $750,000.

The department offered evidence that Kane's bid was unrealistically low, that the company was behind schedule in the work, and that it had encountered unexpected construction problems that were not the department's fault. Department witnesses said that if Kane had actually completed the work as required by the contract, the company would have lost $1,000,000.

1. For the plaintiff, ask the jury for damages of $750,000. Stress the reasons why this or any other contract should be enforced.

2.   For the defendant, tell the jury it should not award damages to the plaintiff. Stress the reasons why the plaintiff actually walked off the job.

3.   For the plaintiff, rebut the defendant's argument.

8.2 DAMAGES ARGUMENT IN NEGLIGENCE ACTION

Three years ago today, Margaret Bone was struck by the defendant Ray Kelly's car as she was crossing Bell Street in a marked crosswalk. The car struck her on the left side, throwing her onto the pavement. She was taken to and examined at a nearby hospital and was released the same day. All X-rays were negative. Her emergency room bill was $1,800.

Miss Bone has testified to suffering continuous back and leg pain since the accident. She testified that the pain, which she described as periodic stabbing or shooting pain down her back and left leg, prevents her from doing activities such as house cleaning and gardening. She has difficulty sleeping and doing other everyday activities. However, Dr. Peter Greenberg, her treating physician, stated at trial that he could find no objective medical findings other than some bruises he noticed on her left leg during the three days following the accident, although he believed then and continues to believe now that her complaints of pain are genuine and were caused by the accident. He has not seen Bone for two and one-half years. He saw Bone in his office five times, and his bill for these services was $2,250.

Bone was not employed at the time of the accident, nor has she since sought employment. She is 63 years old and unmarried. She lives alone.

Six months before trial, Bone was examined by the defendant's specialist, Dr. Andrew Silver. He testified at trial that he also could find no objective medical findings for her complaints of pain and was unable to determine any basis for the complaints.

1. For the plaintiff, ask the jury for substantial money damages. Assume that the defendant is not contesting liability.
2. For the defendant, argue the issue of damages.
3. For the plaintiff, rebut the defendant's argument.

8.3 DAMAGES ARGUMENT IN PRODUCTS LIABILITY ACTION

This is a products liability case. Four years ago the plaintiff, Mark Venner, suffering from mild acne, began taking a drug manufactured by the defendant, Cursory Corporation. The drug, called Kleptocin, was prescribed by Venner's doctor. He did so after reading Cursory's literature that touted the drug for "infections" but said nothing about using it for minor viral or infection problems. The drug had received approval by the Food and Drug Administration (FDA) after testing showed it was effective in fighting severe infections.

The literature contained the following statement:

CAUTION: Reports of paralysis have been received from a small percentage of users after heavy and prolonged use of drug.

INDICATED USE: This drug has proved effective in cases of infection.

The doctor had not passed on the warning to Venner. Only the Cursory Company is being sued. It is the law of this jurisdiction that the manufacturer's duty to make and distribute a reasonably safe product cannot be delegated to another.

Venner claims that after taking the drug for three months he became paralyzed in both legs. Doctors have testified that he never will walk again. The plaintiff's expert witnesses have testified that Kleptocin was the proximate cause of the paralysis. They told the jury that the drug was useful in cases of severe infection, but that it never should have been used for something like mild acne. The plaintiff's theory of liability centers on the failure of Cursory to warn users that the drug should be used only in cases of severe infection.

The plaintiff also presented evidence to support his claim that Cursory engaged in the minimum testing possible under FDA guidelines and that a competing company, Klurg Pharmaceutical, was testing a new antibiotic at about the same time Kleptocin was being tested. The defense presented witnesses who said that Cursory acted reasonably and in accord with the state of scientific knowledge at the time of ingestion. Kleptocin was a new drug when Venner used it.

The plaintiff is now 20 years old, is single, has only a high school diploma, and is unable to find work.

Cursory is a Fortune 500 company traded on the New York Stock Exchange, with a net worth of $100 million.

1. For the plaintiff, tell the jury why it should award substantial compensatory and punitive damages to the plaintiff.

2. For the defendant, tell the jury why a verdict should not be brought against the company.

3. For the plaintiff, rebut the defendant's argument.

8.4 IDENTIFICATION ARGUMENT IN ROBBERY CASE

Six months ago today, at approximately 10:00 P.M., William Jones was robbed at knifepoint in an alley in the 600 block of Congress Street. The defendant, Frank Smith, has been charged with the robbery, and the case is now on trial.

Jones testified during the trial that he had been in a local tavern, the Blarney Stone, for about one hour just before the robbery occurred. He admitted to drinking "about two beers" while there. He was taking a shortcut to his parked car when the robbery occurred.

Jones testified that he was walking down the alley and was about 50 feet from Congress when a man suddenly came from nowhere and blocked his path, held a knife in his face, told him not to move, and with his other hand reached into Jones's pocket and removed his wallet. The man also took Jones's wristwatch, then ran down the alley away from Congress and disappeared.

Jones stated that the entire episode took about 30 seconds. There was a streetlight on Congress at the entrance to the alley but no lights in the alley itself. Jones described the robber to the police as a "white male, 18 to 25 years old, 5′9″ to 6′ tall, medium build, wearing blue jeans and jacket, with no unusual characteristics." Jones described the knife as a "long hunting-style knife, with a blade about 6″ long, sharpened on one edge only, with a bone handle."

The morning after the robbery Jones went to the police station, where a robbery detective asked him to look through a mug book to see if he could recognize anyone as the man who had robbed him the night before. The mug book contained about 200 photographs, each photograph being the face and shoulders of a different white male between the ages of 18 and 30 of varying heights and weights. After Jones had looked at about 50 photographs, he pointed to a photograph of Frank Smith, the defendant, and said, "that looks like him," but that he "wanted to see him in person to be sure."

One week later, following Smith's arrest, Jones was again asked to return to the station to view a lineup. When he arrived, the police had already placed five men, one of whom was the defendant, in a lineup. Each man in the lineup was a white male between 18 and 25 years old, between 5'8" and 6'2" tall, and weighing between 150 and 190 pounds. The detective asked Jones if he recognized anyone, and Jones stated that he recognized the defendant as the man who had robbed him the previous week. No photograph was taken of the lineup. None of the other men in the lineup was included in the photographs shown to Jones at the police station.

At trial, Smith testified on his own behalf. He denied committing the robbery. He stated that he was 19 years old, was 5'9" tall, and weighed 150 pounds. He said his mug shot had been taken when he was arrested for being a minor in possession of alcohol when he was 18 years old. He pleaded guilty to that charge and was placed on one year's probation.

1. For the prosecution, tell the jury why Jones's identification of Smith is credible and is sufficient to convict him of the robbery charge.
2. For the defense, argue the identification issue.
3. For the prosecution, rebut the defendant's argument.

8.5 IDENTIFICATION AND ALIBI ARGUMENT IN ROBBERY CASE

This is an armed robbery case. The defense is mistaken identification and alibi. The only identification witness, Rita Brown, saw a man who robbed her at gunpoint for about 60 seconds. She was held up six months ago at 2:00 P.M. on Sunday on the street in front of her home. The weather was dry and clear. She called police at once but was unable to identify anyone in the photos shown to her at the police station. She says she saw the robber again three weeks later, on a Monday at 8:00 A.M., waiting for a bus one block from the scene of the robbery. She called the police. They arrived minutes later and arrested the man, Marshall Jonas, at the bus stop. He lived one-half block from the bus stop at the time. No lineup was conducted.

Testifying at the trial, Jonas said that at the time of the crime he was at his cousin's house, eating chicken with his cousin, William Marshall, and his girlfriend, Shirley Gregory. Jonas called Marshall as an alibi witness at the trial but did not call Gregory. There is nothing in the record to indicate why she was not called.

Jonas also testified that he arrived at the bus stop each weekday morning at about 8:00 A.M. He worked at a Chicken King restaurant downtown. He said that he never saw Rita Brown before the day he was arrested. He has no criminal record.

1. For the prosecution, argue the reliability of the eyewitness identification.
2. For the defense, argue the weakness and defects of eyewitness identification.
3. For the prosecution, rebut the defendant's argument.

8.6   SELF-DEFENSE ARGUMENT IN MURDER CASE

This is a murder prosecution. The defense is self-defense. The defendant, Marsha Jones, and the victim, Elmer Jones, were married and living in a one-bedroom apartment in a two-flat building. Both were 30 years old, had been married for eight years, and had no children. Elmer Jones was employed as a guard in the county jail; Marsha Jones worked as a part-time secretary.

Testifying at trial, Marsha Jones stated that on the day of the shooting, six months ago today, she was in the living room of the apartment watching television when her husband came home about 11:00 P.M. He had been drinking and promptly got into an argument with her. He was yelling that the house was a mess and that as usual she hadn't done a thing about it. She stated that she tried to calm him down, but he just got worse, started threatening her, and then began punching her in the stomach. She tried to protect herself but couldn't. In desperation, she ran to the bedroom where she knew her husband kept his revolver that he used for work at the jail. She then returned to the living room and told her husband to leave her alone. She testified that her husband laughed, told her she wouldn't use the gun, and suddenly lunged at her. She then pulled the trigger of the gun twice. Her husband then fell down in the living room.

Immediately after the shooting she called the police. When the police arrived she told them what had happened. The police did not notice any bruises on her body.

Marsha Jones also testified that her husband often came home drunk and often threatened her and beat her. She said that her husband was about 6′2″ tall and weighed about 210 pounds. She is 5′4″ tall and weighs 120 pounds.

On cross-examination, the defendant admitted she had not told the police of the earlier threats and beatings and admitted she had never called the police about them or told anyone. She said Elmer had threatened to kill her if she told anyone. She said there was a telephone in the living room and bedroom, but she never called anyone.

Ballistics evidence showed that the victim was shot from over three feet away and that his body had two bullet-entry wounds. The first bullet entered his body in the chest at the left nipple and exited his back at the same level as the entry wound. The second bullet entered his body at the left rib cage just below the armpit and exited the body below the right armpit. The expert was unable to determine which shot had been fired first.

The autopsy report also disclosed that the victim's blood contained alcohol in an amount slightly in excess of the state's presumption-of-intoxication level.

1. For the prosecution, tell the jury why it should convict the defendant and not believe the defendant's testimony.
2. For the defense, argue why the killing was justifiable self-defense.
3. For the prosecution, rebut the defendant's argument.

IX

TRIALS

Introduction

General Jury Instructions

General Civil Jury Instructions

General Criminal Jury Instructions

Suggested Verdict Forms

INTRODUCTION

Each of the trials in the resources section of this book on CasebookConnect illustrates factual situations and issues commonly found in civil and criminal trials. Their lengths make them possible to be tried effectively in three or four hours. The civil cases [9.1 to 9.5, 9.12, 9.14(B) and (C), 9.15, and 9.16] and criminal cases [9.6 to 9.10, 9.13, and 9.14(A)] are arranged in approximate order of increasing complexity. The 9.11 file can be tried as either a civil or a criminal case.

Your instructor will give you specific additional instructions and ground rules for each trial. However, you should prepare your case as though it were a real case with all the formalities and procedures of an actual trial. Backgrounds of witnesses have usually been intentionally limited or omitted entirely. Be prepared to develop realistic, credible backgrounds for them. Unless instructed otherwise, you should call each witness allocated to your side. If impeachment prove up becomes necessary, call a prove up witness or prepare an appropriate stipulation.

To keep this book from becoming overly large, the trial files themselves are included in the resources section of this book on CasebookConnect, and this chapter contains only brief overviews. You should use the exhibits in the case files found in the resources section of this book on CasebookConnect. You may also prepare additional appropriate exhibits, such as enlargements of diagrams or anatomical drawings, or obtain suitable objects shown in photographs, such as weapons or clothing.

Prepare elements instructions for the claims and defenses, definitions of any critical concepts and terms, and verdict forms. The general jury instructions that follow may also be used. Be prepared to present your proposed jury instructions to the court before trial.

Presenting your case persuasively requires both adequate preparation and the execution of effective techniques. This is where all the specific techniques you have practiced in the preceding chapters should come together so that your side of the issues can be effectively and persuasively presented to the jury.

The suggested background reading is Mauet & Easton, *Trial Techniques and Trials*, especially Chapters 1, 2, and 11.

General Jury Instructions

(for use in civil and criminal trials)

[1]   Members of the jury, the evidence and arguments in this case have been completed, and I now will instruct you as to the law.

[2]   The law that applies to this case is stated in these instructions and it is your duty to follow all of them. You must not single out certain instructions and disregard others.

[3]   It is your duty to determine the facts and to determine them only from the evidence in this case. You are to apply the law to the facts and in this way decide the case.

[4]   Neither sympathy nor prejudice should influence you. [You should not be influenced by any person's race, color, religion, or national ancestry.]

[5]   From time to time it has been the duty of the court to rule on the admissibility of evidence. You should not concern yourselves with the reasons for these rulings. You should disregard questions [and exhibits] that were withdrawn or to which objections were sustained.

[6]   Any evidence that was received for a limited purpose should not be considered by you for any other purpose.

[7]   You should disregard testimony [and exhibits] that the court has refused or stricken.

[8]   The evidence that you should consider consists only of the testimony of the witnesses [and the exhibits] that the court has received.

[9] You are the sole judges of the believability of the witnesses and of the weight to be given to the testimony of each of them. In considering the testimony of any witness, you may take into account the witness's ability and opportunity to observe, [the witness's age,] the witness's memory, the witness's manner while testifying, any interest, bias, or prejudice the witness may have, and the reasonableness of the witness's testimony considered in the light of all the evidence in the case.

[10] You should consider all the evidence in the light of your own observations and experience in life.

[11] Opening statements are made by the attorneys to acquaint you with the facts they expect to prove. Closing arguments are made by the attorneys to discuss the facts and circumstances in the case and should be confined to the evidence and to reasonable inferences to be drawn from the evidence. Neither opening statements nor closing arguments are evidence. Any statement or argument made by the attorneys that is not based on the evidence should be disregarded.

[12] Faithful performance by you of your duties as jurors is vital to the administration of justice.

[13] When you retire to your jury room at the end of the trial, you will first select one of your number to act as your presiding juror to preside over your deliberations.

[14] You will then discuss the case with your fellow jurors. Each of you must decide the case for yourself, but you should do so only after you have considered all the evidence, discussed it fully with the other jurors, and listened to the views of your fellow jurors.

[15]   Your verdict[s] must be agreed to by each juror. Although the verdict must be unanimous, the verdict should be signed by your presiding juror alone.

General Civil Jury Instructions

[1]   When a party has a burden of proof on any issue, that means you must be persuaded, considering all the evidence in the case, that the issue on which the party has the burden of proof is probably more true than not true.

[2]   [(One) (Both)] of the parties in this case [(is a corporation) (are corporations)]. A corporation must be considered in the same way you would consider an individual party in this case.

General Criminal Jury Instructions

[1]   The defendant[s] [(is) (are)] charged with the offense[s] of _____ [which include(s) the offense(s) of _____]. The defendant[s] [(has) (have)] pleaded not guilty.

[2]   The [(information) (indictment) (complaint)] in this case is the formal method of accusing the defendant[s] of an offense and placing [(him) (her) (them)] on trial. It is not any evidence against the defendant[s] and does not create any inference of guilt.

[3]   [(The) (Each)] defendant is presumed to be innocent of the charge[s] against (him) (or) (her). This presumption remains with (him) (or) (her) throughout every stage of the trial and during your deliberations on the verdict, and is not overcome unless from all the evidence in the case you are convinced beyond a reasonable doubt that the defendant is guilty. All of you must agree on the verdict [for each defendant].

[4]   The State has the burden of proving the guilt of the defendant beyond a reasonable doubt, and this burden remains on the State throughout the case. The defendant is not required to prove (his) (or) (her) innocence.

[5]   You should give separate consideration to each defendant. Each is entitled to have his case decided on the evidence and the law that applies to (him) (or) (her).

[Any evidence that was limited to (one defendant) (some defendants) should not be considered by you as to (any) (the) other defendant(s).]

[6]   The fact that [(a) (the)] defendant[s] did not testify must not be considered by you in any way in arriving at your verdict.

[7]   You are not to concern yourself with possible punishment or sentence for the offense charged during your deliberation. It is the function of the trial judge to determine the sentence should there be a verdict of guilty.

Suggested Verdict Forms

(Edit to suit the circumstances of each case and the law in your jurisdiction.)

[Caption]

Verdict

We, the jury in the above case, find in favor of _____

(party)

and against _____.

(party)

We find that plaintiff was damaged in the amount of _____ dollars.

(dollar amount)

We find _____ _____% responsible, and _____

(party)   (percentage)   (party)

_____% responsible, for plaintiff's damages.

(percentage)

_____

Presiding Juror

[Caption]

Verdict

We, the jury in the above case, find defendant _____

                                                                  (name of defendant)

_____ of the charge of _____.

(guilty or not guilty)   (crime charged)

                               _____

                                    Presiding Juror

9.1 FALSE ARREST, MALICIOUS PROSECUTION, AND DEFAMATION

KAREN ADAMS

v.

CHANDLER DEPARTMENT STORE

Introduction

The Chandler Department Store is a large department store in a shopping mall in this city. It is a corporation and its only place of business is the mall store.

Karen Adams is a doctor specializing in pediatrics. She is single and lives and has her medical office in this city.

On November 1, [-2], Dr. Adams was shopping in the cosmetics department on the first floor of the Chandler Department Store. A sales clerk saw Dr. Adams put a container of Paris spray cologne in her purse and walk away from the counter. The clerk signaled a store detective, an off-duty police officer, who was standing nearby.

The detective stopped Dr. Adams by a store exit and told her she had not paid for an item from the cosmetics department. Dr. Adams denied it. The detective then escorted Dr. Adams to the store security counter, where her purse was searched, revealing the Paris spray cologne container. Dr. Adams claimed that the cologne was hers.

The store manager was called, and s/he talked to Dr. Adams in the security office. The manager then called the police. Dr. Adams was arrested and taken to the police station, where she was processed and released the next day.

Three weeks later the criminal charges against Dr. Adams were dropped by the local prosecutor's office. Accounts of Dr. Adams's arrest, and the later dismissal of the charges, were reported in the local newspaper.

Dr. Adams then brought this lawsuit.

Pleadings

Plaintiff Adams sues defendant Chandler Department Store on three theories:

1. False arrest. Plaintiff claims that the Chandler Department Store caused her to be falsely arrested because there was no reasonable basis for the arrest.
2. Malicious prosecution. Plaintiff claims that Chandler Department Store's insistence that she be arrested for shoplifting was malicious and was done because plaintiff refused to sign a waiver of liability.
3. Defamation. Plaintiff claims that she was defamed when the store's security guard called her a "shoplifter" in front of other store customers.

Plaintiff seeks all damages allowable under applicable law, including punitive damages for willful and wanton misconduct.

Defendant denies each of plaintiff's allegations. Defendant also asserts as a defense this jurisdiction's shoplifter detention statute, stating that its detention of Dr. Adams was proper under the law.

Witnesses

Plaintiff may call the following witnesses:

1. Dr. Karen Adams
2. Bailey Williams
3. Dr. Jesse Lee

Defendant may call the following witnesses:

1. Kelly Jackson
2. Kaden Flannigan
3. Pat Curran

If impeachment prove up becomes necessary, the parties must prepare an appropriate stipulation to admit the prove up evidence.

Exhibits and Materials

The following may be available:

1. *Daily Gazette* articles dated 11/2/[-2] and 11/22/[-2]
2. Misdemeanor complaint and summons
3. City Police Department general incident report dated 11/1/[-2]
4. City Police Department general incident report dated 11/2/[-2]
5. City Police Department general incident report dated 11/20/[-2]
6. Chandler Department Store shoplifting incident report
7. Sample sticker
8. Photograph of Paris spray cologne bottle prepared by plaintiff for use as a demonstrative exhibit at trial
9. Drug prescription from Dr. Lee
10. Dr. Lee's patient notes
11. Diagram of cologne counter

A statute in this jurisdiction provides as follows:

Any retail establishment that has reasonable grounds to believe that any person has taken any item of merchandise without paying for that merchandise may detain the person for a reasonable period of time, under reasonable circumstances, to determine whether such merchandise has in fact been taken without being paid for.

The parties must stipulate to the following:

1. The city police department reports are, under FRE 803(8), certified public records.

2. The misdemeanor complaint and summons are, under FRE 803(8), certified public records.

3. The two newspaper clippings from the *Daily Gazette* on 11/2/[-2] and 11/22/[-2] are actual clippings from the newspaper on those dates.

9.2 CONTRACT

WHITNEY THOMPSON

v.

THERMORAD CORPORATION

Introduction

This case involves the adequacy of an electric baseboard heating system that was installed in plaintiff's apartments. Two years ago, plaintiff Whitney Thompson was building a 50-unit apartment complex. S/he advertised for bids and contracted with defendant, Thermorad Corporation, the low bidder, to install an adequate baseboard heating system. Thermorad selected and installed its Model I system in the apartments.

The Model I failed to heat the apartments adequately when the weather turned cold. Thompson claims that Thermorad did not select an adequate system for the apartments. Thermorad claims that the problem was caused by Thompson's insulating the apartments with only six inches of fiberglass insulation in the ceilings, instead of twelve inches, the industry standard.

When the parties could not agree on a solution, Thompson contracted with another heating contractor, Peerless Heating, to remove the Thermorad Model I system and replace it with a Peerless system.

Pleadings

Plaintiff's suit raises two theories. First, plaintiff sues defendant for breach of contract. S/he seeks to recover the $100,000 s/he paid Thermorad, the $25,000 that represents the difference between Thermorad's price and the amount later paid Peerless, and the lost rental income.

Second, plaintiff sues defendant for misrepresentation. Plaintiff claims that defendant misrepresented the ability of the Model I system to heat the apartment units adequately, and that this was done to induce plaintiff to enter into a contract with the defendant. S/he seeks consequential and punitive damages.

Defendant claims it performed its part of the contract and owes plaintiff nothing. Defendant says plaintiff's defectively insulated building was the reason for the heating problem, and that plaintiff misrepresented the amount of insulation s/he would install in the apartment units. Defendant also claims that plaintiff failed to mitigate damages.

The case is being tried in your state and your jurisdiction's contract and tort law applies.

Witnesses

Plaintiff may call the following witnesses:

1. Whitney Thompson
2. Sandy Hatch
3. Cory Turner

Defendant may call the following witnesses:

1. Emery Jacobs
2. Jaime Woods

If impeachment prove up becomes necessary, call a prove up witness or prepare an appropriate stipulation.

Exhibits and Materials

The following may be available:

1. Excerpts from depositions of:
   (a) Whitney Thompson
   (b) Emery Jacobs
   (c) Jaime Woods
   (d) Sandy Hatch
   (e) Cory Turner

2. Thermorad memo dated March 15, [-2]

3. Whitney Thompson letter to John Smith

4. Advertisement for bids

5. Thermorad Model I brochure

6. Thermorad's letter response to advertisement

7. Contract

8. Other correspondence and memos of Thompson and Thermorad

9. Canceled checks to Thermorad and Peerless

10. Photograph of Thermorad Model I system

11. Blueprints of apartment unit

Assume that the trial judge will allow admission of all relevant evidence to determine the intent of the parties and the meaning of the contract. Both parties must stipulate that:

1. The apartment blueprints called for six inches of fiberglass insulation in the ceiling of each apartment.

2. The construction industry insulation standard for this area is R-19 in the walls and R-38 in the ceilings, which is six inches of fiberglass insulation in the walls, twelve inches in the ceilings.

3. There is no applicable building code requirement for any insulation in buildings.

9.3 NEGLIGENCE (CONTRIBUTION CLAIM)

JORDAN MINOR CONSTRUCTION COMPANY
v.
MID-AMERICAN CONCRETE COMPANY

Introduction

This is a contribution action. The plaintiff, Jordan Minor Construction Company, paid a sum of money to settle a negligence claim against it, filed by Antonio Giovanni. Minor Construction now claims it is entitled to contribution from Mid-American Concrete Company for a percentage of the amount of money paid. The jury will be called on to determine the relative percentage of fault among Minor Construction, Mid-American, and a nonparty, Accurate Steel Company.

This case involves an 1,800-pound steel staircase that was installed between the first and second floors of the Madonna High School, part of a $40 million construction project. On June 19, [-2], the staircase fell through the floor and crashed into the basement. Antonio Giovanni, a cement finisher (employed by Steiger Construction Company, which is not a party) who was working in the basement, was pinned under the staircase and lost his arm as a result of this accident.

There are three contracts involved in this case. The first is between Madonna High School and Jordan Minor Construction Company, the general contractor on the project. The second is between Minor Construction and Mid-American Concrete Company, the manufacturer and installer of concrete flooring known as Flexistan. The third is between Minor Construction and Accurate Steel Company, the manufacturer and installer of the steel staircase. Each company is incorporated under the laws of this state.

Flexistan is a trade name for structural concrete floor blocks. Mid-American, for this project, decided to manufacture the blocks with each block having three hollow cores filled with foam. When the blocks were manufactured, the process was done in such a way that it resulted in concrete covering the outsides of the hollow cores so that the Flexistan blocks appeared to be solid. Mid-American delivered and installed the Flexistan in the staircase area of the first floor of the Madonna High School during the morning of June 16, [-2].

Accurate Steel delivered the steel staircase in the early afternoon of June 16, [-2]. However, contrary to plans, Accurate Steel did not manufacture or deliver a steel channel on which the bottom of the staircase was to rest. The channel is designated to distribute the weight of the staircase on the floor. The staircase was then installed with the bottom resting directly on the middle of a Flexistan block.

Three days later, on June 19, [-2], the Flexistan block on which the staircase was resting suddenly shattered, causing the staircase to fall into the basement where Giovanni was working.

Pleadings

Antonio Giovanni sued Jordan Minor Construction Company but not Mid-American Concrete Company or Accurate Steel Company. Shortly after the staircase collapse, Accurate Steel declared bankruptcy. It is without assets or insurance. Minor Construction then filed a third-party claim for contribution against Mid-American. While the case was in the discovery phase, Minor Construction settled its case with Giovanni for $1.5 million. That left Minor Construction as the plaintiff against Mid-American in the contribution action. As plaintiff, Minor Construction has the burden of proof.

Minor Construction contends Mid-American was at fault and negligently created a dangerous condition because: (1) Mid-American did not tell anyone that it was installing Flexistan blocks with hollow cores, and (2) the Flexistan blocks that Mid-American delivered to the job site contained no warnings or notice that they were hollow core.

Mid-American denied Minor Construction's allegations and denied it was negligent in any way. Further, Mid-American claims the injury to Giovanni was caused by the negligence of Minor Construction and/or the negligence of Accurate Steel.

Applicable Law (Jury Instructions) and Pretrial Rulings

It is the law of this jurisdiction that a party who has paid a sum of money for causing an injury to another may be entitled to recover a percentage of that sum from a third party. In this case, Minor Construction has paid a sum of money to Antonio Giovanni in settlement of his claims for his injuries and damages. Minor Construction now claims it is entitled to contribution from Mid-American Concrete Company for a percentage of that sum paid.

550

To apportion damages, the jury must determine from all the evidence the relative degrees of fault of Minor Construction, Mid-American, and Accurate Steel. To make that determination, the jury should consider the duty owed by each company to Antonio Giovanni, the extent to which the conduct of each company deviated from the duty owed to Antonio Giovanni, and the extent to which the negligent conduct of each company proximately caused Antonio Giovanni's injuries and damages.

In pretrial rulings, the trial court has held:

1. The negligence, if any, of Antonio Giovanni is not relevant to this case;
2. The jury is not to be told that Accurate Steel went into bankruptcy and is without assets;
3. The jury is not to be told the dollar amount of Minor Construction's settlement with Antonio Giovanni; and
4. Antonio Giovanni is unavailable as a witness, for purposes of Rule 32 of the Rules of Civil Procedure, and all parties to this case had reasonable notice of the deposition of Giovanni (though Mid-American did not participate). Thus, the court has ruled that either or both parties to this case may present Giovanni's testimony via the reading of his deposition transcript. As with other testimony, the court will consider objections, other than Rule 32 objections and objections that are waived by virtue of not being raised at the deposition, to this testimony.

The verdict form to be given to the jury is to read as follows:

We, the jury, apportion responsibility as follows:

Minor Construction Company	_____ %
Mid-American Concrete Company	_____ %
Accurate Steel Company	_____ %
TOTAL	0% or 100%

If you find that any of these companies was not at fault in a way that proximately caused Antonio Giovanni's personal injuries, then you should enter zero percent as to that company. The percentages you find must total 0% or 100%.

Witnesses

Minor may call the following witnesses:

1. Antonio Giovanni (by deposition)
2. Jordan Minor
3. Terry Henderson

Mid-American may call the following witnesses:

1. Harper Stark
2. Archie Tubbs

Exhibits and Materials

The following may be available:

1. Deposition of Giovanni
2. Deposition of Minor
3. Deposition of Stark
4. Deposition of Tubbs
5. Deposition of Henderson
6. Contracts
7. Memorandum of Mid-American
8. Memorandum of Accurate Steel
9. Photograph of steel channel
10. Diagram of Flexistan blocks
11. Diagram of steel staircase

9.4 PRODUCTS LIABILITY AND WRONGFUL DEATH

SHIRLEY HARTE,
Administrator of the Estate of Marion Harte, Deceased

v.

ACME MANUFACTURING CO.

Introduction

This is a wrongful death and survival action arising from a fire in Marion Harte's apartment on July 31, [-2]. The fire started when Marion Harte used a mechanical cigarette lighter, the Acme "Magic Lite." The lighter was a gift from Marion Harte's son/daughter, Shirley, who had bought it just that day at the Flint Hardware Company.

When Marion Harte attempted to light her cigarette, the lighter exploded, enveloping her in flames, causing extensive burns on her face, chest, and arms. She was taken to a hospital by paramedics, but died about one hour after the accident.

The plaintiff is Shirley Harte. S/he brings this product liability action against Acme Manufacturing Company, the maker of the Magic Lite. S/he seeks money damages for the wrongful death of his/her mother and for his/her mother's pain and suffering during the one hour she lived after the accident.

Pleadings

Plaintiff claims the Magic Lite manufactured by Acme was unreasonably dangerous because: (1) it was defectively designed; (2) warnings on the lighter were inadequate; and (3) there were no warnings or instructions in the box containing the lighter. Plaintiff proceeds solely on a strict liability theory.

Plaintiff seeks damages under the wrongful death claim for the primary loss that resulted from Marion Harte's death, which may include the loss of money, goods, services, and society. S/he seeks damages under the survival claim for any conscious pain and suffering Marion Harte experienced between the time of her injuries and her death and any medical and funeral expenses incurred as a result of her injuries and death.

Acme Manufacturing Company admits designing and manufacturing the lighter, but contends its design was not defective and that the warnings on the lighter and in the box were adequate. Acme further asserts the affirmative defenses of assumption of the risk, contributory negligence, product misuse, and other "fault" or other theories that are viable under the facts and the applicable law. In essence, the defendant contends that the fire was caused by Marion Harte's failure to follow the instructions on the lighter and in the box.

Flint Hardware Company had been named as a defendant in the original lawsuit. The plaintiff contended that Flint knew or should have known the lighter was being sold without the insert warnings in the box. The claim against Flint was settled 60 days ago. Plaintiff and Flint entered into a covenant not to sue. Under the covenant, plaintiff agreed to dismiss Flint as a defendant, and Flint agreed to pay plaintiff $25,000 and agreed that its store manager, Cassidy White, would be available to testify at trial and that his/her testimony would be consistent with his/her deposition.

The case is being tried in your state and your jurisdiction's tort law applies.

Witnesses

Plaintiff may call the following witnesses:

1. Shirley Harte
2. Fran Wilson
3. Dale Berg

Defendant may call the following witnesses:

1. Cassidy White
2. Rowan Mercer
3. Meredith Swan

If impeachment prove up becomes necessary, the parties must prepare an appropriate stipulation to admit the prove up evidence.

Exhibits and Materials

The following may be available:

1. City Fire Department paramedic report

2. Mercy Memorial Hospital autopsy report

3. Flint Hardware receipt

4. Two photographs of Magic Lite

5. Diagram of Magic Lite

6. Magic Lite instructions

7. Two letters to Acme Manufacturing Co.

8. Letter from Rowan Mercer to Cassidy White

9. Letter from Consumer Products Laboratory to Mercer

10. Resume of Meredith Swan

11. Memorandum to Plaintiff's Lawyer

12. Excerpts of depositions of

    (a)   Shirley Harte

    (b)   Fran Wilson

    (c)   Cassidy White

    (d)   Rowan Mercer

    (e)   Meredith Swan

The parties must stipulate to the following:

1. The present life expectancy for a woman 51 years old is 30.3 years.

2. The City Fire Department Paramedic Report is a certified public record, under FRE 803(8).

3. The autopsy report from the Mercy Memorial Hospital is a business record of the hospital, under FRE 803(6).

9.5   GENDER DISCRIMINATION, WRONGFUL TERMINATION, AND DEFAMATION

SHARON DONALDSON

v.

EMPIRE CAR RENTAL COMPANY

Introduction

Empire Car Rental Company is a small car rental company that began in [-7]. It is located only in this city and presently has two offices; the downtown office, opened in [-6], and the airport office, opened in [-4].

Sharon Donaldson is a lifelong resident of this city. She graduated from the local state university in [-6] and began working for Empire, which had recently opened the downtown office. She worked as a rental agent after completing her training period.

When Empire opened the airport office in [-4], it hired Lou Smith as its manager. Donaldson was transferred to the airport office and promoted to assistant manager. A few months later Smith decided to leave Empire, and Donaldson was promoted to manager of the airport office.

In [-3] Empire created a new management position, the city manager, who would be in charge of both offices and any future ones in this city. Richard Jackson was hired as the new city manager.

Jackson and Donaldson did not work well together. The friction between the two came to a head in September [-2] when Jackson called Donaldson into his office and fired her, effective immediately. Jackson gave as his reason that Donaldson had violated company policy by authorizing the rental of a car with unlimited mileage to a personal friend.

Donaldson was out of work for approximately one year. She contacted an employment agency, Career Placements, to find her a new job. Donaldson finally received and accepted a job offer with another company, Equipment Leasing. Her salary at that job is substantially lower than her salary at Empire.

In November [-2], Donaldson filed a discrimination claim with the Equal Employment Opportunity Commission (EEOC). The EEOC investigated the claim, determined that Title VII had been violated, and issued a right to sue letter. Donaldson then brought this lawsuit.

Pleadings

Plaintiff Donaldson sues defendant Empire Car Rental Company on three theories:

1. Title VII employment discrimination. Plaintiff claims that she was subjected to disparate treatment by Empire. To prove a claim of disparate treatment under Title VII, plaintiff must prove that her gender played a motivating part in a particular employment decision. If plaintiff proves this by a preponderance of the evidence, the burden of presenting evidence shifts to the defendant, who may avoid liability only by providing a nondiscriminatory reason for the plaintiff's treatment. Plaintiff then has the burden of proving the employer's reason is pretextual.
2. Breach of contract. Plaintiff claims that the personnel manual issued by Empire was part of her employment contract and that Empire breached it by firing her without taking the procedural steps required by the manual.
3. Defamation. Plaintiff claims that Richard Jackson, Empire's city manager, defamed her when he called her "dishonest" in a letter to Career Placements.

Plaintiff seeks all damages allowed under applicable law, including lost wages and commissions, lost future income, and punitive damages.

Empire denies each of plaintiff's allegations. Empire says that the personnel manual's procedures permitted Donaldson's firing. Empire also asserts an affirmative defense to the defamation claim, stating that Jackson had a qualified privilege to repeat his evaluation of Donaldson to her employment agency and prospective future employers.

The case is being tried in the local U.S. District Court. No jurisdictional issues have been raised.

Witnesses

Plaintiff may call the following witnesses:

1. Sharon Donaldson
2. Dana Ripley
3. Sandy Hoffman

Defendant may call the following witnesses:

1. Richard Jackson
2. Chris Steele
3. John Kinney

If impeachment prove up becomes necessary, the parties must prepare an appropriate stipulation to admit the prove up evidence.

Exhibits and Materials

The following may be available:

1. EEOC investigative file, which includes:
   (a) Interviews of witnesses
   (b) Empire's records
   (c) Empire's personnel manual
   (d) EEOC right to sue and determination letters
   (e) Career Placements' records
   (f) Jackson's letter to Hoffman

2. Excerpts of depositions of:

    (a) Sharon Donaldson

    (b) Richard Jackson

    (c) John Kinney

    (d) Dana Ripley

    (e) Chris Steele

    (f) Sandy Hoffman

Stipulations

The parties must stipulate to the following:

1. The EEOC witness interviews, right to sue letter, determination letter, and any other EEOC records are all certified public records, under FRE 803(8), of the EEOC.

2. The court has previously ruled as a matter of law that the Personnel Manual is a binding contract between the parties.

9.6 MURDER

STATE
v.
MERLE RAUSCH

Introduction

This case involves a shooting that occurred on June 15, [-1], on the 3300 block of North Clark Street.

The defendant, Merle Rausch, and the victim, William Jones, were in the Red Apple tavern that evening. Around 11:00 P.M. they got into an argument, which was broken up. Rausch then left the tavern, followed by Jones. The shooting occurred on the street a short while later.

Pleadings

The State has filed murder charges against Rausch. He has entered a plea of not guilty and served notice on the State of his intended defense of self-defense. The case is being tried in your state and your jurisdiction's criminal law applies, including the law on lesser-included offenses.

Witnesses

Prosecution may call the following witnesses:

1. Nicky Felton
2. Freddy Martin
3. Officer Taylor Connor
4. Dr. Sidney Burns

Defense may call the following witnesses:

1. Merle Rausch

2.   Finley Williams

If impeachment prove up becomes necessary, the parties must prepare an appropriate stipulation to admit the prove up evidence.

Exhibits and Materials

The following may be available:

1.   Police report
2.   Preliminary hearing transcript
3.   Report of interview
4.   Pathologist's report
5.   Diagram
6.   Photo of street and sidewalk
7.   Gun
8.   Box containing five cartridges and one empty casing
9.   Photo of five cartridges and one empty casing

Both sides must agree to the authenticity of John French's Report of Interview with Finley Williams.

9.7   MURDER AND ATTEMPTED ARMED ROBBERY

STATE

V.

JOHN HUDSON

Introduction

This case involves an attempted robbery and shooting that occurred in Lazar's Clothing Store on February 14, [-1]. The store was owned and managed by Sidney and Sara Lazar. Ms. Lazar was shot and killed during the attempted robbery. Two men were involved in the crime.

After the shooting, police arrived and interviewed Mr. Lazar and a bystander, Ryan Green. That afternoon, Mr. Lazar looked through a stack of photographs and tentatively identified photographs of John Hudson and Dale Buckner as photos of the two men who had killed his wife.

That night, after checking the two suspects' arrest records and obtaining an arrest warrant for Hudson and Buckner, the police went to their apartment and arrested them. The police also found certain physical evidence in the apartment. Outside they saw a car matching the description of the getaway car.

The police then called Mr. Lazar and the bystander, Green. At the police station, both Lazar and Green participated in several identification procedures.

The police records show that Hudson was convicted of aggravated assault seven years ago and was sentenced to two years in the penitentiary.

A ballistics expert at the police crime lab examined a gun found in the apartment and concluded that it had been recently cleaned. Because of this, he was unable to determine whether it had been recently fired. The ballistics expert also examined the bullet that was removed from Sara Lazar's body. The expert concluded the bullet was a .38 caliber bullet, but because it was too damaged he could not determine if it was fired from the gun.

A pathologist who performed the autopsy on Sara Lazar's body determined that death was caused by a single gunshot wound to her head, which entered her brain.

A custodian of the records of the state motor vehicle department looked through the records and found that a [-8] black Cadillac sedan was registered to John Hudson on February 14, [-1].

Pleadings

Hudson and Buckner were formally charged with murder and attempted armed robbery. Both entered pleas of not guilty. They were held in custody without bond. Buckner was stabbed to death in a jail fight three weeks before trial. Hudson is being tried. The case is being tried in your state, so your jurisdiction's criminal law applies. The trial court has denied all motions to suppress evidence based on constitutional grounds.

Witnesses

Prosecution may call the following witnesses:

1. Sidney Lazar
2. Ryan Green
3. Investigator Sam Reilly

Defense may call the following witnesses:

1. John Hudson
2. Whitney Barr

If impeachment prove up becomes necessary, the parties must prepare an appropriate stipulation to admit the prove up evidence. Prosecution and defense must agree to stipulations for the following:

1. Pathologist, as to the cause of Mrs. Lazar's death
2. Ballistics expert, as to the examination of the gun and bullet
3. Custodian of records, as to the vehicle registration for Hudson's car

4. The distance between Lazar's Clothing Store and Sam's Chicken Shack is five miles, and the normal driving time between them in mid-afternoon is approximately 15 minutes

5. The defendant's prior conviction (if admissible for impeachment and not admitted by the defendant)

6. Barr's time card is a business record of Lester's Auto Repair

Exhibits and Materials

The following might be available:

1. Police report

2. Transcript of preliminary hearing

3. Albert LaRue memorandum

4. Whitney Barr statement

5. Whitney Barr time card

6. Gun

7. Box for bullet

8. Bullet

9. Black leather jacket

9.8 AGGRAVATED SEXUAL ASSAULT

STATE

v.

MICHAEL MILLER

Introduction

This case involves an alleged aggravated sexual assault that occurred during the night of January 8, [-1]. The victim, Shirley Thompson, claims that the defendant, Michael Miller, abducted her at knifepoint in an alley while she was walking home from work and raped her twice. The defendant admits that he had sexual intercourse with Ms. Thompson, but claims that it was with her consent.

Pleadings

The State has filed aggravated sexual assault charges against Miller. He has entered a plea of not guilty and served notice on the State of his intended consent defense. The case is being tried in your state and your jurisdiction's criminal law applies.

Witnesses

Prosecution may call the following witnesses:

1. Shirley Thompson
2. Ralph Thompson
3. Detective Rich
4. Dr. Reyes Perez

Defense may call the following witnesses:

1. Michael Miller
2. Sam Collins

If impeachment prove up becomes necessary, the parties must prepare an appropriate stipulation to admit the prove up evidence.

Exhibits and Materials

The following may be available:

1. Rich's report
2. Miller's statement
3. Collins's statement
4. Map
5. Dr. Perez's report
6. Grand jury transcript
7. Photographs

Both parties must agree on the following written stipulations:

1. Dr. Perez's report is a business record of the Williams Memorial Hospital, in accordance with FRE 803(6).
2. The two vehicle photographs attached to this case file are of the defendant's car and accurately show how the car looked on January 8 and 9, [-1].
3. The gas station photograph attached to this case file is of Eddie's Service Station. It accurately shows how the station looked on January 8 and 9, [-1].

9.9 MURDER

STATE

v.

FRANK FLETCHER AND ARTHUR MORRIS

Introduction

This case involves a killing of a police officer on July 2, [-1]. Officer William Kane was shot while he was sitting in his parked squad car. A witness, Shelby Green, reported what s/he had seen to the police.

Two weeks later Richard Edwards was arrested for a burglary. Green identified Edwards as one of the three men who were involved in the Officer Kane shooting. At first Edwards denied being involved in the shooting, but he later changed his story following an agreement with the prosecutors. He then implicated defendants Fletcher and Morris as the other persons who committed the shooting. On July 26, the police arrested defendants Fletcher and Morris at their apartment.

Police records show that Fletcher had been convicted of armed robbery, receiving a two-year sentence, six years ago. Morris had been convicted of burglary two years ago and received one year of probation.

Edwards has been charged with the burglary, for which he was arrested, but that charge is still pending at the time of the trial in this cause. He has not been charged with the killing of Officer Kane. Police records show Edwards was convicted of burglary six years ago and served a sentence of one year in the state penitentiary.

The autopsy report from the county medical examiner's office disclosed that Officer William Kane was killed by a gunshot that entered his head at the right temple and exited his head at the left temple, lacerating the brain. The autopsy was performed on July 3, [-1], by Dr. David Dodd, a county medical examiner's pathologist. No pellet was recovered from the body.

Pleadings

The state has filed murder charges against Fletcher and Morris as direct actors and as aiders and abettors. Both have entered pleas of not guilty. The case is being tried in your state and your jurisdiction's criminal law applies.

Witnesses

The State may call the following witnesses:

1. Richard Edwards
2. Shelby Green
3. Investigator Quinn Kelly
4. Sergeant Lee Williams

The defense may call the following witnesses:

1. Frank Fletcher
2. Arthur Morris
3. Madison Sampson

If impeachment prove up becomes necessary, the parties must prepare an appropriate stipulation to admit the prove up evidence.

Exhibits and Materials

The following may be available:

1. Edwards's statement to Kelly
2. Edwards's grand jury testimony
3. Kelly's arrest report
4. Preliminary hearing transcript
5. Sampson's statement to Daniels
6. Ballistics report

7. Fingerprint report

8. "Off the Heat" sign

9. Photograph of the squad car

10. Diagram of intersection

11. Box of .38 caliber shells (photographs)

Both sides must agree on written stipulations for the following:

1. Cause of Officer Kane's death

2. Prior convictions of Fletcher, Morris, and Edwards (if admissible to impeach and not admitted during examination)

3. The box of .38 caliber shells in this file is the box of shells Investigator Kelly says s/he found in Morris's dresser

4. The photograph of a police squad car in this file is a photograph of Officer Kane's car, taken by a police photographer on the day of the shooting

5. Edwards has been in police custody since his arrest on July 16

6. Fletcher and Morris have been in custody since their arrest on July 26

7. The ballistics report qualifies as a Rule 803(8) public record

8. Admissibility of the fingerprints report

Fletcher and Morris have filed a Notice of Alibi in which they state they were at their apartment watching "*Jurassic Park*" at the time of the killing. No one else was present in the apartment at that time.

The trial court has denied the defendant's motions to suppress their statements and the items found in their apartment.

9.10 BRIBERY

STATE

v.

AVERY WENTWORTH AND CHRIS BENSON

Introduction

This case involves an alleged bribery of two police officers following their arrest of Reed Foster for possession of heroin.

Reed Foster was stopped by the defendants, Officers Avery Wentworth and Chris Benson, on January 10, [-1], for running a red light. A subsequent search uncovered heroin. Foster was taken to the station. S/he called his/her lawyer, Taylor Johnson, who came to the station and met with one of the arresting officers.

Two days later Johnson presented a motion to suppress on Reed Foster's behalf. Officer Benson testified at the hearing. The motion was granted and the heroin charges were dismissed.

On January 23, Reed Foster went to the district attorney's office and complained that his/her lawyer, Taylor Johnson, and the two police officers, Wentworth and Benson, had shaken him/her down for money.

Taylor Johnson was called before the grand jury and initially denied Foster's charges. Following discussions with the district attorney and after receiving a grant of immunity, Johnson appeared a second time before the grand jury and changed his/her story.

On February 6, the defendants' lockers at the station were searched. At this time the defendants made statements and physical evidence was found.

Police records indicate that Reed Foster pled guilty on January 5, [-7], to burglary and was sentenced to one year in the penitentiary. On February 1 of last year, Foster was arrested on a burglary charge. That charge is still pending at the time of this trial.

The State has obtained a deposit slip from the First State Bank. It shows that Avery Wentworth deposited $400 in cash in his/her savings account on January 13 of last year.

Pleadings

Benson and Wentworth are charged with bribery. Both have entered pleas of not guilty. The case is being tried in your state and your jurisdiction's criminal law applies.

Witnesses

Prosecution may call the following witnesses:

1. Taylor Johnson
2. Reed Foster
3. Morgan Goodman

Defense may call the following witnesses:

1. Chris Benson
2. Avery Wentworth
3. Bobby Hall

If impeachment prove up becomes necessary, the parties must prepare an appropriate stipulation to admit the prove up evidence.

Exhibits and Materials

The following may be available:

1. Police report of January 10, [-1]
2. Transcript of January 12, [-1]
3. Statement of Reed Foster
4. Grand jury testimony of Taylor Johnson on January 28, [-1]
5. Immunity order
6. Grand jury testimony of Taylor Johnson on February 4, [-1]
7. Memo of Morgan Goodman
8. Interview of Bobby Hall

9. Deposit slip
10. Three $100 bills

All parties must agree on written stipulations for the following:

1. Business records foundation for the deposit slip.
2. Prior convictions of Reed Foster (if admissible to impeach and not admitted during examination).
3. Investigator Tom Johnson's report, which is an authentic and complete copy of the original, had to be disclosed by the defense to the prosecution under the applicable discovery rules.
4. There have been no disciplinary proceedings initiated by the state bar against Taylor Johnson as of this date.

9.11   CRIMINAL MAIL FRAUD OR CIVIL FRAUD

UNITED STATES OF AMERICA OR ROCK INSURANCE CO.
v.
CHRIS MANNING

Introduction

This case can be used as a criminal mail fraud prosecution or as a civil fraud case with compensatory and punitive damages.

Chris Manning, a lawyer, is charged with defrauding the Rock Insurance Company by being part of a fraudulent scheme in which a car accident was staged and a false claim was submitted to Rock Insurance.

The government/plaintiff alleges that Manning organized the scheme with another person, Lynn Stone, and that Stone recruited a driver who was instructed in how to stage a rear-end collision, then claim s/he received neck and back injuries, and then go to Manning to file a claim against the other driver's insurance company. Manning would collect a contingency fee from the settlement amount and would give Stone 20 percent of his/her contingency fee as a finder's fee.

Manning denies s/he paid Stone a finder's fee and says that s/he believed each case s/he filed was a legitimate case in which his/her client had been injured and that s/he obtained a reasonable, good-faith settlement for his/her client.

Pleadings

The United States has obtained an indictment of the defendant, charging him/her with one count of mail fraud under Title 18, § 1341. The indictment alleges that Manning devised a scheme to obtain money from the Rock Insurance Company by means of false and fraudulent representations (that a legitimate accident had occurred, and that Manning's client had actually been injured and incurred substantial expenses), and that Manning knowingly used the U.S. mail system for the purpose of executing the scheme. The case is in the local U.S. District Court.

Rock Insurance Company has filed a civil fraudulent misrepresentations complaint against Manning. The complaint alleges that Manning made a claim to the Rock Insurance Company that contained intentional and material misrepresentations of facts (that a legitimate accident had occurred and that Manning's client had actually been injured and incurred substantial expenses), that Manning knew they were false when made, that Manning intended to induce the Rock Insurance Company to pay on the claim, that plaintiff reasonably relied on Manning's misrepresentations, and that plaintiff was consequently damaged. Rock Insurance Company seeks all damages allowed under applicable law, including punitive damages. Jurisdiction is based on diversity of citizenship, since Rock Insurance is an out-of-state company and Manning is a citizen of this state. The case is in the local U.S. District Court.

Defendant in the criminal case has entered a plea of not guilty. Defendant in the civil case denies the plaintiff's allegations.

When trying the criminal case, assume the civil case has been stayed until the criminal case is concluded. When trying the civil case, assume the criminal case was dismissed and never tried. All materials in this case file are available in both the criminal and civil cases.

Witnesses

Plaintiff may call the following witnesses:

1. Randy Carlson
2. Lynn Stone
3. Sandy Adams

Defendant may call the following witnesses:

1. Chris Manning
2. Sean Brent

If impeachment prove up becomes necessary, the parties must prepare an appropriate stipulation to admit the prove up evidence.

Exhibits and Materials

The following may be available:

1. City Police accident report
2. Mercy Hospital emergency room report
3. City Towing repair estimate
4. Albertson's Food Store letter
5. Super Call Telephone Company records search report
6. FBI reports
7. Manning's office records
8. Manning's checking account records
9. Dr. Sandy Adams's office records
10. Rock Insurance Company records
11. Express Money Center letter
12. Rock Insurance Company check
13. Grand jury transcripts
14. IRS memo

The parties must stipulate to the following:

1. Business records foundations for all business records.
2. All checks and deposit slips are authentic.
3. Manning's demand letters and Rock Insurance's settlement check were placed in the U.S. mail and mailed in interstate commerce.
4. The transcripts of recorded telephone conversations in the FBI reports are accurate verbatim transcripts of the conversations.

9.12   MEDICAL NEGLIGENCE

JENNIFER SMITH

v.

KELLY DAVIS, M.D.

Introduction

In February, [-2], Jennifer Smith went to Dr. Sandy Johnson, an internist, for an annual examination. Dr. Johnson recommended that Smith begin having annual mammograms and referred her to Dr. Kelly Davis, a radiologist. Dr. Davis's mammogram revealed that Smith had a small lump in her right breast, which Dr. Davis found to be consistent with a probable fibroadenoma, a non-cancerous tumor. Dr. Davis sent the report to Dr. Johnson, who discussed the report with Smith. However, Smith did not have any follow-up procedures done to verify the diagnosis or treat the tumor.

In November, [-2], Smith noticed a lump in her right breast and again saw Dr. Johnson, who referred her to Dr. Chris Tucker, another radiologist. Dr. Tucker's mammogram revealed that Smith had a larger mass in her right breast, which Dr. Tucker found highly likely to be cancerous. A later biopsy confirmed the diagnosis.

In December, [-2], Smith had a partial mastectomy of her right breast, which was followed with radiation and chemotherapy.

Pleadings

Plaintiff's suit raises one claim, medical negligence, against Dr. Johnson and Dr. Davis, for failing to properly diagnose and timely treat her breast cancer.

Before trial, Dr. Johnson settled with the plaintiff for $500,000. Plaintiff's claim against Dr. Davis is now being tried, and both liability and damages are in issue.

The case has been filed in your federal district court as a diversity action (plaintiff moved to another state before she filed the action) and your state's tort law and relevant jury instructions apply.

Witnesses

Plaintiff may call the following witnesses:

1. Jennifer Smith
2. Dr. Chris Tucker

Defendant may call the following witnesses:

1. Dr. Kelly Davis
2. Dr. Sandy Johnson

Your instructor may impose other requirements and limitations on the issues to be tried, the witnesses that can be called, and the evidence that can be presented.

If impeachment prove up becomes necessary, call a prove up witness or prepare an appropriate stipulation.

Exhibits

The following may be available:

1. Medical records of:
    (a) Dr. Sandy Johnson
    (b) Dr. Kelly Davis
    (c) Dr. Chris Tucker
    (d) Dr. Terry Barnes
    (e) Good Shepherd Regional Medical Center
2. American College of Radiology BIRADS Codes
3. Stages of Breast Cancer information
4. Dr. Kelly Davis expert report (including curriculum vitae)
5. Dr. Chris Tucker expert report (including curriculum vitae)
6. Settlement agreement between plaintiff and Dr. Sandy Johnson

7. Depositions of:

    (a)   Jennifer Smith

    (b)   Dr. Sandy Johnson

    (c)   Dr. Chris Tucker

    (d)   Dr. Kelly Davis

Stipulations

The parties must stipulate that:

1. The medical records of the doctors and hospital in this case file are business records under FRE 803(6).

2. The life expectancy of a 42-year-old woman in the United States is 39.1 years.

3. Plaintiff has incurred the following medical expenses to date:

    (a)   Dr. Sandy Johnson: $1,200

    (b)   Dr. Kelly Davis: $600

    (c)   Dr. Chris Tucker: $1,400

    (d)   Dr. Terry Barnes: $10,000

    (e)   Good Shepherd Hospital (surgery & post-op): $30,000

    (f)   Good Shepherd Hospital (chemo & radiation): $40,000

4. Dr. Chris Tucker and Dr. Kelly Davis are, through their education, training, and experience, qualified to give expert opinions concerning the radiological diagnosis, treatment, and prognosis of breast cancer.

9.13 DRIVING WHILE INTOXICATED AND CARELESS AND IMPRUDENT DRIVING

STATE
v.
BRAD SMITHTON

Introduction

This is a criminal driving while intoxicated (DWI) and careless and imprudent driving (C & I) case. The various states have assorted structures for driving while intoxicated (sometimes known as "driving under the influence" or "impaired driving") offenses. The materials in this trial use the basic structure from the state of Missouri. Therefore, the jury instructions here are based on Missouri law. Many, but by no means all, other states would have similar jury instructions. Your instructor might ask you to ignore the law outlined here and use the structure and jury instructions of your state.

In the early morning hours of July 1, [-1], Brad Smithton left a party and drove his Jeep to pick up his girlfriend, Sara Twist. After picking up Twist, Smithton took a shortcut through a remote part of the Central State University campus on a street called "Prominence Point." The northern and southern portions of this short street are paved, but the middle portion is a dirt road (i.e., essentially a pair of tire ruts). Lieutenant Rocky Roberson of the Central State University Police Department arrested Smithton on suspicion of DWI, C & I, and an alleged offense related to his vehicle license plate.

The arresting officer and another officer filled out official paperwork. That official paperwork is included in this file. [You should assume that the defense made the appropriate discovery request and that the prosecution complied by providing the materials included in this trial file.]

The instructor will give the defense attorney(s) information for the defendant, Brad Smithton. Only the defense attorney(s) and the defendant himself are allowed to see this information. The prosecutor(s) cannot.

Pleadings

The three citations ("tickets") are noted in the Exhibits and Materials listed below. The DWI and C & I citations constitute the pleadings for this case. The prosecutor dropped the third charge, regarding Smithton's alleged driving of a vehicle that did not have a front and rear license plate visible to other drivers.

Witnesses

The prosecution may call the following witnesses:

1. Lieutenant Rocky Roberson
2. Officer Bernie Fine

The defendant may call the following witnesses:

1. Defendant Brad Smithton
2. Otis Campbell (Brad Smithton's fraternity brother)

Either party may call the following witnesses:

1. Sergeant Kim Donaldson [The prosecutor(s) should find a person to play this role.]
2. Sara Twist [The defense attorney(s) should find a person to play this role.]

The witnesses are not necessarily loyal to the attorneys who call them. To recreate the dynamics that would be present in a real trial as closely as possible, the prosecutors should find volunteers to play the roles of Lieutenant Rocky Roberson, Officer Bernie Fine, and Sergeant Kim Donaldson, and the defense attorney(s) should find volunteers for the roles of Sara Twist, Brad Smithton, and Otis Campbell.

If impeachment prove up becomes necessary, the parties must prepare an appropriate stipulation to admit the prove up evidence. The parties must stipulate that the deposition transcripts and transcripts of interviews accurately reflect what was said. No witness is allowed to claim any transcription error.

Exhibits and Materials

The following items are available:

1. Lieutenant Rocky Roberson's original report (7/1/[-1]), including a hand-drawn map by Roberson
2. InfoMaster Evidence Ticket
3. 7/1/[-1] Supplemental Report by Officer Bernie Fine, with photo of Jeep
4. 7/10/[-1] Supplemental Report by Officer Bernie Fine, with Transcript of Interview of Otis Campbell
5. 9/22/[-1] letter from Scott W. Gregory, the defense attorney who previously represented Brad Smithton, with its enclosure, the affidavit of Sara Twist [The lead prosecutor did not respond to this letter. Therefore, attorney Gregory's attempts at plea negotiations were not successful.]
6. The deposition of Sergeant Kim Donaldson [This deposition was taken to preserve Donaldson's testimony, because s/he anticipated being out of the country at the time of the trial. However, the trip was cancelled, because the Central State University Police Department could not come up with the funds to pay for it. As a result, Sergeant Donaldson is available to testify at trial.]
7. Refusal to Submit to Alcohol/Drug Test Form
8. Alcohol Influence Report Form
9. DWI Citation (Count I at trial)
10. C & I Citation (Count II at trial)
11. Vehicle License Citation (dropped by prosecutor before trial)
12. Driving Record (for Brad Smithton)
13. Jury Instructions

Statutes in this jurisdiction provide for DWI and C & I offenses. The required elements are outlined in the jury instructions at the end of the set of trial materials in the resources section of this book on CasebookConnect. [Note: Your instructor might ask you to craft your own set of jury instructions, based on your jurisdiction's statutes.] Another statute in this state also makes it a traffic offense to operate a vehicle without both a front and rear license plate that are visible to other drivers.

9.14(A) MISDEMEANOR BATTERY AND ASSAULT OF A LAW ENFORCEMENT OFFICER

STATE

v.

TODD WEARL

Introduction

This trial is somewhat different from traditional hypothetical trials in trial advocacy classes. Usually, witnesses are asked to read a set of instructions that tell them what they "know" and then to testify based on that knowledge. In this trial, witnesses will observe the event in question (via a video on the Internet) and then testify based on their actual observations. Thus, the witnesses will be relying on their own observations of the event and their recollections of those observations.

The events that led to this litigation occurred in your city, which will be called "University" for purposes of this trial, on August 14, [-1], just outside the Library/ Museum Building, which is also sometimes referred to by its formal name of "Hulston Hall." The diagram included in these trial materials shows the outline of the Library/ Museum Building. The outline is accurate. The north half of the building is the Museum portion. The south half is the Library portion. The door from which two of the three participants in the incident (one of the men in civilian clothing and the police officer) exited the building is between the Museum portion and the Library portion.

Two males were walking in opposite directions outside the Library/Museum building. George Otta, who was wearing a white T-shirt, was leaving the building. Todd Wearl, who was wearing a red T-shirt, was walking toward the building. They ran into each other and a disagreement ensued. A uniformed policeman, Officer Dan Kinger, saw these events from inside the Library/Museum Building, then responded. He eventually pepper sprayed Mr. Wearl.

Those playing witness roles will view a video recording of the incident. Each ordinary witness will watch a specifically designated video once, then testify based on his or her recollection of what he or she saw and heard. To give those playing the roles of the participants in the incident (George Otta, Todd Wearl, and Officer Dan Kinger) a somewhat more comprehensive perspective of what occurred, each of them will be allowed to view two videos, but they will be allowed to watch each video only once.

All participants should assume that Otta, Wearl, and Kinger had never met each other before this incident. This was a chance encounter between the three of them. They have no "history" with each other.

Special Instructions

The attorneys in this case should carefully follow these instructions:

Witness Instructions. Your instructor will give you links to PDF files that contain the instructions for each of your witnesses. As an attorney in the case, you are *not* allowed to look at these instructions at any point before trial. Instead, get the appropriate link to each of your witnesses and ask him or her to read *all* of the enclosed instructions before watching the videotape(s) assigned to that witness.

Finding Volunteers to Serve as Witnesses. As a student attorney, you will be expected to find volunteers to play the witness roles.

The prosecutor(s) will have to find "volunteers" for

1. George Otta [Must be male.]
2. Officer Dan Kinger [Must be male.]
3. Witness 1 [Note: Witness 1 was talking on a cell phone when the incident occurred.]
4. Witness 8

The defense attorney(s) will have to find "volunteers" for

1. Todd Wearl [Must be male.]
2. Witness 4A
3. Witness 4B [Note: Witnesses 4A and 4B were standing in location 4, talking to each other, when the incident occurred. Therefore, you should

find people for these roles who would have some reason to be talking to each other. In other words, find two people who know each other.]

4. Witness 2

After you find persons willing to fill these roles, you should give them the links to their witness instruction packets, as noted above. Ask them to review all of the instructions before watching the assigned videos. Then wait for them to watch the videos on their own—that is, without you being present. After this occurs, you should interview them. All of this should occur before the witnesses are deposed.

You are not required to call every witness in this case. Instead, you should choose those witnesses you wish to call. You are allowed to call witnesses who were "found" by your opponent.

Additional Special Instructions are in the trial file.

Exhibits and Materials

The following may be available:

1. Diagram of Library/Museum Building [Note: This diagram is of unknown origin. Someone apparently copied the basic outline of the building from a map and inserted numbers on it. It was probably someone who worked for the University Police or for one of the law firms involved in the case, but nobody now knows who created the diagram. Some, but not necessarily all, of the numbers on the diagram show the approximate locations of witnesses. Attorneys should ignore all numbers that are not relevant to their case (and, if they plan to offer the diagram as an exhibit in some form, should probably remove some or all numbers and other writing from the diagram).]

2. University Police Uniform Incident/Offense Report (six pages, including two pages on the traditional uniform report form, two pages of typed narrative, and a two-page "Use of Force Report")

3. River City Hospital Discharge Instructions (re: George Otta)

4. River City Hospital Radiology Department Report (re: George Otta)

5. River City Hospital Emergency Department Report (re: George Otta)

6. River City Hospital Work/School Excuse (re: George Otta)

7. Jury Instructions (including Verdict Form) [Note: Your instructor might ask you to draft your own set of jury instructions, based upon the law in your jurisdiction.]

Stipulations

The parties must stipulate as follows:

1. All medical records are the originals of these records, created and kept in the regular course of business of the medical institution that created and kept them.

2. All statements of observations in medical records are accurate reflections of the observations made by the person recording the observations in the records, made at or near the time of these observations.

3. To the extent that the medical records contain opinions of medical professionals, these opinions are the conclusions of persons qualified as experts to reach those conclusions. The opinions are based upon adequate bases. The methods the experts used to reach the conclusions are sufficient under the applicable standards of the jurisdiction.

9.14(B) INTENTIONAL TORT (BATTERY)

GEORGE OTTA
v.
TODD WEARL

Introduction

This trial is somewhat different from traditional hypothetical trials in trial advocacy classes. Usually, witnesses are asked to read a set of instructions that tell them what they "know" and then to testify based on that knowledge. In this trial, witnesses will observe the event in question (via a video on the Internet) and then testify based on their actual observations. Thus, the witnesses will be relying on their own observations of the event and their recollections of those observations.

The events that led to this litigation occurred in your city, which will be called "University" for purposes of this trial, on August 14, [-1], just outside the Library/ Museum Building, which is also sometimes referred to by its formal name of "Hulston Hall." The diagram included in these trial materials shows the outline of the Library/ Museum Building. The outline is accurate. The north half of the building is the Museum portion. The south half is the Library portion. The door from which two of the three participants in the incident (one of the men in civilian clothing and the police officer) exited the building is between the Museum portion and the Library portion.

Two males were walking in opposite directions outside the Library/Museum building. George Otta, who was wearing a white T-shirt, was leaving the building. Todd Wearl, who was wearing a red T-shirt, was walking toward the building. They ran into each other and a disagreement ensued. A uniformed policeman, Officer Dan Kinger, saw these events from inside the Library/Museum Building, then responded. He eventually pepper sprayed Mr. Wearl.

Those playing witness roles will view a video recording of the incident. Each ordinary witness will watch a specifically designated video once, then testify based on his or her recollection of what he or she saw and heard. To give those playing the roles of the participants in the incident (George Otta, Todd Wearl, and Officer Dan Kinger)

593

a somewhat more comprehensive perspective of what occurred, each of them will be allowed to view two videos, but they will be allowed to watch each video only once.

All participants should assume that Otta, Wearl, and Kinger had never met each other before this incident. This was a chance encounter between the three of them. They have no "history" with each other.

Also, you should assume that the local prosecutor decided NOT to pursue the criminal case against Wearl. Thus, you should assume that this intentional tort suit for battery by Otta against Wearl is the only litigation that has arisen out of this incident.

Special Instructions

The attorneys in this case should carefully follow these instructions:

Witness Instructions. Your instructor will give you links to PDF files that contain the instructions for each of your witnesses. As an attorney in the case, you are *not* allowed to look at these instructions at any point before trial. Instead, get the appropriate link to each of your witnesses and ask him or her to read *all* of the enclosed instructions before watching the videotape(s) assigned to that witness.

Finding Volunteers to Serve as Witnesses. As a student attorney, you will be expected to find volunteers to play the witness roles.

Plaintiff's counsel will have to find "volunteers" for

1. George Otta [Must be male.]
2. Officer Dan Kinger [Must be male.]
3. Witness 1 [Note: Witness 1 was talking on a cell phone when the incident occurred.]
4. Dr. Alex Tintinalli

The defense attorney(s) will have to find "volunteers" for

1. Todd Wearl [Must be male.]
2. Witness 4A

3. Witness 4B [Note: Witnesses 4A and 4B were standing in location 4, talking to each other, when the incident occurred. Therefore, you should find people for these roles who would have some reason to be talking to each other. In other words, find two people who know each other.]

4. Witness 2

After you find persons willing to fill these roles, you should give them the links to their witness instruction packets, as noted above. Ask them to review all of the instructions before watching the assigned videos. Then wait for them to watch the videos on their own—that is, without you being present. After this occurs, you should interview them. All of this should occur before the witnesses are deposed.

You are not required to call every witness in this case. Instead, you should choose those witnesses you wish to call. You are allowed to call witnesses who were "found" by your opponent.

Additional Special Instructions are in the trial file.

Exhibits and Materials

The following may be available:

1. Diagram of Library/Museum Building [Note: This diagram is of unknown origin. Someone apparently copied the basic outline of the building from a map and inserted numbers on it. It was probably someone who worked for the University Police or for one of the law firms involved in the case, but nobody now knows who created the diagram. Some, but not necessarily all, of the numbers on the diagram show the approximate locations of witnesses. Attorneys should ignore all numbers that are not relevant to their case (and, if they plan to offer the diagram as an exhibit in some form, should probably remove some or all numbers and other writing from the diagram).]

2. University Police Uniform Incident/Offense Report (six pages, including two pages on the traditional uniform report form, two pages of typed narrative, and a two-page "Use of Force Report")

3. River City Hospital Discharge Instructions (re: George Otta)

4. River City Hospital Radiology Department Report (re: George Otta)

5. River City Hospital Emergency Department Report (re: George Otta)

6. River City Hospital Work/School Excuse (re: George Otta)

7. Jury Instructions (including Verdict Form) [Note: Your instructor might ask you to draft your own set of jury instructions, based upon the law in your jurisdiction.]

Stipulations

The parties must stipulate as follows:

1. All medical records are the originals of these records, created and kept in the regular course of business of the medical institution that created and kept them.

2. All statements of observations in medical records are accurate reflections of the observations made by the person recording the observations in the records, made at or near the time of these observations.

9.14(C) 42 U.S.C. § 1983 SUIT

TODD WEARL

v.

DAN KINGER

Introduction

This trial is somewhat different from traditional hypothetical trials in trial advocacy classes. Usually, witnesses are asked to read a set of instructions that tell them what they "know" and then to testify based on that knowledge. In this trial, witnesses will observe the event in question (via a video on the Internet) and then testify based on their actual observations. Thus, the witnesses will be relying on their own observations of the event and their recollections of those observations.

The events that led to this litigation occurred in your city, which will be called "University" for purposes of this trial, on August 14, [-1], just outside the Library/ Museum Building, which is also sometimes referred to by its formal name of "Hulston Hall." The diagram included in these trial materials shows the outline of the Library/ Museum Building. The outline is accurate. The north half of the building is the Museum portion. The south half is the Library portion. The door from which two of the three participants in the incident (one of the men in civilian clothing and the police officer) exited the building is between the Museum portion and the Library portion.

Two males were walking in opposite directions outside the Library/Museum building. George Otta, who was wearing a white T-shirt, was leaving the building. Todd Wearl, who was wearing a red T-shirt, was walking toward the building. They ran into each other and a disagreement ensued. A uniformed policeman, Officer Dan Kinger, saw these events from inside the Library/Museum Building, then responded. He eventually pepper sprayed Mr. Wearl.

Those playing witness roles will view a video recording of the incident. Each ordinary witness will watch a specifically designated video once, then testify based on his or her recollection of what he or she saw and heard. To give those playing the roles

597

of the participants in the incident (George Otta, Todd Wearl, and Officer Dan Kinger) a somewhat more comprehensive perspective of what occurred, each of them will be allowed to view two videos, but they will be allowed to watch each video only once.

All participants should assume that Otta, Wearl, and Kinger had never met each other before this incident. This was a chance encounter between the three of them. They have no "history" with each other.

Also, you should assume that the local prosecutor decided not to pursue the criminal case against Wearl. Thus, you should assume that this civil rights suit by Wearl against Officer Kinger is the only litigation that has arisen out of this incident.

Special Instructions

The attorneys in this case should carefully follow these instructions:

Witness Instructions. Your instructor will give you links to PDF files that contain the instructions for each of your witnesses. As an attorney in the case, you are *not* allowed to look at these instructions at any point before trial. Instead, get the appropriate link to each of your witnesses and ask him or her to read *all* of the enclosed instructions before watching the videotape(s) assigned to that witness.

Finding Volunteers to Serve as Witnesses. As a student attorney, you will be expected to find volunteers to play the witness roles.

Plaintiff's counsel will have to find "volunteers" for

1. Todd Wearl [Must be male.]
2. Witness 2
3. Dr. Pat Stevens
4. Plaintiff's Liability Expert

The defense attorney(s) will have to find "volunteers" for

1. George Otta [Must be male.]
2. Officer Dan Kinger [Must be male.]

3. Witness 1 [Note: Witness 1 was talking on a cell phone when the incident occurred.]

4. Defendant's Liability Expert

After you find persons willing to fill these roles, you should give them the links to their witness instruction packets, as noted above. Ask them to review all of the instructions before watching the assigned videos. Then wait for them to watch the videos on their own—that is, without you being present. After this occurs, you should interview them. All of this should occur before the witnesses are deposed.

You are not required to call every witness in this case. Instead, you should choose those witnesses you wish to call. You are allowed to call witnesses who were "found" by your opponent.

Additional Special Instructions are in the trial file.

Exhibits and Materials

The following may be available:

1. Diagram of Library/Museum Building [Note: This diagram is of unknown origin. Someone apparently copied the basic outline of the building from a map and inserted numbers on it. It was probably someone who worked for the University Police or for one of the law firms involved in the case, but nobody now knows who created the diagram. Some, but not necessarily all, of the numbers on the diagram show the approximate locations of witnesses. Attorneys should ignore all numbers that are not relevant to their case (and, if they plan to offer the diagram as an exhibit in some form, should probably remove some or all numbers and other writing from the diagram).]

2. University Police Uniform Incident/Offense Report (six pages, including two pages on the traditional uniform report form, two pages of typed narrative, and a two-page "Use of Force Report")

3. University Eye Care Associates letter by Dr. Pat Stevens (re: Todd Wearl)

4. Excerpts from University Police Department Manual Re Use of Force

5. Jury Instructions (including Verdict Form) [Note: Your instructor might ask you to draft your own set of jury instructions.]

Stipulations

The parties must stipulate as follows:

1. All medical records are the originals of these records, created and kept in the regular course of business of the medical institution that created and kept them.

2. All statements of observations in medical records are accurate reflections of the observations made by the person recording the observations in the records, made at or near the time of these observations.

9.15   OIL AND GAS: CLAIM FOR USE OF PORE SPACE

KIT AND REESE LANIK
v.
DAUNTLESS OIL AND GAS, INC.

Trial file written by

Tara Righetti, Professor,

University of Wyoming College of Law and School of Energy Resources

and

Stephen Easton, President,

Dickinson State University

with

Charles Nye, Geologist and Research Scientist, *and*

Dr. J. Fred McLaughlin, Director

University of Wyoming School of Energy Resources,

Center for Economic Geology Research

Introduction

    Ranchers Kit and Reese Lanik assert that Prataria state statutes require Dauntless Oil and Gas, Inc., to compensate them for injecting produced water into the pore space beneath their ranch. The Lanik ranch is what is called a "split-estate," meaning the mineral and surface estates have been severed. When this occurs, the mineral estate is considered to the "dominant" estate, meaning that the owner of the mineral estate has the right to reasonable use of the surface estate as is necessary to production of the minerals.

    The Laniks own the surface estate, which many state statutes, including Prataria's, have clarified includes the non-hydrocarbon rock and pore space in the subsurface.

601

Pore space is the space within rocks that collectively can create a reservoir. It can be used as a place to dispose of the saltwater produced as a byproduct of the production of hydrocarbons, as a place to store hydrocarbons or carbon dioxide, or as a pathway for pressurization of wells.

When an operator like Dauntless successfully drills for oil and gas, the materials that come to the surface almost always include saltwater. Operators separate this saltwater from the desired hydrocarbons at the surface. Sometimes they dispose of this saltwater by injecting it into the pore space beneath the earth's surface. Injection of produced water into the subsurface is a lawful activity and is permitted pursuant to the Underground Injection Control program of the Safe Drinking Water Act. Subsurface injection of produced water has been found to be part of the mineral owner's implied servitude to make reasonable use of the surface of split estates. Accordingly, an oil and gas operator does not need the surface owner's agreement to dispose of salt water.

The common law implied servitude did not require a mineral owner to compensate the surface owner for reasonable use of the land for mineral development. However, many states, including Prataria, have passed statutes that require compensation to surface owners for certain types of harm resulting from mineral development. The Laniks have made a claim under Prataria's Split Estate Act for damages to their pore space. Dauntless asserts that it is not required to compensate the Laniks for use of the pore space, because the Laniks have not suffered any compensable harm, as defined by the statute. It also asserts that, even if separate payment is due to the Laniks pursuant to Prataria statutes, the Laniks' damages are substantially lower than they claim.

For an overview of the legal issues involved in this type of suit, see Tara Righetti, *Unseen Injury: Does Wyoming's Split Estate Act Create a Statutory Right to Compensation for Subsurface Harms?*, WYO. LAW., Dec. 2017, at 26.

Witnesses

The plaintiffs may call the following witnesses:

1. Kit Lanik

2. Arjun Kaur (as an adverse witness)

3. Scout McCandless (as an adverse witness)

4. Robin Górski

The defendant may call the following witnesses:

1. Armistice Wheeler

2. Sky Soung

3. Cody Cavendish

4. Any of the witnesses identified above as plaintiffs' witnesses

Exhibits and Materials

The following items are available:

1. Patent under 1862 Homestead Act to Ondrej Lanik, 8/23/1927

2. Enlarged Patent under 1909 Enlarged Homestead Act to Antonia Lanik, 6/16/1931

3. Mineral Deed to Huttleson Mineral Trust, 5/16/1936

4. Plugging and abandonment report on Wildcat 34-67-34, 7/12/1941

5. Decree of Distribution (from probate) conveying property to Kit Lanik, 11/1/[-40]

6. Oil and Gas Lease from Huttleson Mineral Trust to Prodigo, 9/14/[-17]

7. Prataria Split Estate Act, § 33-9-201 et seq. [-16]

8. Surface Use Agreement from Laniks to Prodigo, 1/12/[-15]

9. Cover letter from Prodigo to Laniks re Check Nos. 1025, 1026, and 1027 for 34-67- 34 #1, #2, and #3 surface damage agreement payments, 3/3/[-15]

10. Prodigo Check No. 1025 for 34-67-34 #1 SDA payment, 3/3/[-15]

11. Prodigo Check No. 1026 for 34-67-34 #2 SDA payment, 3/3/[-15]

12. Prodigo Check No. 1027 for 34-67-34 #3 SDA payment, 3/3/[-15]

13. Cover letter from Prodigo to Laniks re Check No. 2204 for roads, pipelines, and powerlines payment, 12/14/[-14]

14. Prodigo Check No. 2204 for powerline, pipeline, and roads payment, 12/14/[-14]

15. Cover letter from Prodigo to Laniks re Check No. 3107 for 34-67-34 #4 surface damage agreement payment, 4/18/[-13]

16. Prodigo Check No. 3107 for 34-67-34 #4 SDA payment, 4/18/[-13]

17. Cover letter from Prodigo to Laniks re Check No. 3468 for 34-67-34 #5 surface damage agreement payment, 7/3/[-13]

18. Prodigo Check No. 3468 for 34-67-34 #5 SDA payment, 7/3/[-13]

19. Prataria Pore Space Ownership Statute, § 26-1-37 [-12]

20. Cover letter from Prodigo to Laniks re Check No. 4623 for 34-67-34 #6 surface damage agreement payment, 12/26/[-11]

21. Prodigo Check No. 4623 for 34-67-34 #6 SDA payment, 12/26/[-11]

22. Dauntless 34-67-34 #6 Well Log, 12/30/[-11]

23. Email correspondence between Arjun Kaur and Scout McCandless re 1940s wildcat well, 1/[-10]

24. Purchase and Sale Agreement between Prodigo and Dauntless, 2/1/[-10]

25. Assignment of Oil, Gas, and Mineral Leases from Prodigo to Dauntless, 2/22/[-8]

26. Cover letter from Dauntless to Laniks re Check No. 1638 for livestock damage payment, 1/23/[-3]

27. Dauntless Check No. 1638 for livestock damages, 1/23/[-3]

28. Kit Lanik letter to editor in Utica Herald, 3/14/[-3]

29. Prataria University news release re funding for CCUS feasibility research, 4/1/[-2]

30. Envision Energy Alliance letter to Dauntless re award for Excellence in Sustainable Surface Management, 6/10/[-12]

31. Prataria Dept. of Environmental Quality report re produced water and crude oil spill due to lightning strike, 6/12/[-2]

32. Dauntless notice letter to Laniks re intent to convert 34-67-34 #6 well to injection, 12/3/[-2]

33. Permit for conversion of 34-67-34 #6 well to injection, 2/14/[-1]

34. Notice of intent to convert 34-67-34 #6 well to injection, 6/1/[-2]

35. Mechanical integrity test on injection well 34-67-34 #6, 2/24/[-1]

36. Email correspondence between Kit Lanik and Armistice Wheeler re damages for injection, 4 and 5/[-1]

37. Internal email correspondence between Armistice Wheeler and Sky Soung re damages for injection, 5/[-1]

38. Nodak Times article re spill near Medora, North Dakota, 7/13/[-1]

39. Deposition of Kit Lanik, 10/22/[-1]

40. Robin Górski report and résumé, 10/30/[-1]

41. Marion Souterre appraisal and résumé, 11/26/[-1]

42. Photo of Lanik Ranch showing 34-67-34 #5, 1/28/[0]

43. Surface ownership map, 1/30/[0]

44. Lanik Ranch wells cross-section, 1/30/[0]

45. Lanik Ranch wells cross-section showing potential flow path, 1/30/[0]

46. Report of monthly injection to 1/31/[0] via 34-67-34 #6, 2/5/[0]

47. Cody Cavendish report and résumé, 2/9/[0]

48. Deposition of Sky Soung, 2/12/[0]

49. Deposition of Robin Gorski, 12/12/[-1]

50. Complaint, 6/12/[-1]

51. Answer, 7/3/[1]

52. Denial of Summary Judgment Motion, December 20, [-1]

53. Proposed Jury Instructions and Verdict Form

9.16   PRODUCTS LIABILITY (SEMESTER-LONG EXERCISE)

RILEY JOHNSON

v.

BEST HELMETS

Introduction

This case involves a fatal accident that occurred in the dry riverbed of the Ronson River in Springdale on October 1, [-1]. The deceased, Ash Johnson, a recent college graduate, was riding his/her motorcycle in the dry riverbed when it hit a large rock. Johnson was ejected from the motorcycle, landing face down in the riverbed. His/her head was thrown down into his/her torso, breaking his/her neck and killing him/her.

At the time of the accident Johnson was wearing an open-face motorcycle helmet with a 3-inch stiff visor made by Best Helmets. Johnson's father/mother, Riley Johnson, will bring a lawsuit against Best Helmets, claiming that the Best helmet was unreasonably dangerous and caused Ash Johnson's death. Best Helmets will deny this claim and further claim that Johnson's own negligence caused his/her death. Best Helmets is a corporation with its principal place of business in a state other than the state where Riley Johnson resides.

Special Instructions

The attorneys in this case should carefully follow these instructions:

Finding Volunteers to Serve as Witnesses. As a student attorney, you will be expected to find volunteers to play the witness roles.

The plaintiff(s) will have to find volunteers for

1. Riley Johnson (plaintiff)
2. H. Smith (eyewitness)
3. Dr. T. Barr (pathologist)

4. P. Newsome (plaintiff's engineering expert)

5. S. Cohen (plaintiff's engineering expert)

The defense attorney(s) will have to find volunteers for

1. B. Miller (eyewitness)

2. A. Wilder (defendant's engineering expert)

3. G. Sommers (defendant's engineering expert)

Witness Instructions. Your instructor will give you links to PDF files that contain the instructions for each of your witnesses. As an attorney in the case, you are *not* allowed to look at these instructions at any point before trial. Instead, be sure each witness has the correct link and ask him or her to read and follow the instructions in the PDF.

Attorney Trial Files. In a similar fashion, the instructor will provide a trial file for your use as an attorney for the plaintiff or for the defendant. Plaintiff's case file has all the documents contained in Riley Johnson's file, including a copy of the police department's accident report. Defendant's case file has all the documents contained in Best Helmets' file, including a copy of the police department's accident report.

Determining What Witnesses Know. The attorneys trying this case, like practicing attorneys, will have to interview witnesses, depose them, or review required disclosures to determine what the witnesses know. Some witnesses, of course, might decide not to talk to some of the attorneys, just as some witnesses in real cases do.

Disclosures and Discovery. Your instructor will set a disclosure and discovery schedule. In deference to the reality of going from start to finish (or, at least, to jury verdict) in a short period of time, these deadlines and limitations will be much more severe than in real world trials. You may assume, though, that each witness who could be subpoenaed to a deposition has indeed been subpoenaed by the "other side" to a deposition.

Deposition Transcripts. When you take a deposition, you should record it in some form, presumably using your smart phone. The attorney taking the deposition will be responsible for transcribing it, then providing the witness and opposing counsel an opportunity to review the transcript, to identify any errors in the transcript. If there are errors, please resolve them amicably. Deposition transcripts should include line numbers. [Warning: Transcribing from audio or video will take you much longer than you think.]

Damages Stipulation. If the case goes to trial, the parties will stipulate that the total damages suffered by Riley Johnson are $250,000. Of course, if comparative fault applies, and Johnson recovers, the net award to Johnson might be less.

X

HISTORIC TRIALS

Introduction

Using Historic Trials to Teach About History and Trials

Rules for Historic Trials

INTRODUCTION

Each of the historic trial files in the resources section of this book on CasebookConnect is based on actual historic events, but the events did not lead to a trial when they occurred. The length of the files makes it possible to try the case in two or three hours, if time limits are strictly enforced.

When trying to find historical events for these trials, the authors look for circumstances (a) with historical significance, (b) that did not result in trials when they occurred, and (c) where there is a fighting chance for each party to secure a favorable verdict. These are not recreations of trials that actually took place, because such recreations would not present students with the challenges of formulating theories and themes, outlining opening statements and closing arguments, and determining how best to conduct direct and cross-examination.

You should prepare your case as though it were a real case with all the formalities and procedures of an actual trial. Although the trials are based on historic events, current law, including current evidence law, will be used. The rules for historic trials are outlined below. In addition, there may be special rules for your trial, as outlined in your trial file or as articulated by your instructor.

To keep this book from becoming overly large, the trial files themselves are included in the resources section of this book on CasebookConnect, and this chapter contains only brief overviews. You should use the exhibits in the case files found in the resources section of this book on CasebookConnect. You may also prepare additional appropriate exhibits, such as enlargements of diagrams or drawings, or obtain suitable objects shown in photographs, such as weapons or clothing.

As with the trials in Chapter 9, presenting your case persuasively requires both adequate preparation and the execution of effective techniques. This is where all the specific techniques you have practiced in Chapters 1 through 8 should come together so that your side of the issues can be effectively and persuasively presented to the jury.

The suggested background reading is Mauet & Easton, *Trial Techniques and Trials*, especially Chapters 1, 2, and 11.

USING HISTORIC TRIALS TO TEACH ABOUT HISTORY AND TRIALS

STEPHEN D. EASTON

WITH ELIZABETH E. O'HANLON

Photo Credits: J. R. Swanegan and Dylan Crouse

If you are looking for a new approach to conducting jury trials in trial advocacy courses or a way to promote your law school or bar group, think about conducting a trial based on a historic event. In addition to serving as a solid mechanism to teach about history and trials, these trials, if promoted, can present your law school or bar group—and our profession as trial lawyers—in a very positive light. This primer is intended to give you a bit of guidance, should you decide to present a historic trial.

Private Silas Goodrich (Caleb Jones) salutes his co-defendant and commanding officer, Captain Meriwether Lewis (Professor John Mollenkamp), on his way to the witness stand. [Photo credit: JR Swanegan]

BASIC CONCEPT

The concept we used in the Spence Law Firm Historic Trials at the University of Wyoming College of Law (and that we used at the University of Missouri-Columbia School of Law) is to take an event from history that did not result in a trial, then create a triable case from that event. We do not replay trials that did occur, because doing so does not challenge the attorneys to create their own trial strategy.

For maximum educational value and ease and effectiveness of presentation, we use historic facts, but modern law and technology. Think of the time machine that is so popular in fiction. Your judge, attorneys, witnesses, jurors, and audience will enter the time machine and pretend that they are being transported to a date in the past. But take today's law and technology with you on the time machine ride.

ADVANTAGES

Why a trial based on history? Several reasons.

Truth Is Stranger than Fiction. First, as opposed to the typical, purely fictional, set of mock trial "facts," something actually happened—or did not happen, as the case may be—when you try a case based on history. That provides an element of drama and emotion that is present in many actual trials but missing from most mock trials.

That adds realism to the case, which makes it easier for all involved, especially the attorneys, to get into their roles. Of course, you will not have the real Meriwether Lewis or the real John Wilkes Booth in your courtroom. But you will have actors playing those roles, trying their best to testify as the actual historic figures would have. If my experience is any indication, the witnesses and lawyers will very much get into their roles, as if they were indeed trying a case of historic significance.

History Is Fun. Lawyers in our historic trials have conducted direct and cross-examinations of well-known historic figures like assassins, mob bosses, heroes and heroines, governors, and even presidents. How many lawyers get the chance to do that? Doing it in front of a live audience makes it even more fun, though risky, for those trying the case. Those playing the witness roles also have fun assuming the character of historic figures.

All rise as President Thomas Jefferson (Professor Frank Bowman) enters the courtroom to testify on behalf of his friend, Meriwether Lewis. [Photo credit: JR Swanegan]

At the two law schools where I have overseen them, the annual historic trials have become much anticipated events in the law school and legal communities. In many ways, they are a community rallying event akin to the spring musical at high schools and universities.

Teaching the Importance of Investigation. The traditional purely fictional mock trial exercise does not give younger attorneys the chance to learn the value of digging for "the facts," because the "facts" in these cases are limited to those presented in the trial file itself. As Professor Irving Younger noted, it is important for younger lawyers to learn that "[f]acts do not grow on trees. . . . They must be investigated and proved." Irving Younger, *The Facts of a Case*, 3 U. ARK. LITTLE ROCK L.J. 345, 346 (1980). New and future lawyers working on historic trials get the chance to investigate the facts, if they are willing to conduct research beyond the trial file they receive.

U.S. Attorney Liz Ahsmuhs impeaches Captain Meriwether Lewis (Professor John Mollenkamp) with an entry from the Journals of the Lewis and Clark Expedition. [Photo credit: JR Swanegan]

It is a somewhat different "investigation" than in an actual trial, of course, because it involves digging in archives and newspaper morgue files, but it is a factual investigation nonetheless. One of the trials I supervised was based to a significant extent on a book about that event that is correctly considered "the" book about that event. The book's author, who exhaustively researched the incident for his book, served as a witness in the trial. He was shocked when a student attorney used a letter from one of the other witnesses that she found deep in the historic archives. Neither he nor any of the other half dozen authors of books about this incident had ever found this important letter. This was the most dramatic, but not the only, example I have seen of students learning the value of digging for facts to prepare for historic trials.

Teaching History. A trial based on a historic event gives everyone involved, from the attorneys to those who simply watch from the audience, a chance to learn a bit of history.

If you or someone working with you invests the time and effort to publicize your trial, your audience will include not only law students and lawyers, but members of the community. Through partnerships with university history departments, high school and community college history teachers, local history groups, and others, we have enticed many people who would ordinarily never set foot in a law school to watch and learn from our trials. Because a hotly contested trial is a good vehicle for teaching, they learn quite a bit about history.

Publicity for Your Law School or Bar Group. Although the primary benefit of historic trials is the education they provide, they might also help you to generate positive publicity for your law school or bar group. We have seen our historic trial attorneys invited to radio shows, and the trials have generated several newspaper stories. Historic trials produce great pictures—shots of Thomas Jefferson, Meriwether Lewis, or John Wilkes Booth on the stand—and media outlets love pictures. In our profession, with its often dismal reputation among the public, opportunities for positive public relations are important.

Joel Defebaugh opens for the defense in *Emi v. Kawai*, the Japanese-American internment defamation trial. [Photo credit: Dylan Crouse]

Fabulous Partnership Opportunities. As with real trials, there are many ways to staff historic trials. It is possible for historic trials to feature one lawyer per client, though this would create a substantial workload for that lawyer. It is also possible for a law school to pair two students together as a trial team or for a bar group to pair two experienced trial attorneys as a trial team.

But we prefer pairing a third-year law student or recent graduate with an experienced attorney on each trial team. Then we require each trial team to split the work load evenly, with the less experienced attorney handling either the opening or the closing and examining half of the witnesses. Working in such a partnership is a tremendous opportunity for a younger attorney, who will probably have to wait quite a while to assume a similar role in a real jury trial. The older attorney will also learn a thing or two from the younger attorney, who is likely to know the history better (via more research effort) and to know how to use technology to present information at trial.

DISADVANTAGES

Like anything in life, the historic trial also has some inherent disadvantages. Happily, with a bit of planning and execution, you can turn some of the disadvantages into advantages or at least minimize the disadvantage.

It Takes Time. You cannot put on any trial, even a small one, without spending quite a few hours in trial preparation. Do not allow an attorney to try the case, no matter how strong that attorney's reputation, unless he or she is willing to devote the time needed to prepare for trial and meet with his or her trial partner and the witnesses assigned to that team. You will also need to find folks who are willing to invest the effort to serve as witnesses and in the other roles outlined below.

It Takes Time, Part II. The trial itself takes time, too. Indeed, the single biggest challenge in conducting a historic trial is getting it completed in the two-hour time frame that an American audience trained by movies of that length expects. It is difficult, if not impossible, to get a case to the jury that quickly. Indeed, while two hours has always been my goal, I have never accomplished it.

Terry Mackey and his client, Fair Play Committee leader Frank Emi (actor Darrell Kunitomi, whose parents were interred at Heart Mountain), enjoy a light hearted moment after the Heart Mountain Trial libel trial. [Photo credit: Dylan Crouse]

That confession having been made, my experience does tell me that the key to getting the case tried in about two and a half hours is to have a student or other volunteer whose sole job is to keep the attorneys on schedule by cutting them off when their opening statements, direct and cross-examinations, and closing arguments last too long.

The best system for keeping the trial to a limited time is to require the attorneys to file a Time Budget 24 hours before trial (as outlined in the *Rules for Historic Trials* below), then to have someone at the trial (often in the role of bailiff) keep the attorneys on this time budget. Seat the timekeeper near the jury box for opening and closing and between the judge and the witness stand during witness examinations, so the attorneys can clearly see him or her. Instruct that person to raise one finger in the air when the attorney has one minute left, then to look at the judge and raise his or her hand with the palm forward (in the universally recognized symbol for "stop"). Instruct the judge to say "Thank you, counsel" when s/he sees the timekeeper's hand raised. If the judge has no mercy the first time an attorney buts up against the time limit, the attorneys will adjust. They won't like it, because attorneys always want to go longer then they should. But they will adjust if the timekeeper and the judge send a clear message that time limits will be strictly enforced.

It Takes Money. While it is of course possible to conduct a historic trial like any other mock jury trial at the end of your trial advocacy course, to put on a memorable historic trial before an audience, your law school or bar group will have to spend some money. Not a lot, but a little. Conducting the research for the trial might require investing some photocopying or printing fees at the archives holding the historic records. You might need to donate a few dollars to a local university drama department or community theatre group to facilitate borrowing of costumes and props; you might also need to buy a few costume items and props. You should consider giving small gifts to the folks who invest the time to put on the show. And you should host a cast party after the trial. All of that adds up, but perhaps you can find a trial lawyer or law firm to sponsor your historic trial.

Plaintiff's attorney Mikole Soto cross-examines Heart Mountain Project Director Guy Robertson (Professor Alan Romero) in the Japanese-American internment defamation trial. [Photo credit: Dylan Crouse]

Knowledge Imbalance Between Attorneys and Witnesses. If your attorneys research the actual history, they might know more about the witnesses they examine than the volunteers who are playing those witnesses. To minimize this problem, the attorneys should agree to strictly follow the "good faith basis" rule whereby no attorney is allowed to suggest the existence of any fact unless there was a solid basis in the historic record for that fact. Creative adversarial attorney "gap filling" regarding items missing from the historic record should not be allowed.

Some Civil Attorneys Fear Criminal Cases. Although you could do a civil historic trial, many will be criminal cases. Some attorneys who concentrate on civil work, including some of the experienced attorneys who would be wonderful trial partners for law students and newer lawyers, are deathly afraid of criminal cases.

This disadvantage can be overcome with a bit of salesmanship. Within most civil attorneys—admittedly sometimes deep within—lies an inner prosecutor or criminal defense attorney. A historic trial might be that famous civil trial attorney's only chance to be Vincent Bugliosi, Gerry Spence, or Atticus Finch.

Close Enough Has to Be Good Enough. No matter how extensive the historic record regarding an event, you will have to fill in some gaps. For example, even though few events are documented as extensively as the Lewis and Clark Expedition, we had to invent newspaper articles, other journal entries, and a letter. For the John Wilkes Booth trial, we had to turn actual historical figures into composite witnesses who observed what three or four real people saw, to save time.

History purists might object to this. To us, that seems rather silly, because we believe we filled the gaps in reasonable ways and that the exercise gave everyone the chance to learn a bit of history. But you might get a bit of flack from the history snobs.

The Chapter 10 trial files reflect the modifications we had to make to the historical record to get the case tried in limited time. If you have an audience at your historic trial, use the time the jury is deliberating to tell the audience what those modifications were.

"IT'S SHOW TIME, FOLKS"

If you are going to use your trial as a show, i.e., a theatrical production, somebody has to be in charge of each of the following roles.

The cast and crew for the 2017 Spence Law Firm Historic Trial, *Emi v. Kawai* (the Heart Mountain libel case). [Photo credit: Dylan Crouse]

Trial Director. Somebody has to find people to do the other tasks listed below and do the tasks that others said they would do, but do not in fact do (an inevitable feature of any project involving multiple volunteers). And somebody has to run the show. It is very helpful to have one or more stage managers to assist the Trial Director in putting on the show.

Researcher/Author. Unless you are using one of the Chapter 10 trial files, somebody has to take on the job of being the historian who researches the events and writes the trial file for the attorneys and witnesses. This is the hardest job on the list. It is also thankless, so you need to find someone who is dependable, capable of both research and writing, fair, creative, and willing to work hard outside the spotlight. If possible, the trial file should contain a series of documents that can be used as prior inconsistent statements or exhibits, including real, and if necessary, created investigators' reports, letters, journal entries, newspaper articles, business records, etc.

The good news is that there is now a small inventory of historic trial files in Chapter 10. We hope to grow this inventory in future editions of MATERIALS IN TRIAL

ADVOCACY. Therefore, except when you decide to do a historic trial based on a locally significant event, you will not have to undergo the considerable expense and workload of researching and drafting a trial file.

Casting Agent. If the Trial Director would prefer not to take full responsibility for filling all of the other roles, you should find someone to "cast" some of the roles, including the attorney, witness, and volunteer roles. Due to inevitable last minute "resignations," try to find a casting agent who has plenty of connections and chits to call in, if necessary.

Prosecutor Steve Easton points an accusatory finger at John Wilkes Booth (Nathan Ridgeway) during opening statement. [Photo credit: Dylan Crouse]

Judge. In terms of advance preparation, the presiding judge's role is among the easiest, if someone prepares a bench book containing a full set of jury instructions and all exhibits. You might want to get a law student to volunteer to serve as the judge's law clerk. If you have a law clerk, ask him or her to write a bench memorandum to the judge regarding evidentiary issues that are likely to arise at trial. ["Historical Trial Law Clerk" is actually a pretty decent line on a résumé. The "law clerk" part adds prestige, while the "historical" part will often be the subject of conversations at job interviews.]

Attorneys. The attorneys are crucial to putting on a good trial, so you must select them carefully. For senior attorneys, you want skilled, entertaining trial lawyers—i.e., hams with talent. But you need hams who are willing to share the spotlight with junior attorneys.

For junior attorneys, you want law students or new lawyers who have demonstrated both skills and guts in their trial advocacy classes, not those who, even if they graduated (or are about to do so) at the top of their class, have not demonstrated the ability to handle the stresses of trial. Trying a case in front of a room full of prominent judges and attorneys is not for the faint of heart.

In both categories, you need attorneys who will put in the time needed to try the case effectively. Historical trials are very much like real trials in requiring many hours of advance preparation for reading, meeting with witnesses, discussing trial strategy with trial partners, drafting outlines, and practicing. When you recruit potential trial attorneys, do not sugarcoat this. Make sure the attorneys are aware that your historical trial is not a scripted event. Instead, as in a real jury trial, many hours of trial preparation are needed for an attorney to be effective for a few minutes in front of the jury.

Witnesses. Speaking of hams, you need some of those in witness roles, too. You could go to the community theater group and cast non-lawyers as witnesses. But do remember—part of the fun for law students or bar group members is seeing lawyers, law students, law professors, and perhaps even judges in costumes, playing their parts for all they are worth.

Also, community theater actors will be used to memorizing a script. You need folks who are willing to do much more than memorize a script. Your witnesses will need to read the entire trial file and, in many instances, other background materials about their figure from history. They need to do this reading to get themselves into character for trial. This requires a considerable investment of time by your witnesses.

Costume and Prop Directors. Without witness costumes, the "time machine" concept will not work. With them and, if possible, a few key props (i.e., exhibits other than pieces of paper), you can effectively pretend that you have moved back in time several decades—or even a couple of centuries.

For our first historic trial, the Meriwether Lewis case, the attorneys dressed in contemporary courtroom dress, rather than historically accurate courtroom attire. Feedback from audience members convinced us to put the attorneys in period appropriate attire, too. Of course, this adds to your Costume Director's workload. In historic trials based on events over half a century old, it also adds the challenge of trying to determine period appropriate courtroom attire for female attorneys, because female trial attorneys are a relatively recent phenomenon. But good Costume Directors can figure this out.

John Mathews (J.L. Wilkins), Booth's fellow actor and friend, inspects the knife that he found after the assassination on the stage of Ford's Theater. [Photo credit: Dylan Crouse]

Costuming perfection is not necessary. In our *Meriwether Lewis* trial, our Captain Lewis had a sergeant's, not a captain's, uniform, though no more than three people realized this, and our Captain Clark was dressed, as his partner (Mariam Decker, attorney for Silas Goodrich) said, "like the lead singer from Paul Revere and the Raiders," but he looked the part of an early 1800s gentleman and former officer. If you make a good faith effort on the costuming front, the audience will forgive minor inaccuracies.

From rather bitter experience, allow us to share a piece of surprising information about costumes. It will be a lot harder to get costumes than you think it will be, because many theater groups have had bad experiences lending costumes to folks who either never return them or return them in horrible condition.

You need a Costume Director who has the ties or the sales skills and the patience to overcome the likely initial resistance of the university drama department or local community theater group. It is a good idea to give that person the authority to promise a donation in exchange for use of the costumes. Also, before you return the costumes, have them cleaned and, if necessary, repaired.

Do not assume that theater groups will be able to supply all the costumes you need. Your Costume Director should also have the creativity and persistence to find costume items at thrift stores and costume shops. Be careful about costume shops, though, as they are not all created equal. Avoid the ones that cater to the Halloween and costume party clientele, because their costumes are often flimsy and non-authentic. Use the costume shops that cater to theater companies.

Start the search for costumes early, because there will be bumps in the road. Be sure you "hire" the right person as Costume Director. You need someone who is dependable, indefatigable, and difficult to discourage. There will be problems.

Jury Coordinator. After conducting hundreds of mock trials, including half a dozen historic trials, it is my firm belief that you should try to avoid seating lawyers, and even law students, as jurors whenever possible. Your jury's deliberation will be more realistic if that jury is not dominated, or even infiltrated, by lawyers and future lawyers.

If you are trying your first historic trial, you will probably want to assign a Jury Coordinator to find jurors in advance. After your historic trials become regularly expected events, you might not have to get jurors in advance. Instead, your Jury Coordinator can simply look for volunteers in the audience. Don't try this system, though, until you are confident that you will have enough non-lawyers in your audience to fill the jury box. Of course, you can also use a combination of these two systems.

You might want to film your jury deliberations. If so, make sure your Jury Coordinator makes the jurors aware of this in advance. Indeed, if you videotape or otherwise record the trial, get signed waivers from all attorneys, witnesses, jurors, etc.

Head Bailiff/Clerk. Find someone to locate and supervise bailiffs and clerks in the following roles:

John Wilkes Booth (Nathan Ridgway) glares at his attorneys. [Photo credit: Dylan Crouse]

Timekeeper: You cannot run a short trial without enforcing time limits.

Witness Grabber: To maximize the "fun" of the costumes, you should sequester witnesses, so the audience sees them one at a time. Have someone get the witnesses quickly after they are called. [Note: In your program, you probably want to identify this person as your "Witness Coordinator." But they are really a witness grabber.]

Oath Giver and Exhibit Clerk: Trial lawyers have an uncanny ability to lose paper and other items while the bullets are flying in court. If possible, have a court clerk whose sole, or at least primary, responsibility is to keep track of the exhibits.

Jury Coordinator: In addition to gathering jurors, the Jury Coordinator (or, if you prefer, Jury Bailiff) should work with the jury during trial. You will save time if you have someone guiding the jury in and out of the courtroom as needed.

Ushers: These good folks can distribute programs, help the inevitable late arriving audience members find seats, and guard the historic artifacts you have on tables outside the courtroom (if any).

Clara Harris (Professor Tara Righetti), one of the Lincolns' guests at the theater, demonstrates how Booth entered the presidential box by using a recreation of the vestibule that led to the box. [Photo credit: Dylan Crouse]

Refreshment Coordinators: If you are going to serve refreshments to your audience at intermission, you have to have a few folks setting up your refreshment table(s) during the first half of the trial. Do not set up the refreshment table before trial, because audience members will help themselves on the way into the courtroom. To keep the trial moving, you need to have enough space for several lines of audience members. Just as you need to keep things moving in the courtroom, you also need to keep things moving during your intermission.

Consider using junior high, high school, or college students in these roles, to maximize the educational value of your historic trial and generate positive feelings for your law school or bar group—and the profession.

Chronicler(s). Try to locate a volunteer photographer, videographer, and perhaps even court reporter. After the trial, buy prints for your attorneys and witnesses. A photograph of an attorney examining Thomas Jefferson is almost sure to make the wall of that attorney's office, where it will generate discussion about your law school or bar group.

Arrangements Committee. Get volunteers to find a place for the trial, to arrange for food, to purchase and wrap small historic trinkets as thank you gifts for trial participants, and to put together a post-trial cast party for all trial participants, including the judge, attorneys, witnesses, bailiffs, clerks, jurors, chroniclers, etc.

If possible, hold your trial in a courtroom. Be aware, though, that evening trials in working courtrooms could be pricey, because you might have to pay overtime to security personnel. Also, audience space is often limited in courthouses. Consider holding the trial in a law school's courtroom, because you can invite all law students and others to attend.

During final argument, prosecutor Emily Williams Simper demonstrates Booth's actions leading up to his shooting of President Lincoln, including peering through a peephole to check on Lincoln's seating position. [Photo credit: Dylan Crouse]

Publicity and Public Relations Staff. You will want people to contact junior high, high school, or college teachers to invite attendance and perhaps to arrange for bailiffs and clerks; prepare posters, e-mails, and other communications inviting target audiences to attend; prepare press releases and otherwise attempt to arrange coverage by local news media outlets (and perhaps state bar publications); produce a program for distribution the evening of the trial; and perhaps coordinate with local history groups.

Ideally, you should have a different person in each of the roles described above, with committees of several people in some roles. This is not essential, though. In the first historic trial I conducted, my student co-author, who was also my co-counsel, and I filled most of the roles listed above. But we are not recommending this approach. As comedian Chris Rock likes to say, you can steer a car with your feet, but it is not a good idea. Find a group of folks committed to putting on your historic trial.

FINDING A HISTORIC EVENT FOR YOUR TRIAL

Using one of the trial files in Chapter 10 substantially reduces your time commitment in conducting a historic trial. But if you are willing to invest the time to do the historical research, find the documents you need to create the core of a trial file, and create enough other elements of the trial file to give your attorneys and witnesses a solid basis to put on a historic trial, consider creating your own historic trial file.

What kind of historic event makes for a good trial? Look for one with as many of the following characteristics as possible.

Close Legal Issues. If your trial will be criminal prosecution, look for an incident where the defendant has a plausible, but not lead-tight, defense or one where the prosecution has substantial proof problems. If it is a civil case, look for one where both the plaintiff and the defendant have decent arguments.

Correct Size. An incident that is too "small" will not generate much interest, but it is also a mistake to take on an event that is too "big." It might be fascinating to try Lee Harvey Oswald for the assassination of President Kennedy, but it is going to be pretty difficult to do it in two hours.

To downsize a historic event for your trial, you can assume some of the facts and remove the related elements of the crime or claim from the jury instructions. For example, in the Meriwether Lewis trial, we assume that the canoe in question was of sufficient value to meet the statutory threshold for a felony.

Defense attorney Kent Spence pleads his client's case during final argument. [Photo credit: Dylan Crouse]

Accessible Historic Record. To give those eager new attorneys the chance to use their research and investigation skills, look for an event that left some footprint that can be researched at state, local, university, or other archives and in the morgue files of newspapers. Some events generate stories, including "anniversary" coverage, by magazines, television and radio stations, and other outlets. A few even find their way into books.

No Actual Trial. For the type of trial described here, it is best if there was no actual trial. If there was a trial, your trial is going to look a lot like that trial, because the attorneys will research that trial. You can create a fun and educational program out of a trial that did take place, but that is a different type of program.

Look for an event that theoretically could have, but did not, generate a trial. Perhaps the defendant avoided capture, escaped, or died. Maybe there were jurisdictional, venue, or logistical issues that made a trial a legal impossibility. For your trial, you will simply ignore these concerns. For example, in the Meriwether Lewis trial, we combined military and civilian law, ignored the fact that the event in question happened outside any state, and pretended that we could somehow magically transport a variety of witnesses to the same place, which we assumed to be St. Louis of Louisiana Territory, for a trial. If you can imagine a time machine, you can imagine a machine that will help you solve geographic problems, too.

Event of Interest. Look for an event from history that involves people or occurrences that still generate interest. An event of national interest, like the Lewis and Clark expedition or the assassination of Abraham Lincoln, works well. If there is a local tie, so much the better.

How do you find an event with these characteristics? Keep watching and listening to reports of historic events, looking for possible trial candidates. Then get lucky. I "found" the event for the Meriwether Lewis trial several years ago, while watching the PBS Ken Burns miniseries about Lewis and Clark, seeing a minute or two about the canoe incident, and thinking "that might make for a good mock trial exercise."

CONCLUSION

While no historic trial, like no actual trial, will happen without a few glitches, in my experience historic trials are very well received. All of those I have overseen or watched have included both high drama and a few moments of widespread laughter. The attorneys, witnesses, and volunteers work hard, but have a lot of fun, too. Even the jurors seem to relish their roles.

Many of the historic trials I have overseen have resulted in hung juries. Audience members find this frustrating. [Note: To counteract this audience frustration, I have started having audience members vote on the verdict, too. To make things simple, I ask those voting "guilty" to sign their name to a red card and those voting "not guilty" to sign their name to a green card. After the ushers collect the cards, they tally the audience vote. To encourage audience voting, select door prize winners from the collected cards. Include a space on the cards for email addresses for those willing to provide them, as you can use those addresses to build an audience invitation list for future historic trials.]

John Wilkes Booth (Nathan Ridgway) with his counsel, Kent Spence and Macrina Sharpe, after his trial. [Photo credit: Dylan Crouse]

But a hung jury is in many ways a good result (or "non-result"). It confirms that the trial file was fairly written, with ammunition for both sides. Also, it allows the many people who work so hard on the case, including attorneys and witnesses, to leave the trial without the sour taste of losing. After all, hard as the attorneys will work to win the case, winning and losing are not the point of a historic trial. Education is.

RULES FOR HISTORIC TRIALS

Subject to modification due to special rules applicable to your historic trial or modification by your instructor, the following rules apply to historic trials.

1. The (Partial) Time Machine

You should assume that the trial is taking place on the date noted in your trial file, which will be shortly after the historic events outlined in the trial file. For purposes of FACTUAL information, all trial participants will travel in a time machine back to that date.

We will, however, use CURRENT law (i.e., law as of the date your trial actually takes place). Said another way, you will take current substantive and evidentiary law back with you on our time machine trip. Also, as noted below, attorneys will be allowed to use current technology.

2. Exhibits

The attorneys are allowed to produce copies of the exhibits without page numbers and footnotes. All such copies will be deemed to be original documents.

All exhibits contained herein are deemed authentic, and attorneys are encouraged to stipulate to foundation as much as possible. Any witness who is asked to do so is required to admit that s/he wrote the document. If a witness refuses to do so or if otherwise appropriate, all attorneys are required to stipulate that the individual wrote the document.

The attorneys are encouraged to create demonstratives and other visual aids to help their presentations. Such exhibits, such as enlargements of exhibits from the trial file, must be shown to opposing counsel at least twenty-four (24) hours prior to trial.

Attorneys are permitted to create their own exhibits, and enter them as evidence, subject to the discovery rules mentioned below. However, exhibits created by attorneys that do not appear in this trial file MUST be consistent with the information in this trial file and cannot unfairly sway the case toward one side. For example, it would be impermissible for an attorney to create an audio recording in which the opposing party admits contested facts. However, it would be permissible for an attorney to create a timeline of events, then attempt to introduce it into evidence.

3. Applicable Law

Unless there is a clear reason not to do so, the case will be tried under current federal law. This includes the current Federal Rules of Evidence.

4. Time Crunch

To present this case within the limited time available, each side will have only one hour for opening statement, direct examination of witnesses, cross-examination of witnesses, and final arguments. By 24 hours before trial, each side must submit its time budget for the trial to the instructor. This means that both sides must decide how to budget their time.

For instance, the Defense might submit a time budget of "Opening, 5 minutes. Cross of ____, 4 minutes. Direct of Defendant, 10 minutes" and so forth. It will be the responsibility of the bailiff to keep time during the trial. The bailiff will do his or her best to hold you to your time limits (and warn you when you are running out of time).

5. Jury Instructions and Verdict Form

The trial file includes a set of jury instructions to be used for the trial, along with a verdict form. It will be assumed that both sides submitted their proposed instructions and that these are the instructions approved by the Court. If both sides agree that a particular instruction should be removed or changed, or if one side wishes to argue for an alteration of the instructions, such changes may be made at the discretion of the Judge.

6. Rules for the Trial Itself

    a. Teamwork. Each team is expected to divide the workload and trial presentation as evenly as possible. Team members should equitably share direct and cross responsibilities. One attorney should do the opening, and the other should do the closing. [For the plaintiff or prosecution, the attorney who does the opening is allowed to do the rebuttal closing, but not the initial closing.]

b. No Re-Cross. For each witness, there will be an opportunity for direct examination, cross-examination, and redirect examination. There will be no re-cross.

c. Good Faith Basis. Attorneys are allowed to ask questions based on the facts in the trial file. We cannot expect our witnesses to actually know everything that the persons they are portraying would know. Therefore, they should be entitled to assume that there is some basis in the trial file for the questions they are asked.

d. Witness Rules. Witnesses need to be aware of the following rules:

    i. Historical Accuracy. Witnesses should testify in a manner that is consistent with what actually happened, except where we have deliberately modified history a bit to get the case tried in a reasonable time, as reflected in the trial file. Thus, in addition to the "reasonable extrapolation" rule applicable to all mock trials, discussed below, all attorneys and witnesses should keep witness testimony consistent with history, using the language of the day.

    ii. Reasonable Extrapolations. Inevitably, there will be items of information that witnesses and attorneys will need that are not contained in this trial file. Witnesses are allowed to make "reasonable extrapolations" from the facts to fill the gaps, when needed. However, witnesses should keep their testimony consistent with their character, and witnesses are NOT permitted to invent facts that are so one-sided as to be unreasonable.

    iii. Impeachment with Prior Statements. Each witness is expected to read and be familiar with the document(s) related to that witness and to testify consistently with the materials in the trial file. Each witness is required to admit that the document(s) related to him/her accurately reflect his/her statements on the date that the document was created. This is a time-saving mechanism: We do not have time to call a newspaper reporter, for example, to testify that Witness A said what he is quoted as saying in the article. Thus, Witness A will have to admit that he said what he is quoted as saying. [He can claim that the reporter "took it out of context" or the like, but he cannot claim that he did not say it.] If any attorney believes that one of these documents becomes admissible as a prior inconsistent statement, the other parties stipulate to foundation. [In other words, you do not have to call the newspaper reporter to the stand to say what is in the article if the witness quoted in the article refuses to admit he said what is in the article. But the other side can object on other grounds, such as relevance or hearsay.]

iv. **Weapons.** If you use firearms or other weapons as exhibits, use them with care. Follow all firearm safety rules. Never point any firearm at another human being. Use trigger locks. If possible, use non-functioning or facsimile weapons—all trial participants can simply pretend they are the real thing. If you are on a campus and you use a firearm or other weapon as a trial exhibit, you might want to notify campus police that you plan to do so in advance.

e. **Technology.** Although the trial will take place in a past era, attorneys are permitted, indeed encouraged, to make full use of all technology available in the courtroom.

f. **Background.** Your instructor might provide some or all of the background information in the trial file to your jurors.

7. Additional Rules

a. There may be special rules applicable to your historic trial, as outlined in the file for your trial in the resources section of this book on CasebookConnect.

b. Your instructor may modify any of these rules or the special rules in your trial file.

HISTORIC TRIAL 10.1
LEWIS AND CLARK CANOE HEIST

UNITED STATES

v.

MERIWETHER LEWIS

and

SILAS GOODRICH

Original trial file by Elizabeth E. O'Hanlon & Stephen D. Easton

© 2019 [No copyright protection claimed for the works of others.]

Background

This trial focuses on a little-known event during one of the most well-known historical adventures, especially in the western United States—the Lewis and Clark Expedition. As most know, after the Louisiana Purchase, President Thomas Jefferson appointed his personal secretary, Meriwether Lewis, to explore the Missouri River that drained much of the newly acquired territory, with the hope of finding a Northwest Passage. Lewis asked William Clark to accept joint command of this expedition.

The incident at the heart of this trial occurred in March of 1806, at the end of the winter the Corps of Discovery spent on the coast of what is now northwest Oregon. In anticipation of the Corps' return trip up the Columbia River, Captain Lewis wanted to obtain a large canoe from the Clatsop tribe via barter. When he was unable to purchase the canoe at an acceptable price, he ordered some of his men, including Private Silas Goodrich, to steal it.

The prosecution will have little difficulty establishing that Private Goodrich stole the canoe and that Captain Lewis knowingly received stolen property, because Captain Lewis admitted these facts in his journal. However, both defendants have potentially viable defenses.

Captain Lewis will present the "emergency measures" defense, also known as "necessity." This defense excuses otherwise unlawful conduct if it was necessary to avoid an imminent injury that would have otherwise occurred, as long as the emergency was not created by the defendant. While piggybacking on this defense, Private Goodrich will also probably pursue the lawful orders defense, which permits a defendant to attempt to establish that he or she was acting pursuant to the order of a superior military officer, unless the defendant knew or should have known that the order was unlawful. The two defenses encompass several disputable issues.

What makes this particular set of facts especially interesting—indeed, controversial—is the reality that the underlying events represent one incident in a long string of U.S. government behavior toward Native American (or Indian) tribes. After all, Captain Lewis, acting as an agent of the U.S. government, first tried to reach a mutually acceptable agreement with the Clatsop to purchase the canoe via barter during their winter together. But upon refusing to pay the price the tribe demanded, he simply took the canoe without the tribe's permission. That was not the first, and it certainly was not the last, time the government acted in that manner.

Important Note About Language and Witness Selection. To stay true to the historical record requires the use of language that is no longer appropriate in today's society (and, in many instances, should not have ever been considered appropriate). In addition, some of the witnesses make statements reflecting attitudes that are improper.

We have attempted to reduce the number of these improper statements and words to a minimum. However, to reflect the attitudes of the participants at the time, a few of these inappropriate statements had to be included, to accurately reflect history.

After consultation with the American Indian Studies Program at the University of Wyoming, we removed the roles of Clatsop Natives and Sacajawea from this trial file. Dr. Angela M. Jaime & Dr. Caskey Russell of the American Indian Studies advised of several reasons for this: "Native people are constantly portrayed as figures in the past or frozen in time; having non-Natives playing Native people is problematic: this is known as 'red face' and is viewed by Natives as akin to having white actors in black face. And not having the Clatsop take part in the Mock Trial also illustrates the dynamics of power at play at the time: the judicial system, trial law, and even the predominance of English, all favoring U.S. citizens. At the time of the crime, the Clatsop were not U.S. citizens; moreover, the Clatsop would have had their own judicial system and laws determining compensation for crimes, which wouldn't have been accepted by the U.S. courts.

Ultimately, we want to illustrate the silencing of Native voices, both in the past and in the present, and we take this as an opportunity to educate others on the reality of this historical event, rather than perpetuating stereotypes about 'Natives.'"

Date

Your trial will take place in the year 1807 in St. Louis, Louisiana Territory. You will assume that the trial takes place in that year, on the date when your trial actually takes place. [Thus, if your trial takes place on March 4, you will assume that it takes place on March 4, 1807.]

Allegations

The United States alleges that Captain Meriwether Lewis received stolen property. Captain Lewis will present an emergency measures defense, which excuses otherwise unlawful conduct if it was necessary to avoid an imminent injury that would have otherwise occurred, as long as the emergency was not created by the defendant.

The United States alleges that Private Silas Goodrich committed the crime of stealing without consent. Private Goodrich will follow Captain Lewis's emergency measures defense and will also pursue the lawful orders defense, which permits a defendant to attempt to establish that he or she was acting pursuant to the order of a superior military officer, unless he or she knew or should have known that the order was unlawful.

Witnesses

The United States may call the following witnesses:

1. Private Hugh Hall

Defendant Meriwether Lewis may call the following witnesses:

1. Captain Meriwether Lewis
2. President Thomas Jefferson

Defendant Silas Goodrich may call the following witnesses:

1. Private Silas Goodrich
2. Captain William Clark

Mandatory Stipulations

The parties must stipulate to the following:

1. Exhibit 1, the PBS website map from St. Louis to Oregon (or a similar map agreed to by the parties), is admissible.

2. Exhibit 2, the map of the Columbia River at the Pacific Ocean, is admissible.

Trial Rules

The trial will be governed by the *Rules for Historical Trials* in MATERIALS IN TRIAL ADVOCACY, Chapter 10. However, the following additional rule will apply to this trial unless the instructor advises to the contrary:

Time Limits: The prosecution will have a total of 50 minutes to present its case, defendant Meriwether Lewis 45 minutes, and Silas Goodrich 40 minutes. Please see the *Rules for Historical Trials* in Chapter 10 of MATERIALS IN TRIAL ADVOCACY for information about budgeting your time and reporting your time budget to the instructor.

HISTORIC TRIAL 10.2
LINCOLN ASSASSINATION

UNITED STATES

v.

JOHN WILKES BOOTH

Original trial file by Evynne Fair and Stephen D. Easton

(incorporating and sometimes modifying the works of others)

© 2019 [No copyright protection claimed for the works of others.]

Background

This file presents the opportunity for a trial regarding what is probably the most famous killing in American history that did not result in a trial: John Wilkes Booth's shooting of President Abraham Lincoln at Ford's Theater in the aftermath of the Civil War.

Some might wonder whether it is worthwhile to put Booth on trial. After all, everybody knows he shot Lincoln, right? What is there to dispute?

Plenty, as this trial file establishes. In our system, everyone—even one of the most reviled figures in American history—deserves a trial and a vigorous defense. In this case, that defense will be insanity (or, as some jurisdictions call it, not guilty by reason of severe mental disease or defect).

To make the case triable, all participants have to engage in a thought exercise by assuming that Booth survived the bullet that hit him inside the tobacco barn on the Garrett family farm in Maryland on April 26, 1865, twelve days after the fateful performance of *Our American Cousin*. The trial file includes "A Note About this Trial File's Assumptions Regarding John Wilkes Booth's Life After Nearly Dying." [In actuality, of course, Booth died at the Garrett farm. But we ignore this piece of history to create a triable case against Booth.] To the greatest extent possible, this trial is otherwise consistent with the historical record about the assassination of President Abraham Lincoln.

To make the case triable in a couple of hours, instead of the multiple weeks that a trial of John Wilkes Booth would have almost certainly consumed, we have tried to squeeze as much information as possible into the heads of only a few witnesses. To do this, we have put information into the heads of selected witnesses that actually would have been known to other witnesses. For example, in this file Laura Keene and John Mathews, actors in *Our American Cousin*, know things that other actors, stage hands, or members of the audience actually observed or knew, while David Herold knows a few things that Lewis Powell actually knew. When we have done this, we have noted this in footnotes and sometimes elsewhere. Also, when we have done this, we have done our best to stay consistent with the historical record, by not creating knowledge for any witness that is beyond what the historical record supports.

Of course, for an event like the assassination of Abraham Lincoln, there is more than one version of the historical record. Indeed, the Abraham Lincoln assassination has probably generated more writing, both good and bad and both traditional print and Internet, than any event in American history other than the assassination of President John Kennedy a century later. Our version of the "historical record" that we have tried to stay true to is what might be considered the consensus of professional or otherwise distinguished historians. Where there is disagreement among the best historians (as, for example, whether the Herndon House meeting occurred on Thursday, April 13, or Friday, April 14, whether Booth broke his leg when landing on the stage or in a later horse riding accident, whether the bullet lodged behind Lincoln's left or right eye, etc.), we have simply made a choice about which theory to adopt for this trial file.

This trial file is designed for a trial that takes place about a year after the shooting itself, sometime in 1866. We have Booth surviving the shooting inside the Garrett tobacco barn, but just barely. In our version of the facts, he spends several months in a military hospital, under guard of course, near death. In January of 1866, he is finally healthy enough to be transferred to the old Capitol Prison. In prison, he will be in shackles and a hood (like his alleged co-conspirators, who were tried before a military commission). By the time of his trial in 1866, there will be no hope, even to him, of rekindling a Southern uprising. So he will be pleading not guilty by reason of insanity to attempt to avoid a conviction for first degree murder, which would almost certainly result in his hanging if that conviction occurred in 1866.

This is not the best set of facts in American history for an insanity defense, of course, but that is the best defense that is available to Booth. Crackpot Internet sites and other conspiracy addicts aside, there really is not much doubt about the fact that Booth fired the shot that killed Lincoln. Booth admits — indeed, brags about — this on several occasions after the shooting. As a result, although the prosecution will have to prove Booth's actions and the resultant death of Abraham Lincoln in its case in chief, a straight murder trial would not be very interesting. If Booth had survived the shooting in the tobacco barn, his attorneys would have had no realistic option other than pursuing an insanity defense. Thus, this trial file is written for such a trial.

While that will be the general gist, this trial file leaves it to Booth's defense team, working with their client, to come up with the details of the defense, within the broad parameters outlined in the file. It is possible that Booth will try to use the trial to make some sort of political statement or rail against the American justice system, and perhaps even his attorneys to some extent, as this is not uncommon in insanity defense trials. [As noted below, Booth will be allowed three outbursts during this short trial, should the defense team deem them to be in the best interest of their insanity defense.] As long as he and his attorneys operate within the general parameters outlined here, these approaches are acceptable.

Date

Your trial will take place in the year 1866. You will assume that the trial takes place in that year, on the date when your trial actually takes place. [Thus, if your trial takes place on March 4, [0], you will assume that it takes place on March 4, 1866.]

Allegations

The trial file includes a first degree murder indictment of Booth.

In response to this indictment, Booth has plead not guilty by reason of insanity.

Witnesses

The United States may call the following witnesses:

1. Clara Harris
2. David Herold
3. Laura Keene
4. John Mathews

Defendant may call the following witnesses:

1. John Wilkes Booth
2. Any prosecution witness not called by the United States
3. Psychologist (if you decide to incorporate a psychologist into your trial)

Mandatory Stipulation

Counsel must stipulate to the admission of the autopsy report. [This saves the trial from slowing down to present expert medical testimony.]

Trial Rules

The trial will be governed by the *Rules for Historical Trials* in MATERIALS IN TRIAL ADVOCACY, Chapter 10. In addition, the following rules will apply to this trial, unless the instructor advises to the contrary:

1. To stay true to the historical record is to use language that is unacceptable today, especially terms that refer to African Americans. This file reflects that reality. However, the instructor might want to prohibit the use of certain terms. Also, it might be wise to have someone warn the audience about offensive language before your historical trial starts.

2. With the exception of the recreated letter by John Wilkes Booth that he gave to John Mathews, we will pretend that each handwritten exhibit is in the handwriting of the persons who created it. With the exception of the one letter previously noted, all exhibits contained herein are deemed authentic, and attorneys are encouraged to stipulate to foundation as much as possible.

Any witness who is asked to do so is required to admit that s/he wrote the document. If a witness refuses to do so or if otherwise appropriate, all attorneys are required to stipulate that the individual wrote the document.

3. The prosecutors may NOT speak with, or attempt to speak with, the defendant. The attorneys are allowed to contact other witnesses. Those playing the witness roles should decide whether the persons they are portraying would speak with the attorneys.

4. Booth will be allowed to have three short outbursts during the trial, if he so chooses.

> First, when the judge declares, "The Supreme Court for the District of Columbia is now in session," or something similar, Booth will be allowed to jump to his feet and declare something like, "I do not recognize the jurisdiction of this court. I am a citizen of the Confederate States of America, not the United States of America."

> Second, at some point when David Herold testifies, Booth is allowed to say, "Et tu, Brute? Even you are abandoning me now?" or something like that. Of course, if Booth said something like that, he would get the pronunciation right: [ɛt ˈtu ˈbruti]

> Third, Booth is allowed to have one other outburst at some point in the trial.

5. After each outburst, the judge will bang his/her gavel and say something like: "Order in the court. Mr. Booth, you will sit down immediately. You will only be heard from in this proceeding if you take the stand and testify. Counsel, I expect you to control your client."

HISTORIC TRIAL 10.3
KILLING OF JESSE JAMES

STATE OF MISSOURI

v.

THOMAS T. CRITTENDEN

Original trial file by James S. Atkins

with

Alexandra Goblet, Caleb Jones, and Stephen D. Easton

© 2019 [No copyright protection claimed for the works of others.]

Background

This case features murder, hatred, secret agents, and one of the most ruthless killers in U.S. history . . . as the victim.

The evidence of Governor Thomas Crittenden's involvement in encouraging (to use a polite phrase) Robert Ford to kill Jesse James is pretty strong. Not perfect, because the governor will assert that he never authorized the killing of James, but perfect, completely indisputable, evidence never exists.

Despite the strength of the prosecution's case, the governor has a decent chance of avoiding conviction. Those in authority often do. While the defense team will technically focus on whether the prosecution can prove Crittenden called the hit on Jesse James, the real defense will be the technically improper but nonetheless rather common "he needed killing" defense.

Although this is a historic trial, it raises issues that still haunt us today. The influence of corporate dollars on politics and government. An executive's use of power against perceived enemies. Going outside the limits set by the law in pursuit of an allegedly important objective. Trading freedom and due process for security, due to concerns about terrorists.

This trial is based on historical events, but to make it flow more smoothly, certain liberties have been taken in constructing these materials. For example, some minor character roles have been fabricated entirely (though always with an eye toward logical historical inference), and some "original" documents have been created or reconstructed based, again, on logical historical supposition. The essential facts, however—those pertaining to how and when Jesse James died—are historically accurate. If you are not already familiar with the story of James's death, the materials referenced below will lend context to the matter at the bar.

One of the key factual disputes in this case is whether Governor Crittenden authorized or otherwise encouraged the killing of Jesse James. The governor is likely to assert that he only sought to have James captured, not killed. The prosecution will likely assert that this is simply a clever effort at plausible deniability—i.e., that the governor knew that Robert Ford understood that the governor wanted him to kill James.

Historical Backdrop

The Historical and Theatrical Trial Society of the University of Missouri-Columbia School of Law first tried this case on April 3, 2008. At that trial, the following Historical Backdrop, written by primary trial file author James S. Atkins, then a Mizzou law student, was provided to audience members in the program distributed before trial:

> Missouri was a flashpoint for secessionist and union violence during the Civil War. She was a state deeply divided. Her populous contained both pro-Union Republicans and southern-sympathizing Democrats. In 1861, the Congress of the Confederate States of America admitted Missouri into membership and memorialized the occasion in one of thirteen stars emblazoned upon the Confederate Jack. Missouri's confederate government held sessions 200 miles south of Jefferson City in Neosho, Missouri. During the same period, the pro-Union government, still located in Jefferson City, openly declared its support for the Union and retained its representation in the United States Congress. Missouri effectively had two governments. The tension of a house divided ripped the state in two.

Missouri was a desirable commodity to both the North and the South. Her wealth of resources included: two major waterways, the Mississippi and Missouri Rivers; abundant natural resources; rich farm land, iron ore, and lead deposits; a sizeable population as the eighth most populous state according to the 1860 census; and reliable lines of communication to western outposts—the Pony Express and the Santa Fe, California, and Oregon Trails. Missouri's value was manifested in the number of battles waged on her soil. By war's end, Missouri was host to so many battles and skirmishes that it ranked as the third most fought over state in the country.

Perhaps the darkest chapter in Missouri's Civil War history was the rise of guerilla warfare within and around her borders. Although a number of states had brushes with guerillas from both sides of the conflict, nowhere was the touch of the "bushwhackers" felt as keenly as in Missouri. "Bushwhacking," as it came to be known, was a form of guerilla warfare in which Confederate sympathizers conducted raids against the Union Army, loyalists, and supply lines. Although the term "bushwhacker" was generally used to describe any such group of Confederate lay fighters, the sheer volume of guerilla activity in Missouri eventually caused the term to be associated most strongly with that state. In a similar manner, pro-Union guerillas in Kansas were known as "Jayhawkers," a term identified with Kansans to this day.

Guerilla activity in Missouri was so pervasive it was nearly a war unto itself. Just as in the larger Civil War, the activities of the bushwhackers often pitted neighbor against neighbor, brother against brother, and even father against son. Indeed the violent guerilla actions of the bushwhackers in Missouri left such an indelible mark on the state that their effects were felt for nearly a quarter century after Lee's surrender at Appomattox Court House brought an end to the nationwide conflict.

The most infamous of the Missouri bushwhackers was William Clark Quantrill. Quantrill was so effective in leading raids against the Union that in 1862, following his efforts to help drive the Union Army out of Independence, Missouri, he was made a Captain in the Confederate Army. Notwithstanding his captaincy, Quantrill was never a Confederate Army regular, nor was he subject to any formal chain of command.

Quantrill led his band of bushwhackers for nearly four years. He developed a number of highly sophisticated tactics for conducting successful raids. Quantrill and his "Raiders," as they were known, would plan their attacks ahead of time, assign specific tasks to members during the raid, determine pre-selected escape routes with built-in redundancies, and even set up "relay horses" to aid in their escape. It was the success of such tactics that made Quantrill's Raiders so fearsome and led to the propagation of post-war outlawry by a number of ex-Raiders.

The more notable characters among Quantrill's Raiders included Cole Younger and the brothers Frank and Jesse James. Following the Civil War, these men, along with a handful of others, formed what became known as the James-Younger gang. Over the years, murder, capture, and betrayal combined to continually change the makeup of the gang's personnel, but they could not change its essence. With Jesse James at the helm, the group remained dedicated to stealing as much and as often as it could. So prolific were their exploits that for nearly two decades Jesse James's gang was the gold-standard for outlaw bands in the western United States.

James and his gang were equal parts ruthless killers, romantic heroes, and urban legends. For twenty years, James and his boys rained down an unrelenting torrent of armed robbery upon trains, banks, and stagecoaches. Some said James was a cold-blooded assassin who deserved to be locked up or shot, while others lauded him as a modern-day Robin Hood and elevated him to hero status for his continued fight for the southern way of life. Whatever be the case, it is undisputed that James's calculated implementation of the skills he learned as a Raider into his career as an outlaw led him to become one of the most successful bandits in American history.

So renowned were James and his gang that Missouri was in danger of becoming a pariah. The unchecked proliferation of Jesse James's career in thievery led to Missouri being known in common parlance as "The Robber

State." By the late 1870s, Missouri, formerly a desirable pass-through state for westward settlers, saw travelers begin to seek safer northern or southern routes west rather than pass through the dreaded Robber State. Railroad and stage coach companies endeavored to find ways to avoid Missouri so as not to appear to customers to be at the mercy of bloodthirsty outlaws. The once proud Missouri had become known as a safe haven for thieves and cut-throats. Civilized easterners and entrepreneurs, and their money, were beginning to avoid the state altogether. Such was the state of affairs when Governor Thomas T. Crittenden came to office in 1881.

While previous governors had paid much lip service to ridding the state of outlawry, Crittenden built a campaign on it. In stump speeches from St. Louis to Kansas City, Crittenden decried the James gang and pledged himself to ridding the state of such miscreant outlaws forever. Crittenden was quick to point out the economic devastation that would befall the state if the western settlers and travelers continued to avoid it, and even quicker to hold up James and his boys as the reason for their departure. The railroad companies, too, were obliged to ally with Crittenden, as the prospect of taming the Robber State was far more appealing than the specter of losing the business of the traveling, and ticket buying, public. Thus an agreement was forged between Crittenden and the railroads. Crittenden was elected on the law-and-order ticket, and he had the financial backing of a very big business interest to help him deliver on his campaign promise—to rid Missouri of the James Gang forever.

In securing elected office, Crittenden had placed himself in a precarious position. By the early 1880s, Jesse James was a living legend. He was a touchstone of lingering resentment by vanquished southerners for their "northern oppressors." He was, for those Missourians still sympathetic to the defeated south, their own native son. James was the embodiment of the war they could no longer wage themselves. He was keeping the faith, and they were obliged to protect him. On the other hand, Crittenden had to deliver. He had to come through for both the law-and-order constituency that elected him and the business interests that bankrolled him. Crittenden had to stop James in order to validate his candidacy, and he had to extinguish the James legend to save his beloved Missouri.

In Crittenden's mind the future of both his legacy and his state were imperiled in equal measure. He was under tremendous pressure, and he vowed to prevail no matter what it took. So began a chain of events that led to the demise of the legendary Jesse James.

Date

Your trial will take place in the year 1883. You will assume that the trial takes place in that year, on the date when your trial actually takes place. [Thus, if your trial takes place on March 4, [0], you will assume that it takes place on March 4, 1883.]

Allegations

The State of Missouri has charged Thomas Theodore Crittenden with aiding and abetting the offense of murder.

Defendant Crittenden has pled not guilty.

Witnesses

The state may call the following witnesses:

1. Robert Ford
2. Finis C. Farr (the state might claim Mr. Farr is an adverse witness)
3. Clay County Sheriff James R. Timberlake
4. Major Henry Neill (the state might claim Major Neill is an adverse witness)
5. Samantha L. B. Moores
6. Daviess County Sheriff Richard Johnson

All of the prosecution's witnesses other than Sheriff Johnson (who is appearing voluntarily) have been subpoenaed by the state.

Defendant may call the following witnesses:

1. Thomas T. Crittenden
2. Kansas City Police Commissioner Henry H. Craig II

3. Col. Wells H. Blodgett

4. Any prosecution witness not called by the state

Police Commissioner Craig has been subpoenaed by the defendant.

Trial Rules

The trial will be governed by the *Rules for Historical Trials* in Materials in Trial Advocacy, Chapter 10. In addition, the following rules will apply to this trial, unless the instructor advises to the contrary:

1. **Confidential Witness Instructions**. In this file, confidential instructions to the witnesses play a key role. These instructions are included in the Teacher's Manual, but they are not included in the trial file. The instructor will distribute these instructions to the persons playing the witness roles, but NOT to the trial attorneys. The attorneys may not, under any circumstances, read the confidential witness instructions.

    Because the confidential instructions are critical in this trial, trying this case will teach the attorneys the importance of attorney interviews with, and preparation of, witnesses. The attorneys will have to try to pry information from some witnesses. As in the real world, this will not always be successful.

2. **No Contact Rule**. Pursuant to Model Rule 4.2, the prosecutors are not allowed to have any contact with the defendant, Governor Crittenden. Model Rule 4.2 might also limit contact with other witnesses. In addition, all attorneys should review Model Rule 3.4(f)'s provisions prohibiting them from asking most, though not all, witnesses to refrain from contact with other attorneys.

3. **Firearm Safety.** If you use a facsimile of Robert Ford's pistol as a trial exhibit, all trial participants should carefully follow gun safety rules. Never point any gun at a human being. If possible, use a non-functioning firearm. Nonetheless, use a trigger lock.

4. **Exhibits, Jury Instructions, and Verdict Forms**. The Teacher's Manual contains formatted, clean copies of Exhibits 13 to 18, the newspaper articles. There should be no differences in content from the corresponding items in the Trial File, but the formatting is different. If s/he chooses to do so, the instructor can provide the attorneys with copies of these items.

HISTORIC TRIAL 10.4
JAPANESE-AMERICAN INTERNMENT DRAFT RESISTANCE (ALLEGED DEFAMATION)

FRANK EMI

Plaintiff

v.

NOBU KAWAI

Defendant

Original trial file by Mikole Bede Soto (edited by Stephen D. Easton)

© 2019 [No copyright protection claimed for the works of others.]

Background

It has been said that the most tragic of human stories are not tales of right versus wrong. Instead, the deepest tragedies are conflicts of right versus right, where each side passionately (and, to at least some extent, justifiably and reasonably) believes that it is right and the opposition is wrong. Under that definition, this case is profoundly tragic.

The core tragedy that forms the background for this dispute is the federal government's internment of Japanese-Americans during World War II. To pile additional insult upon that insult, the government initially did not allow Japanese-Americans (with very limited exceptions) to enlist in the armed forces during World War II.

As the war dragged on, the government changed this policy. Indeed, it reinstated the draft of young Japanese-American men, even though they were interred in relocation centers. The dispute leading to this suit concerned how Japanese-Americans should respond to the draft.

The majority of the interred population believed that their young men should allow themselves to be drafted or enlist to demonstrate that Japanese-Americans were loyal to the United States. But at one relocation center, Heart Mountain in remote northern Wyoming, an organization named the Fair Play Committee encouraged resistance to the draft. The Fair Play Committee, including leader Frank Emi, took the position that though Japanese-Americans should enlist if they were released from the camps, they should not be drafted while they were incarcerated by the government that was drafting them.

The dispute between these groups, both of them convinced that their view was the noble one, was intense. Eventually, it spread from Heart Mountain to other relocation centers, though the Heart Mountain Fair Play Committee was always the draft resistance movement's beating heart.

On March 18, 1944, the HEART MOUNTAIN SENTINEL, the camp newspaper, published a scathing editorial condemning the Fair Play Committee entitled "Provocateurs." This lawsuit is based upon that editorial. We have made two minor modifications to the editorial to make this a viable lawsuit. First, we have assumed that Nobu Kawai, the SENTINEL's Associate Editor, wrote the editorial. [While this is not a certainty, it is a reasonable assumption, because Associate Editor Kawai was a strong and vocal supporter of enlistment.] Second, while the actual editorial avoids naming names, we have modified the editorial slightly to include direct attacks on Frank Emi, one of the leaders of the Fair Play Committee. [Again, this is reasonable. In many ways, Mr. Emi was the public face of the Fair Play Committee. Also, there are indications that Mr. Kawai and Mr. Emi clashed over the draft.]

For our lawsuit, we have Mr. Emi filing a defamation suit against Mr. Kawai. Thus, this trial presents an opportunity to learn about one of the many disastrous, but largely unknown or at least forgotten, consequences of President Franklin Roosevelt's internment of Japanese-Americans—a deep divide among the interred community over the draft. For more than a few Japanese-Americans of the World War II generation, this divide lasted for the rest of their lives—i.e., for over half a century. Both sides agreed that internment based solely upon race was wrong. Both believed they were right about the draft. And both were right. This led to the dispute encapsulated in this trial, where nobody is wrong, but sharp conflict nonetheless ensued.

INTRODUCTORY NOTES

While this trial of Fair Play Committee leader Frank Emi suing the author of the HEART MOUNTAIN SENTINEL *Provocateurs* editorial for libel/slander did not actually

660

occur, our goal is to remain consistent with the historical record as much as possible. In particular, there is the hope that the trial will bring forth an accurate representation of the tensions between the draft resisters and the majority of the other internees at Heart Mountain (and, later, in other internment camps).

Since this trial did not actually occur, some changes have been made to historical records to make this trial possible. As noted above, two significant changes were to identify the editorial's author and to have the editorial explicitly criticize Frank Emi by name. Also, we had to fabricate depositions of the witnesses, because such depositions did not actually take place, though they presumably would have (though probably not as quickly as we have imagined) if this case had been litigated under modern discovery rules. While the depositions are our creation, the witnesses deposed in this trial file are actual historical figures. The depositions stay true to the sentiments that were prevalent during the draft resistance controversy.

Attorneys and other trial participants should use the historical background in this trial file to familiarize themselves with important dates and terms, such as *Nisei* and *Issei*. The context of this trial is particularly important to understanding the relationships between the U.S. government, the draft resisters, and the other internees at Heart Mountain.

The authors hope that this trial helps to highlight important events in American history. Generally, and correctly, America's collective memory views the internment camps with negativity, if it notes them at all. However, the decision of the Fair Play Committee to resist the draft and the response of those within the interred Japanese-American community who supported enlistment continue to enlighten differing perspectives on citizenship, citizen obligation and duty, and government responsibility. This is a sad story from our history. But it is one worth knowing.

Important Note About Language. Staying true to the historical record mandates the use in this trial file of language that is no longer appropriate. In particular, the term "Jap" was often used during the World War II era to refer to both individuals who emigrated from Japan and their children, even if these children were born in the United States. This term is now considered derogatory, and some who used it in the World War II era also meant it as a derogatory term. However, because this trial is set in 1944, some witnesses would use this term. It is best, we believe, to avoid this term as much as possible in the trial itself. But avoiding it altogether might not be possible.

Another loaded term is "camp." During its existence, Heart Mountain was referred to as the Heart Mountain Relocation "Camp."[1] In modern discourse about World War II, the word "camp" is often associated with German concentration camps. There is controversy about whether the term camp should be associated with Heart Mountain and the other western facilities used to house Japanese-Americans during the war. Some avoid the term, due to the different treatment that internees in German and American facilities endured. Others, who note that both countries forcibly migrated persons, largely their own citizens, to their camps due to membership in ethnic and other groups, embrace the term "camp" and even "concentration camp" for the U.S. facilities, to emphasize the injustice of such forced migration and incarceration. Because, again, we use the language of the era depicted, this trial file often refers to Heart Mountain as a "camp."

If you will have an audience at your historic trial, you should warn them about the reasons for the use of these loaded terms before the trial begins. Consider using both a notice about language in the program you distribute and a verbal warning before the trial begins.

Date

Your trial will take place on June 1, 1944. [Due to events related to the controversy being litigated in this case, including one of the largest mass trials in U.S. history later that month, where 63 draft resisters were convicted in U.S. District Court in Cheyenne, it is important for you to pretend your trial takes place on June 1, 1944.]

Allegations

This trial file contains both a complaint, sounding in defamation, and an answer. These pleadings outline the allegations in the case.

---

[1]*See* the Heart Mountain Interpretive Center website at http://www.heartmountain.org/history.html.

Witnesses

The plaintiff may call the following witnesses:

1. Frank Emi, Leader of the Fair Play Committee
2. John Nelson, Assistant Project Director of Heart Mountain
3. Gloria Kubota, Fair Play Committee Secretary[2]
4. William ("Bill") Hosokawa, Editor-in-Chief of the HEART MOUNTAIN SENTINEL[3]

The defendant may call the following witnesses:

1. Nobu Kawai, Associate Editor of the of the HEART MOUNTAIN SENTINEL and author of *Provocateurs* editorial[4]
2. Guy Robertson, Project Director at Heart Mountain
3. Sgt. Ben Kuroki
4. Any plaintiff's witness not called by the plaintiff

Mandatory Stipulation

As noted below, it will be assumed that the parties have stipulated that, for purposes of this trial, Frank Emi is a limited public figure.

---

[2]All committee members in Heart Mountain were male. But Gloria Kubota, the wife of a Fair Play Committee member, acted as the Committee's informal secretary. We are using her as a composite witness who is knowledgeable about many matters to eliminate the need to call numerous witnesses.

[3]Plaintiff's counsel might assert that Mr. Hosokawa is an adverse witness. If so, the judge will detemine whether to allow plaintiff's counsel to use leading questions during direct examination of Mr. Hosokawa.

[4]All editorials were published without attribution. As discussed above, we have chosen the historical figure of Nobu Kawai to fill this role, because he openly disagreed with the stance of the Fair Play Committee.

Trial Rules

The trial will be governed by the *Rules for Historical Trials* in MATERIALS IN TRIAL ADVOCACY, Chapter 10. In addition, the following rules will apply to this trial, unless the instructor advises to the contrary:

1. **Applicable Law.** Because this case is being tried in a Wyoming trial court, we will be operating under Wyoming law, including the (current) Wyoming Rules of Evidence. In the main, the key jury instructions provided come from Wyoming pattern jury instructions. We have eliminated some instructions that would ordinarily be given to reduce the length of the instructions (because the reading of jury instructions bores the audience and the jury). Any other legal questions should be answered using current Wyoming or federal law.

2. **Witness Contact.** The plaintiff's attorneys may NOT speak with, or attempt to speak with, the defendant, and the defense attorneys may NOT speak with, or attempt to contact, the plaintiff. The attorneys are allowed to contact other witnesses, unless Model Rule 4.2 or other Model Rules would prohibit such contact. Those playing the witness roles should decide whether the persons they are portraying would speak with the attorneys. [The attorneys are encouraged to review Model Rule 3.4(f)'s provisions prohibiting them from asking most, but not all, witnesses to refrain from communicating with other attorneys.]

3. **A Note About Defamation.** In this case, there is a public controversy in Heart Mountain Camp regarding the draft. Frank Emi voluntarily injected himself into the controversy through his involvement in the Fair Play Committee. Therefore, as noted above, the trial will proceed as if the parties have stipulated that Frank Emi is a limited public figure. The jury instructions in this file are written with this understanding. [In part, this measure is taken to simplify the file, as there is no time for a lengthy debate about Mr. Emi's status under defamation law.]

HISTORIC TRIAL 10.5
ROCK SPRINGS MASSACRE (WRONGFUL DEATH)

MING LEE, on behalf of AH LEE, decedent,

Plaintiff

v.

THE UNION PACIFIC RAILROAD COMPANY, parent corporation,

THE UNION PACIFIC COAL COMPANY, its subsidiary, and DOES 1 through 20,

Defendants

By Student Trial Director Katelyn Krabbenhoft (based on sources noted below),

with the assistance of John Fritz (edited by Stephen D. Easton)

© 2023 [No copyright protection claimed for the works of others.]

INTRODUCTORY NOTES

Editor's Note. Trials are almost always about human tragedies—someone has suffered a horrible injury, been fired, been the victim of a crime, been accused of committing a crime, etc. People don't need trial lawyers when things are going well for them. Instead, they turn to our profession at the worst moments of their lives, and ask us to help them.

This trial concerns a tragedy of monumental proportions. Indeed, the Rock Springs Massacre is the saddest event in the history of the state of Wyoming. And it actually occurred before there even was a state of Wyoming.

In the Rock Springs Massacre, white miners who were upset with their Chinese counterparts pillaged and burned the Rock Springs Chinatown to the ground, killing numerous Chinese miners and others. The number of deaths remains in dispute to this day. Those who search for "the good guys" in this event will search in vain. Your trial will focus on which of "the bad guys," at least as we see them with modern eyes, should be held legally responsible.

Thus, although some prefer to avoid revisiting the tragedies of our past, perhaps even attempting to bury them beneath our collective recollection, this trial is based on the premise that doing so is a mistake. Looking at the worst events of our history provides us the opportunity to learn and—maybe—avoid repeating the mistakes we have made in the past. Indeed, the tensions that brought about the horrors of September 2, 1885, are familiar to us today: Political and cultural disagreement about immigration, labor and management at odds, long hours of difficult work under trying conditions, and, yes, racism.

Thus, as a proud former resident of Rock Springs (Yellowstone Grade School Kindergarten class of 1964!) and descendent of coal miners, the editor believes we can learn valuable lessons from remembering the tragedy of those times, if we have the courage to look for them. The underlying facts make this a gut-wrenching case. But trial lawyers need to learn to handle the raw human emotions at the heart of their cases.

In this trial, the widow of a man killed in the Rock Springs Massacre brings a wrongful death suit against the operator of the coal mine that sparked the riot. We have chosen a non-miner as the plaintiff's decedent to avoid issues related to workers' compensation (a system that did not exist in the 1880s, but one that would cause unhelpful confusion in our system of legal time machine travel, where we largely bring modern law with us when we go back in history to conduct trials). We have chosen the railroad that operated the mine as the defendant in the case to reflect the reality that plaintiff's lawyers need to build cases against defendants who can pay judgments against them, with the resultant reality that an intentional tort suit against the miners who killed the plaintiff's decedent would not provide any monetary relief to the plaintiff.

There are two major legal issues in dispute. First, can the plaintiff establish a causal link between the operation of the mine by the railroad and the resultant death of Ah Lee, the operator of a popular laundry in Rock Springs? If so, the second issue arises: In a comparative fault system, how much fault should be assigned to the miners who actually killed Mr. Lee?

Of course, there are also issues regarding what amount of damages fairly compensates Mrs. Lee. If the trial actually took place in 1888, one would expect racism to play a significant factor. Again, this is a difficult matter that we prefer not to acknowledge, but trial attorneys work in the real world, with all its limitations, not the utopia that we would prefer.

You should assume that your trial is taking place in 1888, on whatever date is applicable (i.e., on the month and day when your trial takes place).

Allegations

This trial file contains both a complaint and an answer. These pleadings outline the allegations in the case.

Witnesses

1. **Mrs. Qui**—Witness for Plaintiff

    Mrs. Qui is the wife of the Chinese boss Soo Qui. Not much is known of her outside her interactions with the rioters. Mrs. Qui lived with her husband on the eastern edge of Rock Springs, but not inside Chinatown. Their house was visited as part of the rioters' goal to chase Union Pacific workers, responsible for the Chinese miners being brought in, out of town. She answered the door in a terrified state and informed the men that her husband had already left town and that she intended to follow. Mrs. Qui later left Rock Springs dressed as a lady of her class, but she was the last to leave. Being the wife of the Chinese boss, she probably felt the way most Chinese did at the time—that they had every right to be there and work the jobs they wanted. She and her husband, however, never returned to Rock Springs.

2. **Ming Lee** (Wife of Decedent)—Plaintiff

    It is not known if the deceased, Ah Lee, had a wife. However, reports are that he was 30 years old at the time of his death. While it was common for Chinese laborers (men) to travel to the United States to save up money to take back home to their families, it was more common for the businessmen to bring their wives with them. For the purposes of this trial, we have assumed that Ah Lee had a wife and that she lived in Rock Springs with him.

3. **Isaiah Whitehouse**—Adverse Witness for Plaintiff

Isaiah Whitehouse was an immigrant miner who became a prominent figure in Wyoming territorial politics. Whitehouse felt the way many miners did at the time, that it was slave labor and damaging to Wyoming as a whole for Union Pacific to bring in the Chinese to work for less pay. Whitehouse believed that the Chinese workers should have joined the Knights of Labor or should have left. He felt that the policies of Union Pacific were abusive, and, as such, wished for the Knights of Labor strikes to be a successful opposition. He knew, however, the strikes would not be successful so long as the Chinese would work for less. The spring prior to the event, Whitehouse had run for and been elected to the territorial legislature. In later accounts, he stated that he had intended to bring change to labor law in the legislature and had planned to bring the Union Pacific abuses to the legislature's attention in the next—his first—session. Whitehouse was one of the most prominent miners involved in the riot, but no one would speak of his actions because most believed in the end goal, even if they did not support the means to that end. Whitehouse is definitely not supportive of the plaintiff in this case. If the plaintiff's attorneys attempt to contact him to discuss the case, he should respond accordingly.

4. **Ah Say**—Witness for Plaintiff

It was said about Ah Say that "the world is better because he lived." Born around 1847 in China, Say traveled to the United States during the 1860s, arriving in Evanston, Wyoming in 1869. Say began his work as a miner, quickly moving up in management as an interpreter and superintendent of the Chinese workers for Union Pacific. Additionally, Say was a local pillar of the Chinese religious community. After the massacre, Ah Say, in his role as a local Chinese leader, demanded Union Pacific give all the Chinese fleeing from Rock Springs free train tickets to leave. After being refused, Say requested two months of back pay owed to the Chinese, but, again, Union Pacific refused.

While the Chinese did not unionize, much to the chagrin of the Knights of Labor, Ah Say was a spokesperson for the Chinese. He likely saw the importance of his relationship with Union Pacific officials but did no more than was necessary to protect the Chinese in Wyoming. Say was a father of at least four, devoutly religious, and a hard worker. He almost certainly believed Union Pacific was at fault for the conditions which sparked the massacre.

[Note: Ah Say is not an essential witness. This trial can be conducted without his testimony. Thus, instructors who wish to shorten the trial might want to delete this witness.]

5. **James** (Jim) **Evans**—Witness for Defendant

James Evans was the mine superintendent of mine Number 6 at Rock Springs. Not much is known of him outside his interactions with the miners leading up to and during the riot. However, he was a Union Pacific manager, and it is likely that he sided with his superiors. After the initial fight in mine Number 6, Evans had attempted to get the miners to go back to work. As mine superintendent, Evans was responsible for closing off old entrances and marking rooms in the entrances. Thus, he was partially responsible for the room assignments that later led to the initial fight. Evans had allowed Whitehouse and his partner Jenkins to move from entry 13 to entry 5, which had more coal. He warned them, however, to only take rooms that had not already been assigned to the Chinese. Evans probably felt that Whitehouse and Jenkins were at fault, and that the riot was unjustified.

6. **Sheriff Young**—Witness for Defendant

Sheriff Young was a man of many trades. It is likely that Young was good friends with many of the Union Pacific foremen and suppliers. He was the first to request troops. He thought there was no justification for the events that occurred. Sheriff Young arrested 16 miners believed to be involved and was disappointed when they were not indicted by the grand jury. Not much is known of Sheriff Young outside his role in getting word out of the events.

7. **Governor Warren** — Witness for Defendant

Various sources point to Governor Warren as having a very close relationship with top Union Pacific officials. Warren was responsible for requesting federal troops and was part of the meetings with the miners after the riot. The Governor sided with Union Pacific officials' decision to not negotiate with the miners after the riot and was also disappointed with the failed criminal case in Sweetwater County. He had no sympathy for the miners but also seemed calloused toward the Chinese. Warren's personal car was attached to the train that was used to haul the Chinese back to Rock Springs from Evanston. The Chinese had been told that they were being taken to San Francisco but instead the train stopped just beyond the burnt ruins of Chinatown. The Chinese, upon arrival, tried to strike against being put back to work and were threatened with being kicked out of the very train cars (their only shelter) that were used to trick them back to Rock Springs in the first place. Governor Warren was present during all of this and never objected to the harsh treatment of the Chinese by Union Pacific.

Trial Rules

The trial will be governed by the *Rules for Historical Trials* in MATERIALS IN TRIAL ADVOCACY Chapter 10. In addition, the following rules will apply to this trial, unless the instructor advises to the contrary:

1. **Applicable Law.** Because this case is being tried in a Wyoming trial court, we will be operating under Wyoming law, including the (current) Wyoming Rules of Evidence. In the main, the key jury instructions provided come from Wyoming pattern jury instructions. We have eliminated some instructions that would ordinarily be given to reduce the length of the instructions (because the reading of jury instructions bores the audience and the jury). Any other legal questions should be answered using current Wyoming or federal law.

2. **Witness Contact.** The plaintiff's attorneys may NOT speak with, or attempt to speak with, the defendant, and the defense attorneys may NOT speak with, or attempt to contact, the plaintiff. The attorneys are allowed to contact other witnesses, unless Model Rule 4.2 or other Model Rules would prohibit such contact. Those playing the witness roles should decide whether the persons they are portraying would speak with the attorneys. [The attorneys are encouraged to review Model Rule 3.4(f)'s provisions prohibiting them from asking most, but not all, witnesses to refrain from communicating with other attorneys.]